Prime Time Preachers

Prime Time Preachers

The Rising Power of Televangelism

JEFFREY K. HADDEN
AND
CHARLES E. SWANN

Introduction by T George Harris

Addison-Wesley Publishing Company, Inc.
Reading, Massachusetts • Menlo Park, California •
London • Amsterdam • Don Mills, Ontario • Sydney

Library of Congress Cataloging in Publication Data

Hadden, Jeffrey K.
  Prime time preachers.

  Includes index.
  1. Evangelists—United States. 2. Television in
religion—United States. I. Swann, Charles E.
II. Title.
BV3773.H32   269′.2′0922   81-3526
ISBN 0-201-03885-4   AACR2

ISBN 0-201-03885-4

ABCDEFGHIJ-DO-8987654321

First printing, May 1981

Cover design by Nason Design Associates.
Book design by Patricia Lowy.

For Joseph H. Fichter, S.J.

Contents

Acknowledgments

It would be impossible to undertake a project of the nature and scope of this one without incurring more debts than one can even begin to acknowledge. We set out to understand the "electronic church," which most people think of as only the syndicated television programs, in the much broader context of religious broadcasting. To achieve that goal, we needed to look at both the history of religious radio and TV broadcasting and the wide variety of its programming and messages.

Before we got very far into the research, it became obvious that we could not properly understand the electronic church if we restricted ourselves to the radio and television broadcasts themselves. The computers that spit out direct mail at lightning speed, the telephone banks that serve to receive pledges as well as offer counsel and prayer to listeners, the cassettes, records, newsletters, and magazines that are available to faithful viewers—these are all integral components of the electronic churches.

Our efforts resulted in spending many hours in front of the TV set. Some days it seemed as though one more program would certainly result in an overdose, but we managed to come back for more. We also spent a lot of time analyzing the direct mail and comparing it with that of other organizations and corporations. But it's not possible to come fully to grips with this broadcasting phenomenon in the comfort of one's living room or study. We spent weeks away from home so that we could gain firsthand knowledge of the electronic churches' operations. To be sure, there are similarities among them, but anyone who says that when you've seen one electronic church operation you've seen them all either hasn't been there or hasn't looked very carefully. One also needs to talk to many people in a lot of sectors of society and in a variety of capacities of religious leadership to grasp why the phenomenon of religious broadcasting has suddenly become so important.

In one sense, our greatest debts are to the people in religious broadcasting who took the time to help us understand what they are all about. In another sense—and we felt this early—it is the audiences of the religious programs who are really the most interesting subjects of all. If people didn't watch, and some of them send in contributions, there wouldn't be an electronic church as it exists today.

Some of our most interesting insights about the electronic churches came from people we encountered en route to interviews. The piles of magazine articles and newspaper clips in our laps almost always betrayed our interest to people who sat beside us on airplanes. We soon discovered that there is hardly anyone in America who doesn't have an opinion about the television preachers, and most people are more than willing to share their views. Their volunteered words of praise or damnation of the televangelists provided invaluable clues of what to look for and what questions to ask. To all those anonymous persons, to casual acquaintances, to old friends and new, go our thanks.

William Fore, assistant general secretary for communication of the National Council of Churches, deserves a special word of thanks for both encouraging and providing the opportunity for us to pursue the research reported here. So also do we owe a significant debt to Ben Armstrong, executive director of the National Religious Broadcasters, for his encouragement as well as his personal hand in opening doors to some of the major religious broadcasters. We came along about the time many religious broadcasters were the targets of critical press, and some, understandably, were hesitant to risk putting their heads on the chopping block again. Armstrong's assurances of our integrity and intentions to produce a balanced and objective account of religious broadcasting no doubt made the difference between getting in and not getting in on several occasions. Without the help of these two men, this project might not have gotten off the ground. The information we obtained is richer than it might otherwise have been without their help.

The personalities who appear on the religious television programs are only the visible portion of the vast organizations they head. We are indebted to those television program leaders who found time in their schedules to talk with us, but an even greater debt is due to the dozens of people on their staffs who answered probing questions and gave generously of their time to help us understand how the electronic churches work. No less important are the insights we gained from church leaders, elected public officials and their staffs, scholars, and journalists who have been covering this story.

Our thanks to the Arbitron Company for permission to publish their audience data on the syndicated religious programs. To the best of our knowledge, this is the first time such data have been published for general consumption. Connie Anthes, manager of Arbitron's communications, made available the organization's resources and graciously helped us understand the company's data-collection procedures. Rachelle Cagner, her very able assistant, patiently helped us locate materials in Arbitron's library and then cheerfully tolerated our presence under her feet while we reproduced vast amounts of material.

Charles Swann wishes to express special thanks to Fred R. Stair, president of Union Theological Seminary in Virginia, who encouraged him to write this book; and to his colleagues at WRFK-FM who never told Fred Stair how many days they had to do Swann's work as well as their own.

I would like to express my deep gratitude to T George Harris. He is widely acknowledged as one of the premier investigative reporters and editors of this country, but few persons have had the opportunity to learn that he is also a great teacher. My gratitude for his interest and counsel on this project from its onset is enormous. More than a dozen years ago, when I was beginning to try to translate sociological jargon into understandable English prose, Harris taught me one of the most important things anyone can know—clarity in communication is requisite to clarity of thought.

I also owe a tremendous debt to Dr. Ralph Ingersoll, associate dean, Baylor College of Medicine in Houston. Ingersoll invited me to spend my sabbatical year at Baylor to finish a book manuscript on medical students and to explore a variety of research possibilities. The idea of studying the electronic church had emerged only a few weeks before my arrival in Texas. When it became apparent that that project was seriously interfering with the medical research possibilities, Ingersoll was more than tolerant of the bind I had worked myself into. He not only encouraged me to turn my full attention to the electronic church project; he provided support for the research as well. So also did I receive support and encouragement from Associate Dean David Mumford.

Upon my return to the University of Virginia, my department chairperson, Jeanne Biggar, provided verbal support for completion of the manuscript as well as tolerance and understanding of my tardiness and neglect of department duties.

Few manuscripts come to fruition without clerical support. In addition to preparation of the manuscript, many hours of interviews had to be transcribed. We express our sincere appreciation to Ruth Malouin, Joycelyn Smith, and Jackie Russell for putting up with both the tedium of the clerical work and, occasionally, a grumpy boss as well. Thanks also to Kate Bonan, an undergraduate at the University of Virginia, for clerical assistance in analyzing the audience data.

Finally, we would like to thank our editors, Doe Coover and Barbara Wood. We hope our occasional pigheadedness had a net positive effect on the substance of the manuscript. We have no doubts that their occasional insistence on doing things their way contributed immeasurably to its clarity.

Jeffrey K. Hadden

Introduction:
Spiritual Terror
in the
Ecstatic Eighties

In *The Lady's Not for Burning,* Judge Tappercoom glared out at a religious riot and fretted over the intrusion of spiritual terrorists and witch burners into the prudent business of the practical world. "Religion has made an honest woman out of the super-natural," he huffed, and did not want her out in the street again.

Religious institutions in our day—the standard-brand temples and churches—do seem like the most honest of women, even antiseptic, like a public health nurse, there to inoculate the children against today's epidemics of spiritual turmoil: against Moonie-style cults, Jesus freaks, meditation movements and body mystics, invading squads of Indian gurus, humanistic psychologists chanting uplift slogans without benefit of collar, est-like seminarians in secular disguise, crusading national organizations of fundamentalists, proud witches and trembling exorcists, tribal shamans and extraordinary believers in Gurdjieff, charismatics speaking in tongues in thousands of Catholic prayer groups, hands-on healers in rich Episcopal parishes, Rosicrucians and out-of-body tourists, dream cultists and psychics of all flavors, and hard-sell evangelists raising millions in cash on TV while claiming decisive power through personal prayer and national politics.

Today's Sunday school boom—Catholic, Jewish and Protestant—owes much of its success in numbers to nervous parents. Millions herd their reluctant young off to church for an occasional hypodermic of traditional serum (presumably a killed virus) to protect them from infection by one of the more virulent strains of spiritual plague.

Such parental worry is understandable. Since parents have raised the kids in a germ-free environment, wherein spiritual fervor is rarer than scarlet fever, the entire population seems to lack immune defenses against just about any religious germ that happens to pop up. And as parents we are seldom prepared to discriminate among the various forms of live spirit so as to reject one and feed the other. One Harvard professor who was a disciple of a ribald black healer felt acute distress when his youngest daughter married into a Jesus sect.

Prudent persons in charge of the establishment in any era have tended to fear sudden change in the routine mixing of religion with the politics of everyday life. They sense, like Judge Tappercoom, that great writhings of the spirit, if allowed to break out of their confining institutions, soon wreak havoc upon the social order. It's been so long since we watched religious fires bend our country's structures that we have only a vague memory of how it happens, but the memory makes us uneasy. As T. S. Eliot reminded us in *Notes Toward a Definition of Culture,* political and economic institutions are but the surface expression of a culture's spiritual base. Religion defines culture, and religious change redefines everything in sight. So the shifting of the spiritual base, either by slow decay or by sudden upheaval, shuffles all the surface structures; spiritual turmoil soon builds up like the early shock waves of an earthquake.

And each new shock hits us without warning. There's nobody much to watch over religion's violent landscape—except those who are trying to sell us some particular piece of it. Our intellectuals are out to lunch. Blinded by the fads of twentieth-century thought, writers and talkers in the universities and in the media are mostly spiritual innocents, as unaware of religion's danger as of its hope. The national data are clear: the University of Chicago's National Opinion Research Center (NORC) has found through opinion polling that our paid brains, more than any other group, are buried in dogmatic materialism. Most suffer from an educated ignorance about religious ferment. So the biggest story of our time gets the poorest coverage.

Chicken Little Panic, Then Silence

Our highly secular academics and journalists tend to flock together and run, now and then, to cover a single spiritual story. When some religious activity at last forces itself upon media leaders, they tend to flock like Chicken Littles in panic over a single raindrop . . . the sky is falling! The authors of this book recount such a cackling in the last months of the 1980 presidential campaign. Having rushed out to scream that fundamentalists were backing Ronald Reagan's bid, months after the main story had been clear, most major-media journalists then ignored the story after the votes were counted, having never scratched below the surface of TV evangelism's giant social movement.

The pale secularists of the press simply have failed to deal with the vivid new spiritualism. And I have to confess my own share of such failures in forty years as a working reporter and editor in national media. My sins of omission are uncommonly serious, since I could often see the fire but generally could not figure out how to explain it clearly enough to sound an effective call or alarm. Indeed, a few of my personal failures serve as a partial checklist on the rising religious turmoil since World War II. Samples:

•Having covered most southern and northern race riots, I somehow failed to explain the profound church involvement (especially from Little Rock onward) clearly enough for us to expect that inevitable confrontation at Selma. There, fired-up white and black ministers risked death to march against Alabama's segregation machinery.

•Black friends more or less forced me to visit Chicago's Elijah Muhammad in the 1950s and to recognize the unique promise of Malcolm X (before the autobiography). But my secular blinders almost made me miss doing the first national report on the Black Muslim sect just when it was becoming the critical new force in American ghettos.

•Theologian Paul Tillich's *End of the Protestant Era,* plus his direct admonitions to me, alerted me to the prospect of "post-existential'' agonies like the rise of the radical right and the violence on college campuses. He spent our last talk just before his death comparing notes with me on the early stages of such movements. Although Tillich's religious analysis drove me to do the first national exposé on the John Birch Society, I was far slower than I should have been to see us heading into the generational riots over fundamental values at Berkeley . . . Columbia . . . Kent State . . . The spiritual crises that flamed up in those struggles have yet to be resolved in years of apparent peace.

•By the mid-1960s, fundamentalist leaders like Billy Graham and Gabe Payne and born-again writers like Keith Miller (author of *The Becomers* and of *Please Love Me*) had shown me the struggles ahead. The Christian right would be far more powerful than the Christian left had been. I did warn in a 1965 article that prudent Americans might yet know "why the prudent Romans fed their lions on Christian meat." But my conviction that religious movements would forge the new political majorities did not lead me to spell out the specifics in time to help anyone understand the situation any better.

•In my long, happy years as the editor of *Psychology Today* magazine, I tracked down and published dozens of systematic probes and surveys that defined a historic shift in U.S. values and beliefs. Theologian Sam Keen helped the editorial staff to patrol the cutting edges of this transformation through the work of seminal thinkers—from mythologist Joseph Campbell to mystic Carlos Castaneda, from the stern Rollo May to the despairing Ernst Becker, from porpoise admirer John Lilly to body mystic Mike Murphy. Researchers helped us trace the new realities. The University of California's sociologists of religion helped us measure the broad shift toward body mysticism, what I called a sense of "God in the gut." Dr. George Gallup helped us identify the mystical beliefs rising inside the standard denominations. Father Andrew Greeley, priest-sociologist at NORC, startled me with his data on the broad public belief in mystical powers: 58 percent of American adults say they've experienced ESP, 27 percent say they've talked with one or more dead friends, and 6 percent have undergone profound mystical encounters very much like St. Paul's blinded fall on the road to Damascus. Some unseen power now unseats our rationalistic certainties. Daniel Yankelovich, soon to publish his most perceptive study of our changing values, has led me through year after year of carefully measured evolution toward today's religious upheaval. Precise as ever, Dan finds about one out of three people rebelling against the cold "instrumental" values that obscure the sacred worth of the whole man or woman.

The Flaming Context of Televangelism

Such data leave no excuse for anyone to doubt that we are well into a religious storm of considerable magnitude. The crude, bold revivalists who invade our homes through the tube are but one indicator of the larger phenomenon. We in the media, however, tend to be like park rangers who report specific blazes in our local field of vision. We do not put various reports together to tell us that the forest is burning. In my case, an unholy fear of standing alone and being misunderstood or laughed at has made me cautious about trying to spell out the general evidence of total religious turmoil. When I try to describe the new decade as the Ecstatic Eighties, I still cannot ignore the fear and trembling that come with knowing that mystical terrors are moving under the surface of everyday events.

My purpose here is to suggest that you read this book on television evangelists with a conscious sense of the broader religious struggle. The stakes are high. If we are headed into a New Reformation, as some theologians argue, it may have a reformation's customary quota of bloody civil strife and of holy wars against fundamentalists of other faiths. That warning does sound shrill, I know, but it only points to obvious potentials. Anita Bryant's war on Florida homosexuals gave the country a foretaste of how savage a political skirmish can get when one side crusades against the personal sins of the other. On the world stage, the Shiite fundamentalists who played ayatollah tricks on fifty-two helpless hostages may have lit the fuse for nuclear war in the hearts of Christian true believers. To ignore such possibilities implicit in religious ferment would be irresponsible.

Such concerns leave no room for the cheap partisanism that has tended to rule both sides of the fight over the "electronic church." Especially during the 1980 presidential campaign, it has been hard to find honest and serious information about the prime-time preachers and their followers. But the authors of this book have a different ax to grind: their emotion, like their wit, arises from scholarly passion, not from partisan politics or church schism. So stop reading now if you are hunting for somebody to confirm your prejudice against the Reverend Jerry Falwell, or on the other hand to help you make a slick case for Moral Majority.

Both authors have been deeply involved in this crisis for many years, one as a top sociologist of religion and the other as a leading Christian communicator and Ph.D. researcher in communications. Dr. Charles E. Swann is a former president and a director of American Protestantism's professional broadcasters (the North American Broadcasting Section of the World Association for Christian Communication). He has also served as an officer of American Catholicism's broadcasting association, *Unda*-USA. An ordained Presbyterian minister and a Doctor of Sacred Theology, Dr. Swann now manages WRFK-FM, the fine-arts radio station in Richmond owned by Virginia Theological Seminary. He has fought for serious research in religious communication and been known as an internal critic of mainline church broadcasting.

Dr. Jeffrey K. Hadden earned his Ph.D. in the sociology of religion from the University of Wisconsin and is now professor of sociology at the University of Virginia as well as former president of the Association for the Sociology of Religion. To Jeff, the biblical admonition to speak the truth with love translates into the passionate objectivity of the dedicated sociologist. So does his need to spot underlying trends that escape the quick-study reporter. Now forty-four, Jeff has devoted his professional life to rigorous research on the belief and behavior of religious groups. By 1968, when I first persuaded him to work with me on a nationwide survey of changing student values, he was just completing one of his six major books, *The Gathering Storm in the Churches*. It was a prophetic analysis of exactly how the civil rights struggle was leaving liberal clergymen morally isolated from the laity. Jeff's knowledge of the literature on religion let us go directly into the hidden beliefs of the protest generation, and one discovery eventually led us both to the underlying theme of this book.

Narcissism or the Heroic Self

While Dr. Hadden and I were probing student beliefs, Harvard's David Riesman talked to me about his concept of "privatization." As author of the noted book *The Lonely Crowd* and of *Individualism Reconsidered,* Riesman worried about lonely individuals who rely less and less on social institutions yet expect more and more of themselves. Such "privatization," as he called it in an interview for *Psychology Today,* exposes the private man or woman to more of a burden than one soul can stand without wobbling.

In the years since then, as you know, major national studies show a strong trend toward still more lonely individualism. Americans are losing faith in corporations, government, schools, churches, medicine, political parties, the press, marriage, parenthood—all the traditional institutions. But while giving up faith in institutions, studies show, they continue to demand more and more of themselves in terms of both achievement and that new obsession with self-fulfillment.

In marriage, for instance, a woman now expects herself to be an accomplished bedmate, an intellectual equal, a wise and loving mother, perhaps a fellow jogger and tennis partner and smart tourist, one who continues to grow, a community organizer and co-host, often a co-professional, and almost always a fellow breadwinner. We expect similar miracles from ourselves at work; aside from earning the highest pay ever known, we expect to be sensitive to co-workers, enlarge our education, make a social contribution, and do very little damage to the environment. The average education of the active worker is now that of a college freshman after Christmas, and still going up.

Social critics have tended to look upon such activities as indicators of rampant selfishness. Tom Wolfe's famous essay on "The Me Decade" and Christopher Lasch's book *The Culture of Narcissism* warned of a hard trend toward such primal selfishness. But there's less selfishness than loneliness in the American psyche today, along with the feeling of being called upon to do heroic things without warm support from good old reliables like the Democratic party, the Catholic Church, or Good Mother Company. The organizational man who lived and died inside

Good Mother has been replaced by the lonely "mobicentric" who jumps fast from job to job, company to company, and city to city in his or her mobility-centered rush to achievement and fulfillment.

It's as if some idiot had raised the ante on what it takes to be a normal human being. Without noticing the overnight change, most of us strive for the new norm. Sexual behavior provides a sensitive indicator of this revolution in nonmaterial expectations. The true sexual revolution has come, not among the public swingers, but in the privacy of the family bedroom. Princeton studies show that American wives make love to their husbands 21 percent more often than they did five years earlier. Yet many feel that they are doing less than their share, not because they feel deprived but because they fear that they are not living up to the norm. As the country expression puts it, Americans by the million feel sent for and can't get there.

The lonely striver comes to feel that the only resource he or she has to develop in this life is the body and mind, that collection of tissue and talent that's often strained to the limit. It's no accident that jogging has become a national obsession—in what Gallup calls the sharpest behavior reversal he has ever studied—or that the drive for health and physical well-being stays at the top of the rising-demand list identified year after year in the Yankelovich monitor of changing values. Nor is it strange, in a nation turned inward to demand heroic effort from the self rather than outward toward reliance on institutions, that today's mystical surge should focus upon the possible interior powers of the God-given body/ mind and especially upon healing. As life comes to feel more and more like that supreme test of self, the marathon run, our national behavior moves further into the "privatization" trend.

Television becomes the inevitable tool for the lonely striver's worship. Just as media campaigns have taken over from the political party, so the prime-time preachers in their powder-blue suits and cocky smiles have stepped proudly up to deliver the church's sermons. They are smart and tough. Ever more sophisticated in their use of the computer as well as of television—the paired technology that raises millions by its combination of exciting programs and direct mail—the preachers have now gained an earthy new sense of power through their Reagan victory. Their audiences are far smaller and more regionally confined, in the South and Southwest, than they care to admit, and their chief targets are still among the elderly, who spend longer hours in front of the tube.

But the research laid out clearly in this work by Dr. Hadden and Dr. Swann points more to the future than to the past. Man proposes; God disposes. But whatever turns our spiritual turmoil takes in the Ecstatic Eighties, these celebrity preachers will be a national force to reckon with for years to come.

T George Harris

The Gathering Electronic Storm

My morning at the Electric Church had been painless and pleasant. The preachers had been prepared, the musicians polished, the order of service precisely timed. And best of all, I had completely avoided any direct involvement with other Christians and those troublesome problems they always seem to have.
William C. Martin, *Texas Monthly*

Martha Bell Childers and Alpha E. Humbard were itinerant preachers who chose each other as life partners while attending a preaching convention in Eureka Springs, Arkansas. Often, in their travels to save souls for the Lord, they worked out of an old ragged tent. When their firstborn was just a lad, he slipped away from the gospel tent compound to watch the raising of the Ringling Brothers' circus "Big Top." As he watched, he clutched his fist and indignantly said to himself, "If God had a tent like that, He'd have a crowd like that."

Rex Humbard has always been a take-charge kind of fellow. From his teens he managed the Humbard gospel enterprises. He initially resisted Dad Humbard's efforts to get him to play a musical instrument, but when the spirit moved, so did Rex. He learned to play guitar in record time and marched down to radio station KTHS in Little Rock, Arkansas, to get the Humbard family group on the air. A few weeks later they were playing on the WLS "Barn Dance" in Chicago for $100 a week.

It took a few years, but Rex got that "Gospel Big Top" for the Lord, a gigantic tent with a seating capacity of 6,000. The Humbards had no trouble filling it, but it wasn't very long after its acquisition that Rex began to envision an even greater challenge to spread the Good News. It happened one balmy summer night in 1952 in Akron, Ohio. Rex spotted a crowd in front of O'Neil's Department Store, close to where the "Gospel Big Top" had been erected. As he worked his way into the crowd, he realized what the source of the crowd's rapture was—a marvelous new gadget called a television set. The crowd was watching a baseball game.

Rex knew it wouldn't be easy. He had struggled through the ups and downs of the radio ministry. But what a wonderful invention this television was. He knew his mission immediately. With the far-reaching capabilities of this new technology, God's word could be spread around the world. Rex knew he would have to stay in Akron, build a church, and go on television.

Fast talk, dogged persistence, and $65 got him a movie theater where he could start a church and a television program. Today, Rex Humbard has come closer than any other human being in history, save perhaps Billy Graham, to preaching the gospel to all the world. His syndicated radio and television programs are broadcast on a total of 650 stations in eighteen countries and are translated into seven languages. His Cathedral of Tomorrow is the only church ever designed especially for television productions. It boasts a hydraulic stage, three audio recording studios, two control rooms, two editing suites, tape duplication facilities, and a video recording studio. Overhead hangs a 50-by-100-foot cross studded with 5,000 red, white, and blue light bulbs that can produce an almost infinite array of lighting effects.

From its modest $65 beginning, the Rex Humbard Ministry is now worth millions. And it is all paid for by private contributions. Still, like those of many of his fellow television colleagues, Rex's ministry appears ever on the brink of bankruptcy. On his April 13, 1980, broadcast he made an impassioned plea for immediate cash contributions needed to stave off disaster. The program was $2.5 million behind in its obligations, and Humbard was running an average of four months behind in payments to stations for TV time.

Humbard's appeals brought in $4 million and wiped out the debt. About the same time, a *Cleveland Press* writer discovered that Rex and two of his sons, who work with him on the television ministry, had purchased a home and condominiums in Florida valued at $650,000 with down payments of $177,500 in cash. A lot of people have long believed that preachers, especially the evangelical variety, have their hands in the offering plate. In light of this belief, the timing of Humbard's corporate debt and personal investment certainly didn't make him look very good. And he didn't help his own cause any when he told the prying *Press* reporter, "My people don't give a hoot what I spend that money for."

He later said that what he meant was that his people don't care how he spends his *own* money, but that's not the way it came across. The wire services and network television quoted old Rex as saying plainly and simply, "My people don't give a hoot what I spend that money for." The implication was that the dollars he had so recently solicited to pay off corporate debts had been used to provide second homes for him and his family in Florida.

It's quite possible that a lot of Rex's loyal followers wouldn't have cared a whole lot if he was dipping into the collection plate just a mite. He and Maud Aimee and the kids and grandkids have brought a lot of happiness into people's lives over the years, and with Maude Aimee being sick now and all, the Humbards ought to be entitled to a few little comforts.

Perhaps Rex's supporters really don't care what he does. But many observers of the American religious scene—from the left and the right—care passionately about what is currently happening in religious broadcasting. It is a social phenomenon so widespread and important that it has acquired a name—the electronic church.

Although religious broadcasting is as old as broadcasting itself, until 1978 most Americans were only vaguely aware of its existence. Of course they knew that there were preachers on radio and television. But since only a fraction of the American population *regularly* hears or views these programs, they received little public notice. Only an occasional scandal or financial problem caused TV religion to be mentioned in the secular media.

Beginning in 1978, however, several mainline Protestant leaders began attacking the electronic church. By early 1979 secular magazine, newspaper, and television reporters were beginning to hear the mainliners and to take an interest in what they were saying. By early 1980 the outpouring of critical commentary on the electronic church had reached flood proportions. It was the critics, thus, and not the religious broadcasters themselves who were responsible for bringing the phenomenon to the attention of a broad spectrum of American society.

Perhaps nothing focused as much attention on the cathode church, however—or drew as much fire from its critics—as the involvement of some of its stars in the political events of 1980. In late 1979 several of them had begun meeting quietly with the prospective presidential candidates. There were perhaps a dozen meetings in all with various members of the electronic church in attendance. As the primaries began and the list of presidential hopefuls shrank, so also did the list of televangelists who were willing to go out on a limb and declare a political agenda. Most who were initially involved fell back to the nonpartisan position that it is a Christian's duty to be an informed and involved citizen—though that in itself was more political than most evangelicals and fundamentalists had previously been. But the few who remained actively political were also highly visible— and the media attention they got made them even more so.

The first evidence of political thunder from evangelical Christians occurred late in April 1980, when about 200,000 of them went to Washington, D.C., for two days of prayer and repentance. Pat Robertson, head of the Christian Broadcasting Network, and Bill Bright, founder of Campus Crusade for Christ, cochaired the Washington for Jesus program. They spent a lot of time trying to persuade a skeptical press corps that the event wasn't political, but several factors made it difficult for these otherwise effective communicators to do so. A highly partisan document called "A Christian Declaration" was rather widely circulated, though it was withdrawn before it became an official statement of purpose of Washington for Jesus. Someone who identified himself as a congressional liaison for the rally sent a letter to all members of Congress which invited them to contact Washington for Jesus to learn how they should vote on a variety of issues. And the rally's leaders had organized the gathering by congressional districts so that people could be better prepared to call on their elected representatives in government. Disclaimers of political intent notwithstanding, there was sufficient appearance of politics to result in a threat by a ranking U.S. senator to investigate the tax-exempt status of the ministries of the program's leadership.

Media consciousness of the involvement of conservative Christians in politics increased severalfold when Jerry Falwell, another TV evangelist, and his Moral Majority showed up in force at the Republican National Convention in Detroit. When some electronic preachers participated in the National Affairs Briefing in Dallas a few weeks later, the media showed up in force—more than 250 strong—and an additional hundred or so members of the press corps arrived with Ronald Reagan when he addressed a screaming crowd of 15,000 at the Briefing on August 22.

Within a matter of days hardly anyone in the media, print or broadcast, didn't know that there was a New Christian Right and that it was moving into politics in force. And the media proceeded to inform the rest of the country, zeroing in on Falwell and the Moral Majority. He appeared on the cover of *Newsweek* and quickly became one of the most sought-after figures in the 1980 campaign. His many guest appearances on television included "Meet the Press," "Today," and "Donahue." He also addressed the National Press Club. When he wasn't present, he was often the subject of conversation—and controversy.

By the time the elections rolled around, the corralling of 1600 Pennsylvania Avenue by a onetime cowboy movie actor wasn't totally unexpected. Ronald Reagan, though long associated with the right wing of the Republican party, was not considered a sufficient threat to excuse the liabilities the Carter administration had amassed. What was not expected on that first Tuesday of November, however, was the virtual annihilation of the liberal leadership of the Congress that was running for reelection. Millions of liberal Americans felt their hearts drop to the pits of their stomachs as they watched the election returns. One by one the liberal senators went down to defeat—Frank Church, Birch Bayh, John Culver, George McGovern, Warren Magnuson, and Gaylord Nelson—all replaced by persons of much more conservative persuasion.

Some analysts saw this housecleaning as a reaction to the incompetence and misfortunes of the Carter administration.

Others saw it as a continuation of a national drift to the right. But what happened was an avalanche, not a drift. And Jerry Falwell, whose name by then had become practically a household word, wasted no time in stepping forward to claim responsibility for the political shift in the name of his Moral Majority and other New Christian Right organizations. Pollster Louis Harris agreed with Falwell's assessment. So did several of the defeated senators and congressmen. It seemed—and the media played up the idea—that the televangelists had created a force to be reckoned with.

What was lost in the furor, however, was the identity of the participants. A myth that emerged from the 1980 campaign was that the New Right and the New Christian Right were one and the same. There is some overlap in their respective rosters, to be sure; but they are distinct. Furthermore, it is not specifically the televangelists' political influence that is significant, but rather, in a broader sense, their power to mobilize masses of everyday Christians. They represent a nascent social movement that has the potential to reshape American culture. Astutely managed, that power will not be easily checked. What the campaign of 1980 actually demonstrated was that this potential is real.

From a long tradition of circuit riders, tent preachers, and Elmer Gantry—like revivalists, the evangelists—now the televangelists—have come a long way. No longer are they simply safeguarding the moral and spiritual character of their private constituencies. No longer are they satisfied with Sister Lou or Brother Jim finding the Lord and being born again. For although salvation is still their goal, the sinner is not you and me anymore; it's America. And saving a nation takes a lot of believers, a lot of money, and a lot of power.

Ben Armstrong, who heads the powerful National Religious Broadcasters, thinks that what he prefers to call the electric church ". . . has launched a revolution as dramatic as the revolution that began when Martin Luther nailed his Ninety-five Theses to the cathedral at Wittenberg." Armstrong's views of the electronic church are wholly and uncritically positive. He foresees that it will result in sweeping changes in how people worship and how they understand their relationship to God. To him television is a miraculous instrument of God which now makes possible the fulfillment of the great commandment to preach the gospel to all the world.

Mainline Protestant and Catholic groups are far less enamored of the religious broadcasting of evangelical and fundamentalist Christians. For openers, the great expansion of paid religious broadcasting all but drove the mainliners, who relied on free time from local stations for their programs, off the air. Add to this the fact that they profoundly disagree with what they consider to be the fundamentalists' simplistic theological messages. The main rub, however, is a growing concern that their own constituencies are deciding to take their religion in the comfort of their living rooms and that they may be sending their offerings to the television preachers instead of dropping them into the local collection plate. When a few TV preachers turned to politics in 1980—a uniformly conservative politics—more fuel was added to an already explosive situation.

In February 1980 a group of about 200 communications specialists from the mainline Protestant and Catholic churches gathered in New York to consider some of the vexing issues raised by the electronic church. Robert Liebert, a psychologist and one of the major speakers at the gathering, told them that the conflict over the electronic church "has every hallmark of an intensifying war of survival among battling Christian groups." He continued: "The forces are gathering ominously, and not even a remote basis for reconciliation is in sight. . . . Today's war is not just another recurring phenomenon. New technology, and particularly communication electronics, has brought an advantage of enormous magnitude for the conservative, fundamentalist side of Christendom's oldest battle."

That's pretty strong language, but the events that unfolded in the year following his presentation seemed to give a great deal of credibility to his assessment. There are others who see the effects of the TV preachers as much broader and more important than a struggle among the major religious groups in America. Writing well before anyone was paying much attention to the television preachers, Jeremy Rifkin stated that there was little doubt but that *"the evangelical community is amassing a base of potential power that dwarfs every other competing interest in American society today''* (emphasis added). How? Through its electronic communications network.

The big-time TV preachers are the generals of this new power base. They are flanked by scores of lieutenants who lead more than sixty syndicated television programs. And more programs are being readied for syndication, to be sent by satellite to cable systems over the Christian Broadcasting Network (CBN), PTL Broadcasting Network, and Trinity Broadcasting Network. But this is only the tip of a vast communications network. More than 300 radio stations broadcast religion full-time. Hundreds more—perhaps thousands—sell many hours of time each week to religious time buyers. There are thirty-six television stations with full-time religious schedules, some of which broadcast twenty-four hours a day. Hundreds of commercial TV stations are completely sold out on Sunday morning—or any other time they are willing to sell to religious telecasters. Sunday evening is fast becoming as lucrative as the morning for those willing to sell to the religious syndicators. There is virtually no home in the United States into which the electronic church cannot send its songs, sermons, and appeals in generous measure. Merely to contemplate its potential power is staggering.

There is no doubt that the electronic church has brought to millions of Americans a new way of experiencing religion. In fundamental ways, the electronic religious experience is affecting the manner in which those same millions view and understand the world they live in. Yet there is nothing very new about religious broadcasting. In fact, the first wireless voice broadcast ever sent out to the world was an informal Christian religious program. From Brant Rock, Massachusetts, on Christmas Eve, 1906, Reginald Fessenden, a Canadian scientist working in the United States, broadcast a program to ships at sea. A. F. Harlow describes the event in *Old Wires and New Waves:* ''Early that evening wireless operators on ships within a radius of several hundred miles sprang to attention as they caught the call 'CQ CQ' in the Morse code. Was it a ship in distress? They listened eagerly, and to their amazement, heard a voice coming from their instruments—someone speaking! Then a woman's voice rose in song. It was uncanny! Many of them called to their officers to come and listen; soon the wireless rooms were crowded. Next someone was heard reading a poem. Then there was a violin solo; then a man made a speech and they could catch most of the words. Finally, everyone who had heard the program was asked to write R. A. Fessenden at Brant Rock, Massachusetts—and many of the operators did. Thus was the first radio broadcast in history put on.'' According to Fessenden's wife, Helen, Fessenden himself played the violin solo, Gounod's ''O Holy Night,'' and read the Nativity passage from the Gospel of Luke. The ''woman singing'' was a phonograph recording of Handel's ''Largo.''

Only two months elapsed after regularly scheduled radio programming began in late 1920 at station KDKA in Pittsburgh before there was a regularly scheduled religious service. Radio exploded in America in the 1920s; within five years there were more than 600 stations, most of which engaged in some form of religious broadcasting.

The second generation of electronic communication emerged during the late 1940s when television was developed. By 1960, nine of every ten households in the United States possessed at least one TV set. Religious telecasting was available almost from the beginning of this marvelous new medium. Its first superstar was Fulton Sheen, the Catholic bishop with a twinkle in his eye, an impeccable delivery—and an angel to clean his chalkboard.

Since only limited air time existed, mainline Protestants and Catholics cooperated with Jews and Southern Baptists in sharing the scarce resource of free network time. But a few evangelical-fundamentalist preachers saw greater possibilities in television and proceeded to buy their way onto the air on local stations.

Rex Humbard wasn't the only evangelical to sense the potential that television offered for preaching God's message. Shortly after Humbard's epiphany in front of O'Neil's Department Store, a young preacher named Oral Roberts brought cameras into his revival tent. Jerry Falwell, who eventually would become another giant of the electronic church, began his ministry in 1956 at the age of twenty-two in an abandoned soft-drink bottling plant. One week after organizing a congregation of thirty-five, he started a weekly radio broadcast. Within a year he was telecasting live from Lynchburg, Virginia. Pat Robertson, son of a U.S. senator from Virginia, filed a charter for the Christian Broadcasting

Network in January 1960 and opened a bank account with a deposit of $3. Today the CBN telecasts religious programming twenty-four hours a day.

At the time they began, each of the television ministers seemed to have a good bit more faith and courage than wisdom or cash. But each of them also believed that the invention of television made available a wonderful new way to spread the Good News of God. Their adventures on the road to TV success read like the "Perils of Pauline"—each, again and again, was rescued from the brink of seemingly certain disaster. The biographies of most of the stars of the electronic church would sound like Horatio Alger novels. To them, the elements of pluck and luck that characterized Alger's heroes have been simply God's interventions in their lives and careers.

Rex Humbard preaches from a church tailored to the requirements of television. "The 700 Club" talk show is produced in studios that are the envy of commercial networks. Robert Schuller's Crystal Cathedral is a soaring, stunning monument in glass and a perfect showcase for one of America's most flamboyant preachers. The parade of guest stars across the stages of some of these shows might make a viewer forget that they are religious programs—except for what is being said. So successfully has the electronic church adapted to television that it reflects secular television's diversity of programming.

Marshall McLuhan once stated that the children of the television age realize intuitively that the classroom is an interruption of their education. Church pastors today are having to face the fact that electronic religion is changing the way millions experience worship, even in church. Even if their people do not stay home to watch the television preachers, the electronic church has altered the expectations both of the role of the preacher and of the content of religious services.

One preacher who has learned the importance of television is Wayne Dehoney, pastor of the Walnut Street Baptist Church in Louisville, Kentucky, and former president of the Southern Baptist Convention. Dehoney has been telecasting his Sunday morning worship services for twenty years, and his telecast is generally acknowledged among Southern Baptists to be one of the very best nonsyndicated programs. He had been on TV for more than seven years before he ever saw a videotape of one of his services. He described his reactions to this viewing to fellow pastors at the Sixth Annual Workshop of the Southern Baptist Radio and Television Commission: "It was the deadest thing I ever saw. . . . It really shook me up. I discovered how slow-moving our church service was. When it's all video, you've got ten seconds with nothing happening, fifteen seconds with nothing happening. Somebody is just taking their time walking up the steps . . . to sing, and picking up the microphone and nodding to the pianist to start, and then turning away for a twenty-second prelude on this tinny piano. It was the slowest-moving thing I ever saw. . . ." Dehoney went on to describe colorfully every dreary detail: the ushers who strutted down the aisle like little generals to take up the offering; the deacon who prayed for three minutes while the camera focused on the top of his bald head; the people in the choir immediately behind the preacher who became restless and scratched their faces and picked their ears. And, of course, that brilliant sermon laced with mental gymnastics that were, Dehoney confessed, of more interest to him than to anyone else.

Dehoney reasoned further that what was dull on the cathode tube was probably dull for those sitting in the pews as well. He discovered that as he took measures to make the telecast more dynamic, the worship service also came alive.

Still, the successful broadcasters face criticism for being too slick, too secular. If television is to be used to communicate the gospel, however, the televangelists believe it needs to be done right. Mike Nason, executive producer of Robert Schuller's "Hour of Power," takes strong exception to those who "feel that low budgets and amateur programming reflect humility as 'Jesus would want.' Christ must be presented in a *first-class* manner."

That point of view is virtually universal among the most successful talents. Most are professionals by the highest standards of the business. They're proud of their studios, their equipment, and their personnel. CBN, sometimes called the Video Vatican of Christian broadcasting, claims to have the best equipment and studios in the world, and the network takes great pride in the fact that television producers from all over come to inspect its facilities—if not to respect its messages.

The electronic churches have imitated the successes of commercial television, the talk-show format being the most successful clone to date; all three Christian networks (CBN, PTL, and Trinity) use it as the cornerstone of their broadcasting. At one point the format of "The 700 Club," flagship show of the CBN, matched "The Tonight Show" of Johnny Carson in almost every detail—band, desk-and-sofa set, sidekick, and appreciative audience. One might even find Hollywood stars as guests, but only those who are born again or Spirit-filled need have their agents book an appearance. Instead of sharing show-biz gossip, guests swap miracles and personal testimonies.

More recently, Pat Robertson of the CBN has smelled the success of the television magazine format and in late 1980 began to move "The 700 Club" in that direction. But other commercial successes are being imitated, or plans are being made to do so. Christian news and game shows already exist, and CBN is developing a Christian soap opera. It takes a lot of money to make a network competitive with the big three, but the Christian three are working on it. With a little help from God and their viewing audiences, it just might happen.

In addition, they are working on the production of Christian communicators. CBN University now has a School of Communications and soon will be exporting graduates who will contribute to the professionalization and proliferation of religious broadcasting. More important, CBN University hopes to produce a graduate who is qualified to compete in the secular communications world, thus broadening the Christian influence in our culture. Broadcasting skills are also being taught at Jim Bakker's Heritage School of Evangelism and Communications, at Jerry Falwell's Liberty Baptist College, and at Oral Roberts University.

But what are the messages of the electronic churches? Here too they have imitated the success formulas of commercial television. Most religious television, like its secular counterpart, deals largely in simple solutions to human problems. Television can't handle complicated material very well. Unless one can afford the luxury of time and money for imaginative illustration, one is limited to what can be *said*. And what is said must be said quickly and extremely simply, or the audience won't understand. Furthermore, audiences also want to be entertained. And they want to be made to feel good. When they are made to feel bad, they turn to another channel. The televangelists preach a message that is supportive of the worth of the individual.

Most TV preachers have gone beyond saying that it is all right to think about yourself. Get right with God, they say, and you won't have to wait until the next life for your rewards. You can expect them now. America has become a privatistic society. Whether this is good or to our ultimate detriment, religion has not escaped the growth of the cult of personhood. Rather, it has developed its own modes of expression. And the television preachers are helping to shape this private religion.

Both motivation theory and the pragmatism born of experience in religious broadcasting dictate that the greatest promise of benefit elicits the greatest response. *Entrepreneurial religious broadcasting cannot survive without audience response that can be converted into contributions.* TV preachers may begin with the simplest and sincerest of motives, but they are inevitably confronted with the budget demands of producing programs, building colleges or cathedrals, and paying for the escalating costs of broadcast time.

The means to generate this income already rests in the televangelists' hands, for if television made the electronic church possible, the computer has made it profitable. With the ability to target direct mail, to poll its constituency, and to put out reams of advertising and public relations copy, the electronic church now has the tools to generate both members and dollars. The computer can acquire, sort, store, and retrieve increasing amounts of information about people on mailing lists with ever accelerating speed and sharply declining unit cost.

Targeting direct mail to viewing audiences is grounded in very sophisticated communications technology. Already it has elevated the electronic churches from an esoteric offering of the television smorgasbord to a powerful force in American culture—this, even though their audience size remains small compared with that of secular prime-time shows. Already the electronic church has blurred traditional notions that television is a one-way communications medium. In the future, the line between personal and parapersonal communication may be virtually abolished as computers develop the capacity to respond with competence and empathy to a greater array of human needs.

Did the televangelists use their technology to influence the 1980 elections? Many chose to believe so, and the shock of the election results and their attribution to Christian zealots set in motion a chain reaction of fear that has not been experienced in the United States in some time. The American Civil Liberties Union sent an urgent appeal to its membership to fight. Everywhere there was a sense that the country was being overrun, not by sensible garden-variety conservatives like Bill Buckley and George Will, but by crazies hell-bent on shoving their brand of Americanism and Christianity down the throats of the rest of the American people.

Christian leaders, both liberal and conservative, took the initiative in speaking out against the born-again politicians. Individual criticism soon became an avalanche of organized attack as large segments of the liberal press and secular organizations jumped on the bandwagon to denounce the New Christian Right. Leaders of fifteen major Protestant denominations, for example, released a statement which they called "Christian Theological Observations on the Religious Right Movement."

In addition to existing organizations that denounced the New Christian Right, new organizations sprang up for the purpose. Norman Lear, creator of "All in the Family" and a lion's share of other successful television sitcoms of the 1970s, hastily assembled a blue-ribbon board of some of the more prominent U.S. liberals in the fields of religion, education, publishing, and entertainment to create People for the American Way. Its stated purpose was to promote religious pluralism, and its first visible effort was a series of television spots that were critical of the televangelists.

Was all this an overreaction? Would the acquisition of real political power by these born-again politicians result in a massive assault on First Amendment rights? Does their view of saving America mean burning books for Jesus, affronting Jews and nonbelievers by restoring Christian prayers in classrooms, and granting the literal biblical story of Creation superior status to the data of science? Does their view of restoring traditional family values mean that a woman's place is in the home? Does "right to life'' mean that women will be forced to have children they don't want—or resort to back-room butchers for abortions? Would the new religious conservatives ban what they call smut from every legal avenue of public acquisition and jail those who get caught publishing or peddling it? Would gays be forced to retreat to the closet or lose every existing opportunity for gainful employment? Would libertine values of all sorts be suppressed? Where would these zealots stop? Where would they draw the line in imposing their values and life-style on the rest of society? Are they really out to establish a theocracy? Would they create a society like Iran's under religious madmen?

Jerry Falwell says the press and the liberal establishment have overreacted and not really heard what he is saying. He claims Moral Majority doesn't want to Christianize the nation. Its members just want their chance—like everybody else—to have their say. He says he believes in religious and cultural pluralism and has no intention of walking on anyone's First Amendment rights. Privately he admits that in his enthusiasm he sometimes overstates his point of view.

We'll have to wait and see whether Jerry Falwell is ''lying through his teeth,'' as one of his more ardent critics puts it, and is deserving of another's protestations that he is ''the most dangerous man in America.'' Some are inclined to think that Falwell's harshest critics have overreacted to his intentions and motivations. But this doesn't alter in the slightest the possibility that in creating Moral Majority he may have reenacted the role of the Sorcerer's Apprentice. The Moral Majority consists of semiautonomous state and local chapters. Whether Falwell is willing and able to control those on the lunatic fringe who will act in the name of Moral Majority remains a question of paramount importance.

There is much restlessness and discontent among U.S. conservatives. Many of them are mobilizable in the name of Christian virtue. Whether their energies will be channeled toward constructive redress of the excesses and mistakes of liberals or toward destructive negation remains to be seen. It is impossible to foresee the ultimate impact of the New Christian Right because the future of this country depends so much on economic, political, and social developments that are only now unfolding.

Some, like our relations with the Soviet Union, are global in character. Others, like our economy and the presence or absence of an energy policy, are national in scope. Other developments are personal in nature, such as whether Jerry Falwell will put his own reputation on the line in defense of the First Amendment in the presence of those who have no regard for the rights of others.

One thing is clear. The televangelists are destined to play a critical role in the shaping of the balance of the twentieth century. They have more undisputed access to the airwaves than any other social movement in American society. Their potential for good should not be overlooked in our current state of apprehension about their sudden presence. They share much in common, but we should not assume they are a monolithic group; their views of society and the public good are not immutable, nor is their theology inerrant. They might just lead to new hopes and possibilities that liberals can only imagine. They might also find themselves disillusioned and frustrated by a system they cannot learn to master.

But neither can this nation afford to take lightly the fears that the sudden bursting of the New Christian Right on the political scene produced. Much of what the televangelists are currently transmitting on the airwaves plays upon the fears and deepest disappointments of Americans. And much of what they advocate is a return to values and life-styles that never were or are inadequate for the complexities of the late twentieth century.

This book is about these televangelists who, even more than they may realize, will play a role in shaping the destiny of us all. Thoughtful Americans, whether they agree or disagree with the messages and agendas of the televangelists, cannot afford to take lightly their impact on American culture. Our task is to help define who these people are, how they got to be so important, to whom they speak, and what will likely be their effect on the future of this country.

The Video Vicarage

*The purpose of every media presentation, whether
television program, newspaper story, training film,
or billboard, is to persuade us to accept as real the
world we see focused through its lens.*
Virginia Stem Owens, *The Total Image,
or Selling Jesus in the Modern Age*

Two or three decades ago, most U.S. Protestant churches held
worship services on Sunday night as well as on Sunday morning,
and many held midweek evening services as well. This pattern
probably was always more pronounced in the southern and
midwestern "Bible Belt" and was strongest among the more
evangelical denominations, where it still survives. But it was
never confined to any geographic area or to evangelical churches.
In fact, the first radio station to broadcast a worship service
picked it up from an Episcopal church in Pittsburgh on a Sunday
night.

Today, few evening services survive in mainline denomination
churches, and their frequency and attendance figures are declining among even the more fervent evangelical sects. Television is
singled out as the principal culprit in the demise of the tradition,
and although it would be impossible to prove this, there is no
question that television has changed American life-styles profoundly. It also has radically changed religious broadcasting.

Those who are old enough to remember when there was no
television will remember that the content of pre-TV radio was a
line-up of soap operas, mysteries, and comedies similar to that
which fills TV today. Despite this similarity of programming,
there are important differences between radio and TV.

Perhaps most obviously, people did not look at radios. They
listened while reading, sewing, working, or looking at each other

and talking about what they were hearing. Radio listening was intergenerational and conducive to community, as family members gathered in one room to listen to the one household radio. Television, on the other hand, destroys community, as each person's eyes *and* ears must remain focused on the box. Even when gathered in the same room (which often isn't the case, because families acquire multiple TV sets to accommodate the tastes of different family members), everyone must line up and face the set.

Just as radio thus required less of its listeners, it imposed no great demands on performers either. Radio was theater of the mind, and listeners created marvelous mental scenes as performers stood around a microphone reading their lines. Similarly, radio religionists were not challenged by the medium to do more than speak into a microphone. The formats of different programs were similar, and the preacher with the best delivery and the most appealing message came out on top in the ratings.

Then came television. No more could the sound-effects artist create a setting in the listeners' minds. No more could the actors merely stand in one place while reading scripts. All the techniques of the movies had to be employed in broadcasting. People could see what they had previously only imagined, and TV producers learned instantly that the "talking head" was the most boring form of television. The screen had to be filled with scenery, actors, motion, and other visually entertaining elements.

Those who wanted to do religious television programs had to come to grips with the nature of the medium. The logic of television is simply that if you want people to watch a program, you must entertain them—visually, aurally, totally. This logic was not lost on television religionists, not even the early ones. David L. Altheide and R. P. Snow tell in their book *Media Logic* of a St. Paul, Minnesota, church called Soul's Harbor that began telecasting its services in the early 1950s: "The minister wore a captain's uniform and preached from a pulpit decorated with nautical artifacts. While the respectable middle class paid little attention, Soul's Harbor became a success. Soon the established denominations were televising their services, but the difference was great. Soul's Harbor adapted to the format of television, whereas the established churches did not. In the established churches there were problems of acoustics, busy color backgrounds that affronted the eyes on black-and-white television, bad camera angles, and the solemn air of the service. In addition, the established churches lacked the single most important ingredient in television—entertainment. In a sense, Soul's Harbor did 'schtick,' and the viewers loved it.''

Today the evangelicals realize full well that they are in hot competition, not only with a lot of secular and a few mainline religious programs (for the formats of all three are strikingly similar), but with each other as well. And they realize that the sophistication and slickness of their productions—in effect, their Hollywood quotient—can determine their success or failure.

Every format of secular television entertainment is being used in the electronic church today, with the possible exception of comedy. Offerings include musical variety shows, news, drama, soap opera, talk shows, and even game shows. Religious programs for children include cartoons, puppet shows, and Christian versions of "Captain Kangaroo."

Chicago viewers, for example, may watch a game show called "Bible Baffle," which features flashing lights, an ebullient host, and excited contestants, just like "The Price Is Right." But on "Bible Baffle" the questions are about the Bible, and the prizes include religious books and vacation weekends at religiously oriented spas. The electronic church has learned that TV writes the rules for its use, and it is following those rules with alacrity.

A few turns of the dial, or a few hours spent watching a religious channel, can bring the viewer religious versions of just about everything in the traditional television gamut. Some are little more than "wallpaper" shows—one taped singing performance after another, interrupted only by a deejay-like host's comments and introductions. Others are full-scale live-audience programs that use all the complexities of video technique to emulate Johnny Carson's format.

As their shows vary, so do the preachers themselves. Their styles of preaching—and entertaining—include everything from the *sotto voce* reassurances of a funeral director to the soft rock of bewigged and bejeweled gospel-singing groups to the hellfire and brimstone of the save-yourself-or-be-damned tearful tirades. Viewers are told how to survive the Second Coming, how to succeed without really trying, and how to be happy without ever crying. One can learn how to get money through giving it, be healed when doctors have failed, and identify the secular, humanistic, ungodly forces that are dragging this nation to destruction. And, not infrequently, an authentic, wholesome godliness shines through.

In the next several pages we present some of the stars (and some who may become stars) of the video vicarage—who they are, where they came from, what their style is like. Their differences are many. Robert Schuller was the son of prosperous midwestern farmers, and Pat Robertson's father was a U.S. senator from Virginia. But many others have strikingly similar backgrounds. Most grew up in the South. Many came from impoverished families of fundamentalist persuasion. Others had parents who were failures and alcoholics. Most, surprisingly, had little or no formal religious education. But at some point in their lives, all felt a call to take their message to the millions.

THE SUPERSAVERS

The elder statesmen of fundamentalist religious telecasting are Billy Graham, Rex Humbard, Oral Roberts, and Jerry Falwell. Collectively, they may have as many viewers as most of the other TV preachers combined. They are all fundamentalist in theology, but there are important differences in their approaches to television and in the messages they preach.

Billy Graham

According to legend, William Randolph Hearst sent out a two-word memo to his nationwide chain of newspapers: ''Puff Graham.'' The year was 1949, and young Billy Graham was conducting an evangelistic crusade in Los Angeles. Reporters and editors obliged Mr. Hearst, and Billy hit the big time.

During the thirty-three years of Billy Graham's worldwide evangelistic crusades he has spoken to 90 million persons face to face. The number who have seen or heard him on television and radio may total in the hundreds of millions. He is unquestionably the most highly visible and preeminent religious figure in the United States. He has his critics, but year after year he appears on the list of America's ten most respected men.

Billy Graham has been so long identified with religious broadcasting that some casual observers are surprised to learn that he has never had a regular long-term television program. Graham's televised crusades are all specials. They appear on an irregular basis in prime time, which Graham purchases on stations around the country for each broadcast.

As a typical crusade telecast opens, cameras pan a rapidly filling stadium or auditorium. Other cameras have caught footage of crowds streaming into the entrances. Song leader Cliff Barrows directs several hundred people in a volunteer choir. Invariably, the choir sings "How Great Thou Art," which has been called the national anthem of revivalism. Warm-up activities have traditionally included solos by George Beverly Shea and by commercial recording artists, with testimonies by those artists and by other famous people.

Finally, Billy preaches. The message is always the same: "You must repent. You must be born again." Billy seldom speaks of social ills, except to point them out as the fruits of sin. He has been criticized by some who would like him to use his enormous influence to address them. His reply is that he was called to be a New Testament evangelist, not an Old Testament prophet. Graham's is a personalistic, privatistic gospel that never wanders from the necessity of individual transformation through accepting Jesus Christ as Savior.

Some critics consider Graham's theology shallow and his methods anachronistic, but they exempt him from the indictment of competing with local churches. Graham will not conduct a crusade in any city unless that crusade is sponsored by the churches; the churches must furnish droves of people to handle local arrangements, supervise the collections, and be responsible for follow-up activities. Lots of local people are also needed to act as counselors at the crusades.

Counselors serve more than one purpose, according to David L. Altheide and John M. Johnson, who studied a Graham crusade in Phoenix: "At the moment of Graham's invitation to 'come forward to Christ,' counselors and choir members begin moving forward. . . . To a naive member of the audience or a television viewer, this movement creates an illusion of a spontaneous and mass response to the invitation. Having been assigned seating in strategic areas of the auditorium or arena and given instructions on the staggered time-sequencing for coming forward, the counselors move forward in such a fashion as to create the illusion of individuals 'flowing' into the center of the arena from all quarters, in a steady outpouring of individual decision. Unless an outsider or observer of these events has been instructed to look for the name tags and ribbons worn by those moving forward, it is all too easy to infer from these appearances the 'charismatic' impact of Graham and his invitation.''

Graham is a fundamentalist, at least to the extent that he has organized his life and ministry around the literal truth of the Scriptures. But he has never displayed any interest in the battle cries of fundamentalism. He is just not an ''aginner.'' Graham is a Southern Baptist but downplays denominationalism. His wife is a Presbyterian, and their home is in Montreat, North Carolina, a Presbyterian conference, vacation, and retirement center.

Graham typifies the evangelicalism that the more traditional and conservative members of nearly all U.S. mainline Protestant denominations have in common. He is the TV preacher of choice for evangelical mainliners, who number many millions.

The finances of the Billy Graham Evangelistic Association have been scrutinized many times. Graham has come out clean, but he was embarrassed in 1977 when the *Charlotte Observer* discovered an undisclosed $23-million fund in Texas, apparently not mentioned in the accountings of the Minneapolis headquarters. Since then, anyone who requests a copy of the BGEA audit is mailed one. Graham's business manager led the formation of the Evangelical Council for Financial Accountability after Graham said on a national telecast, ''. . . there are some charlatans coming along and the public ought to be informed about them and warned against them.''

Oral Roberts

Many Americans still remember Oral Roberts as the man with the ''world's largest gospel tent'' who traveled from city to city from the late 1940s through the early 1960s. During the twenty years of his tent meetings, he established a reputation as a spellbinding preacher and faith healer. Roberts is still a spellbinding preacher, but the healing is much less flamboyant, as he now heals only in crusade meetings; on television he merely promises and prays for it. He has progressed a long way from the shirt-sleeved sweatiness of the gospel tent. These days he wears expensive suits and enjoys preeminence among TV religionists.

Granville Oral Roberts, son of a Pentecostal Holiness minister, grew up in poverty in Pontotoc County, Oklahoma. His father's ministry, according to Oral's own account, was sporadic, and the family was sometimes hungry. In his book *The Call,* Roberts tells of running away from home, only to return when he was stricken by tuberculosis. He also describes a miracle cure, both of the tuberculosis and of the stuttering that had plagued him till then. He certainly doesn't stutter today. He is a powerful preacher with many followers, who send him more than $50 million a year for the support of his TV show, his university, and his hospital.

Oral was licensed to preach as a Pentecostal Holiness minister in 1935. He attended a few college courses but has had no formal theological training. He was pastor of a church in Enid, Oklahoma, in 1947 when he rented a local auditorium and conducted a crusade. In 1948 he conducted his first tent meeting.

Oral's first television program, on January 10, 1954, was broadcast on sixteen stations. It was filmed in a studio, but in early 1955 he began filming in the tent. For a time his sermons were done in a studio, healing lines in the tent. Changing times in TV led to changes in Roberts's approach, however. Seeing that the medium was growing more sophisticated, Roberts dropped his program in 1967, when his tent came down for the last time.

Roberts was seeking new styles in more than one way. By 1966 he was seriously considering joining the Methodist Church. He did so in 1968, although not at the highest level of Methodist ministerial orders. He returned to the air in 1969 with new ecclesiastical credentials and a new television style.

His new television program was at first taped in the NBC studios in Burbank, California, but it is now done in Roberts's own multimillion-dollar studios on the campus of Oral Roberts University in Tulsa. The production facilities at the university are considered to be among the best in the country. The Miss Teen-age America Pageant, country music programs, commercials, and other shows have been produced there when Roberts's own taping schedule permitted renting out the facilities.

Roberts's new program bore no resemblance to those of his sawdust-trail days under canvas. He had adopted the look and the techniques of modern television entertainment programming. Oral's son, Richard, became the singing star of the show, backed up by the World Action Singers of ORU. Guest stars were scheduled frequently on the weekly program, and always on the periodic prime-time specials. Before each taping, a warm-up session helped the audience to relax and clap with enthusiasm. During the warm-up, cameras recorded applause and smiling faces as cutaways to be edited into the program later. Opening and closing program shots featured scenes from the beautiful, ultramodern campus of Oral Roberts University, Roberts's showcase in Tulsa. Recent programs have also featured shots of Oral's huge City of Faith medical complex, which is under construction but in serious financial trouble. The medical center has been attacked by the Tulsa Hospital Council, which complains that the hospital isn't needed because Tulsa already has a surplus of a thousand hospital beds, and the City of Faith would put other hospitals out of business.

In early 1980 "Oral Roberts and You" was being shown on 165 TV stations and had the largest audience of any syndicated religious program. Yet this audience has diminished since Roberts's heyday, as Oral's tremendous financial problems have driven him to devote much energy and program time to fund raising. He preaches and teaches about "seed faith" stewardship, in which money planted in the Oral Roberts ministries will bear fruit in the form of multiple blessings from God. He pleads for financial support so that he can finish his hospital. He proclaims "financial emergencies" that can be met only by immediate gifts from his viewers. It remains to be seen whether he can get more money from fewer viewers, but his audience appears to be shrinking because of his deemphasis of entertainment in favor of fund raising and a more traditional worship service format.

Rex Humbard

The choir and orchestra soar into the theme song, "You Are Loved." Graphics swirl on the screen, followed by a visual extravaganza of colored lights from the stage set. A beaming, bouncing announcer appears and asks the audience to "give a great big welcome to my dad and mom, Rex and Maud Aimee Humbard!'' To prolonged loud applause, Rex and Maud Aimee meet center stage. After a bit of patter, Maud Aimee opens the show with the first musical number.

The atmosphere is Nashville ''countrypolitan,'' right down to the coatless orchestra members in open-neck shirts and unbuttoned vests. The closing credits of the program include stores that have furnished gowns and suits to the fourteen members of the Humbard family. Together, these brothers, sisters, spouses, and grandchildren form various singing ensembles; Rex occasionally strums his guitar in accompaniment. He also engages in patter with family matriarch Maud Aimee, whose middle name was bestowed in remembrance of female evangelist Aimee Semple McPherson. Guests are introduced, who perform or chat with Rex. Humbard's sermons are brief and personal, and they seem barely to interrupt the flow of entertainment. Rex invites letters and prayer requests and usually prays over a pile of them in each program. Professionally produced spot announcements offer to viewers ''You Are Loved'' pins or some other trinket designed to acquire names for the mailing list. Each Christmas he carries the names and prayer requests of all his friends to Calvary, from where his holiday program is beamed back to the United States by satellite.

Humbard's program is normally videotaped at the first church ever designed specifically for the requirements of television. The 5,000-seat Cathedral of Tomorrow is a round building with a domed roof. It contains a huge electronic organ with three sets of pipes—but the organ is never used on the TV show. It doesn't seem to fit the format, for no traditional church hymns are sung on the show. The mood and the music are strictly upbeat contemporary gospel.

Beneath a 100-foot-long cross illuminated with 5,000 light bulbs, the stage is large enough to accommodate TV cameras and crews, choir, orchestra, and the Humbard family. No pulpit can be seen, although Rex sometimes takes his place behind what appears to be a Plexiglas music stand.

Until 1952, Alpha Rex Humbard was one of the Humbard Family Singers in his itinerant preacher father's traveling tent revival entourage. After a successful revival in Akron, Ohio, he decided to leave his father's "Gospel Big Top" and start a church in Akron. He had television in mind from the first.

Rex Humbard had no formal theological training and was ordained by his father. Humbard writes in *To Tell the World,* however, of having studied courses in Bible and religion and being ordained by the International Ministerial Federation, an association of independent, nondenominational ministers. The frantic pace of revival meetings which he and his family conducted, always on the move from one city to the next, makes one wonder just where and when Humbard had time to study. He has never been a member of any denomination.

The church he established in 1953, Calvary Temple, was nondenominational. It met for the first few years in a defunct movie theater purchased by Humbard. Calvary Temple grew until five services had to be conducted every Sunday to accommodate the crowds. In 1958 the Cathedral of Tomorrow was completed.

Humbard's first television broadcasts, live from Calvary Temple, went on the Akron airwaves in 1953, not long after he had observed the crowd watching television in front of O'Neil's. In the days before videotape, programs not on motion-picture film could not be distributed to other TV stations, and motion-picture film production is tedious and expensive. Oral Roberts was willing to bother with it in those days, but Rex Humbard wasn't. Consequently, distribution of his program was limited to a few relatively close stations in Ohio, West Virginia, and Pennsylvania. But with the arrival of videotape in the early 1960s, Humbard began to branch out. He had reached, by his own account, 68 stations by 1968. That number grew to 115 by 1970, to 175 by 1975, and today he is on 207 U.S. television stations.

Rex Humbard is a simple man with a simple message, which he still delivers with a soft Arkansas drawl. He may not succeed in carrying the gospel to all the world, but more than any other syndicated televangelist, he has taken up the challenge. His program is translated into seven languages and shipped to eighteen foreign countries, where it is broadcast on more than 400 television and shortwave radio stations. The Rex Humbard Ministry maintains offices in Canada, Japan, the Philippines, Australia, Brazil, and Chile. The Humbard family also travels the world to conduct rallies. Recently they filled the world's largest stadium (170,000 occupancy) in Rio de Janeiro.

Jerry Falwell

Jerry Falwell grew up listening to Charles E. Fuller's "Old-Fashioned Revival Hour" but had little religious modeling in his youth. His father was a self-made man, successful in a variety of hometown entrepreneurial ventures. He had little interest in religion and little time for his family. A drinking problem resulted in Carey Falwell's premature death at age fifty-five. Helen Falwell, unable to get Jerry and his twin brother to get up and go to church, would leave the radio in their room tuned to the Reverend Fuller's program. Those years of listening to Charles Fuller must have made at least a subliminal impression. After Jerry Falwell became a religious broadcaster in his own right, he called his program "The Old-Time Gospel Hour."

Although something of a hell-raiser in his youth, Falwell experienced a religious conversion at the age of eighteen. Initially it was pretty girls, not religion, that attracted him to the Park Avenue Baptist Church in Lynchburg, Virginia. Several years later the piano player, Macel Pate, would become Mrs. Jerry Falwell. After his conversion, Falwell dropped out of engineering studies, which he was pursuing at Lynchburg College. Upon graduation from Baptist Bible College in Springfield, Missouri, in 1956 he returned to Lynchburg and started a church.

The Thomas Road Baptist Church was started with thirty-five members in an abandoned Donald Duck soft-drink bottling plant. The church grew by leaps and bounds almost from the beginning, and today its congregation of 17,000 is the nation's second largest. As a reminder of his modest beginnings, a bookshelf that lines one side of Falwell's office prominently displays a dozen bottles of Donald Duck soda.

One week after organizing his church, Falwell started a radio program. Six months later he went on Lynchburg television. In those early days Falwell's sights were not on the national scene, but on building a solid local church. This he accomplished in a decade. By the end of the 1960s, Falwell began to have more ambitious goals, having already established a Christian academy and a bus ministry that brought children to church from all over the hinterlands of Virginia, and construction of a new 3,000-seat sanctuary was under way. In 1971 Falwell founded Liberty Baptist College and in 1973, Liberty Baptist Seminary. Also during this period he began a significant expansion of his television ministry.

Today, Liberty Baptist College enrolls 2,900 students, and there are plans for 200 new independent Baptist churches to be founded by graduates of the seminary. But that is just the beginning. During the 1980s Falwell projects that his graduates will found 5,000 new churches, and he envisions that a Liberty Baptist University will one day enroll 50,000 students.

For all the inflamed rhetoric surrounding Falwell's latter-day political activities as leader of the Moral Majority, one might tune into his program expecting to see a fire-eating preacher. But Falwell is far from it. His program is a surprisingly conventional worship service. The music, as the title of the program suggests, is old-time gospel, attractively presented, but not upbeat mod, latter-day music that mimics secular successes. Falwell speaks in measured tones of self-assurance, more like a corporate executive than a thundering, Bible-thumping, fundamentalist preacher.

Nonetheless, Falwell is a self-proclaimed fundamentalist. His doctrine is Baptist, but he is not affiliated with the Southern Baptist Convention or any other denomination. "The Old-Time Gospel Hour" is a bastion of frontier fundamentalism moved uptown. It presents an old-time religion seeking to call a sinful people back to their senses and to their God-inspired beginnings. On his program he may preach about a variety of topics, ranging from "signs of the soon coming of Jesus" to the God-mandated rightness of U.S. support for Israel. Falwell understands Internal Revenue Service rules about political statements made by non-profit organizations, and he saves his best political rhetoric for other platforms. So also is he careful not to attack certain people or segments of society on the air; to do so might leave him vulnerable to a Fairness Doctrine charge before the Federal Communications Commission.

But make no mistake about it; his regular listeners are aware that Jerry Falwell's Bible is against immorality, liberalism, communism, the welfare state, pornography, abortion, sex education in the schools, and the Equal Rights Amendment. His message is a call to return to an America that once was, a simpler America that was guided by biblically inspired moral principles and that knew not the agony of moral ambiguity. His apparent certainty about the rightness of that world has caused many thoughtful Americans rather considerable apprehension about the means Jerry Falwell might employ to impose his views on this nation.

THE MAINLINER

Mainline Protestant and Catholic groups once dominated the air time networks had set aside for religious broadcasting. But that was before the televangelists came along and offered local stations handsome rates for Sunday morning "ghetto" time. Robert Schuller, whose Garden Grove Community Church is affiliated with the Reformed Church in America, is the only mainliner on the marquee of religious broadcasting. His denomination, however, does not sponsor his broadcasts. Like the organizations of the other televangelists, his "Hour of Power" pays for air time on every station on which the program appears.

Robert Schuller

Sunday, September 12, 1980, was a moving day for the regular viewers of the "Hour of Power." Robert Schuller preached his last sermon from the old sanctuary of the Garden Grove Community Church. His topic: "Every Ending Is a New Beginning." Then viewers saw Schuller lead a procession from the old sanctuary to the new Crystal Cathedral, a reflective glass structure in the shape of a four-pointed star. The cathedral spans 415 feet from point to point in one direction and 207 in the other. Its 10,611 panes of glass are supported by white-painted metal trusses.

All over the United States that morning, people were shedding tears of joy as they watched the procession. It was not the eloquence of the sermon, or the magnificence of the ceremony, or even the first glimpse inside the Crystal Cathedral—a stunning panorama—that caused so many to choke up. All over the country there were tens of thousands of individuals who had helped to pay for this "impossible dream" with their $10 and $15 gifts to the "Hour of Power" ministry. It was an architectural triumph. It was also a personal triumph in the life of a man who began his southern California ministry on the roof of the concession stand of a nearby drive-in theater. Most of all, it was a triumph of that man's message of "possibility thinking."

Among the pictures in Robert Schuller's office are those of Bishop Fulton J. Sheen and Norman Vincent Peale. Sheen showed all would-be religious broadcasters that a powerful preacher can make it on television. Peale has preached for decades the very popular "power of positive thinking." It takes no leap of the imagination to understand Schuller's respect for and debt to both men. Schuller is the successor to their mantles; he is a mainline telegenic preacher who skillfully blends psychology and religion.

Schuller freely acknowledges his intellectual debt to Norman Vincent Peale, who once appeared on the drive-in roof with him. "Possibility thinking" is a theology of self-esteem, hope, and positive thinking. Schuller's sermons, as well as his conversational discourse, are loaded with slogans such as "turning scars into stars," "turning stress into strength," "different rules for different roles," and always, positive affirmation of self: "You are a beautiful person" or "God loves you, and so do I." When Schuller mounted the marble podium for the dedication ceremonies of the Crystal Cathedral, he prayed that God would "show us how to turn a monument into an instrument."

Schuller has come a long way since the day in 1955 when he stood atop the sticky, tar-papered roof of a drive-in theater snack bar in Orange County, California, and preached to about seventy-five people in cars. His church, the Reformed Church in America, had asked him to go to California to start a congregation. Schuller did few things conventionally. When the church grew large enough to be housed in a building, he continued to hold services at the drive-in as well. In time he built a church that incorporated the features of both, with glass panels that rolled back so that worshippers in cars in the ramped parking lot could see inside, or persons who preferred to be outside could sit on the grass. In the Crystal Cathedral, also, one arm of the star slides open like a giant airplane hangar door so that those who wish to may worship in the privacy of their autos.

The "Hour of Power" telecast was inaugurated in 1970. Today it is syndicated on 149 stations in the United States and is the only program regularly telecast on the Armed Services Network. The television program is also connected with a nationwide telephone counseling service for both spiritual and psychological problems. A typical show begins with a rising, rousing anthem by the choir. As they sing, the cameras provide a panorama of the beautiful grounds of the Garden Grove church, of the fountains, of soaring gulls and blue skies, of eucalyptus trees swaying in a gentle breeze, and, always, of the happy faces in the congregation.

Then a camera zooms in on Robert Schuller. Clad in a magnificent robe, with arms extended and a broad smile on his face, he booms out, "This is the day the Lord has made! Let us rejoice and be glad in it!" A professional announcer does a voice-over—usually headlining Schuller's "gift of the week," with details on how viewers may get one to come later. Then Schuller is introduced. He preaches dramatically and forcefully. He is a first-rate orator with a great flair for the dramatic.

The "Hour of Power" often includes the appearance of a guest whom Schuller interviews, with a lighthearted touch, about his or her faith. He doesn't believe in using his pulpit to promote any political viewpoint, so a show that features someone who is associated with one side of an issue is balanced by a later visit with someone associated with the opposing side. Liberal Democratic Senator Birch Bayh, for example, was followed a short time later by conservative Republican Congressman Guy Vander Jagt.

Schuller's sermons are usually punctuated with alliteration and mnemonic devices, so that the major points are not lost amid his illustrations and anecdotes. For example, a sermon on how to become a transformed person was built on five concepts: fantasize, analyze, verbalize, organize, and finally concretize. "The words are simple," Schuller tells his listeners, "but they contain profound psychological, theological, and spiritual truth."

Schuller is the only mainline Protestant in the cast of cathode stars. He doesn't like being confused with the other evangelists on TV, some of whom he thinks are charlatans. And he doesn't like people to refer to his television program as a church. On the other hand, Schuller believes that mainline Protestantism is "losing ground because it is failing to meet the deepest emotional needs of the people." He is trying hard to use his television ministry as an instrument of psychological and emotional therapy. There are some who don't care for Schuller's calling his "possibility thinking" Christianity. They say that his theology is as simple as equating sin with negative thoughts and Original Sin with self-doubt. A thoroughly positive man, Schuller has little time to answer critics or engage in intramural quarrels. His response to criticism is an invitation to spend some time at the Garden Grove Community Church and determine whether there is any theological depth to what is taught and practiced there. Television, he argues, is a powerful but limited medium. He is pointing people in the right direction, not giving them the full gospel.

THE TALKIES

The success of Johnny Carson's "Tonight Show" has inspired several religious versions of the talk show. Jim Bakker, in his autobiography *Move That Mountain!,* recalls getting the idea for the format after coming home late at night from a revival meeting. When he went to work for Pat Robertson's Christian Broadcasting Network in 1965, he began developing plans for such a program. "The 700 Club" premiered on local television in Virginia Beach in November 1966, and Jim Bakker was its original host. Since then the talk show has taken a permanent place as a major vehicle of religious broadcasting. A quick look at three of the "talkies" follows.

Jim Bakker

"It's not listed in the Bible," said Jim Bakker in a 1979 article in *Christianity Today,* "but my spiritual gift, my specific calling from God, is to be a television talk-show host. That's what I'm here on earth to do. I love TV. I eat it, I sleep it." Bakker (pronounced "baker") is host of "The PTL Club," a daily talk and variety show distributed by satellite to stations and cable systems all over the country. *PTL* means both "Praise the Lord" and "People That Love." The show emanates from a building at the PTL Network's multiacre Charlotte, North Carolina, complex. On the outside the building looks like a huge colonial church. Inside is a modern multimillion-dollar TV studio.

The live audience is composed of tourists and guests at PTL's campground. Before the show they are warmed up by a speaker who leads them in rousing songs and coaches them on when to applaud during the two-hour show. During the warm-up volunteers are recruited to staff the banks of telephones on the set.

Jim Bakker is introduced in Johnny Carson fashion. He even has a sidekick like Johnny's. Jim's Ed McMahon is Henry Harrison, a robust man several years Bakker's senior, who is usually addressed as Uncle Henry, a sobriquet he acquired when he assisted Jim and Tammy Fay Bakker with a puppet show during Bakker's CBN days. A parade of guests and singing stars moves through the taping session. Jim interviews them about miracle healings, faith success stories, and their own religious lives or ministries. The proceedings are punctuated with lots of exclamations of "Glory!" and "Praise God!" On occasion Jim Bakker preaches a sermonette—especially if PTL is experiencing one of its regular financial crises—and breaks into tears if matters are grave.

Tammy Fay Bakker is also a regular on the show, talking with Jim and singing. Her singing career is getting a big push these days; her records are being distributed to radio stations all over the country in the hope that she will catch on in the burgeoning gospel music market.

Jim Bakker's predilection for speaking in tongues and faith healing is soft-pedaled on camera, although Uncle Henry has been known to break into unknown tongues a couple of times on the air.

Bakker preaches, and presents through the guests he selects, a gospel of shiny-eyed success in the spirit. His health-and-wealth theology holds that God wants to bless believers materially as well as spiritually. He is convinced that Christ can make life work and that his gospel will bring people to higher standards of living. He thought it significant, when he traveled through India and Africa, that the Christians' homes were bigger and more comfortable than the non-Christians'. He preaches a Christianity that is not just a religious experience, but a life-style of success. This life-style is reflected in the extensive PTL Heritage USA, a

1,200-acre campground and vacation complex. PTL also began a full-fledged Heritage University but has had to limit its courses of study to evangelism and communications.

"The PTL Club" has a history of financial mismanagement and crisis, which is perhaps now being brought under control by business managers who have taken the financial reins out of Bakker's hands. The show's finances have received so much publicity that a Charlotte radio station broadcast a parody called "The Pass the Loot Club."

Some of this must at times seem strange and distant to Jim Bakker, the son of a Michigan factory worker. Jim was a poor, extremely shy child. He was small in stature but had a large inferiority complex. As a young adult he once had the misfortune to run over a child. The child recovered completely, but the fright of the accident caused Jim to take seriously his parents' Assemblies of God religion. He entered North Central Bible College to prepare for the ministry but dropped out to marry Tammy Fay. He was ordained anyway, and he and Tammy Fay lived the life of traveling evangelists for several years. Their puppet show for children eventually got them on Pat Robertson's struggling young TV station, where Bakker starred for several years. After leaving CBN, the Bakkers went to California and worked with Paul Crouch at the fledgling Trinity Broadcasting Network station. Bakker claims that relations with Pat Robertson were always good but frankly admits that he and Paul Crouch fell out. It wasn't long before Bakker accepted the invitation of North Carolina laymen to come to Charlotte to be president of PTL. Thus, Bakker became the only person to be involved in the beginnings of all three of America's religious broadcasting networks—not bad for the scared little kid from Muskegon Heights, Michigan.

Indigenous versions of "The PTL Club," using local hosts who engage guests from the countries in which the show appears, are being produced for Japan, Thailand, Australia, France, Italy, Brazil, Haiti, and Mexico, and for distribution in Central and South America and Africa.

Pat Robertson

Marion G. "Pat" Robertson is a Phi Beta Kappa graduate of

Washington and Lee University, was a Marine captain in Korea, graduated from Yale Law School, and was formerly a businessman. He is also an evangelical preacher of the first rank, a faith healer, a speaker in tongues, and a hearer of direct revelations which he calls "Words of Knowledge" from God.

Robertson is the host of "The 700 Club," a ninety-minute daily religious talk show. More than that, however, he is the president and chief executive officer of the Christian Broadcasting Network, which owns four television stations and five radio stations, has a staff of 800, and aims to become, through satellite distribution, this country's fourth commercial television network. CBN already programs a channel twenty-four hours a day with old family sitcom reruns and a variety of religious programs from many sources. The channel is distributed by satellite to any cable TV system in the country that will accept it. But CBN means to stake out a 10-percent share of the total U.S. TV audience with a full schedule of news, drama, sports, game shows, soap operas, variety shows, and commercials. The difference between CBN and the other three networks is that CBN plans to do all this from an explicitly Christian perspective. CBN people have even been developing a Christian soap opera, "The Inner Light"—their answer to "The Guiding Light" and "As the World Turns."

By his own admission, Robertson was a tortured man after finishing Yale Law School. He failed to pass the New York bar exam, claiming his heart wasn't in it. He was engaged in an electronics components business when he felt called to go into the ministry. He chose Biblical Theological Seminary in New York, where he was part of a tongues-speaking fellowship. After graduation in 1959, he was still unsettled and uncertain about his life. For several months he and his wife and children existed in a charismatic commune in a Brooklyn slum. Later that year, Robertson heard about a defunct UHF television station for sale in Virginia Beach. Incredibly, he arranged to buy it for a fraction of its value. Even that was a venture of faith, however, for Pat had no money at all. Somehow he managed to survive for several months by preaching in Virginia churches, and he finally corralled enough donations to put the station back on the air on October 1, 1961. The first broadcast day lasted two and a half hours.

On a 1963 fund-raising telethon, Pat asked for 700 people to pledge $10 a month to meet the monthly operating budget of WYAH. That was the birth of the 700 Club. (Dues today have risen to $15 per month.) Sometime later, CBN employee Jim Bakker started a talk show that was named "The 700 Club." The rest is history. CBN today occupies a $50-million headquarters complex and has an annual budget of about $55 million. All this growth has been accomplished through the generosity of viewers who give according to Pat's "Kingdom Principles," which Pat frequently explains. Basically, the more you give to God, the more God will give back to you. The best and quickest way to get the process started is to send a gift to "The 700 Club."

Robertson is a gentle-voiced, smiling fellow. He teaches more than he preaches, and he prays often on the program. His guests tend to be evangelicals who have stories to tell of miracles in their lives or of ministries they are carrying out with decisive effects on the lives of others. Many are Christian authors touting their books on the salvation circuit, or singers with religious records to hype.

Pat's co-host of "The 700 Club" is Ben Kinchlow, whose role is much like that of the sidekick of secular talk shows— cheerleading and picking up the ball if he senses the host is about to have a lapse. He also sets Robertson up with questions when he thinks that his boss has not yet finished expounding on some particular topic. When Robertson is absent, Kinchlow, a tall, handsome man whose deep black hair is turning gray, hosts the program himself. Kinchlow could one day become the first black to host a syndicated talk show. That this may be in the offing is suggested by the fact that in 1978 CBN asked a sample of regular "700 Club" contributors what they thought about the idea. Robertson's popularity and the still shaky financial foundation of the ever expanding CBN enterprises are not likely to make this a reality soon, however.

Pat Robertson is easily the best educated of the video vicars. So incredible is his command of facts in so many areas that a skeptical viewer would find it difficult to believe that Robertson doesn't work from cue cards after extensive briefings. He is briefed about his guests, but he does his own homework. His spontaneous lecturettes on all sorts of subjects amaze both his guests and his staff, who have worked closely with him for years.

Robertson's political and economic views are conservative, and more frequently than not his guests share his conservative philosophy. By late 1979 Robertson was talking and writing in his newsletter, *Perspective*, like a man who was about to make a move into politics. But he came back from his yearly retreat and told his closest associates that God wanted him to back away from politics.

That wasn't an easy task. He was already committed to being program chairman of Washington for Jesus, a two-day rally for prayer and repentance, which aimed at attracting a million participants. As the rally approached, he worked hard to disavow any political agenda for the gathering. The organization did reject some of the more overt political activities that had earlier been a part of the schedule. Still, everyone knows that no one brings a crowd to Washington, save the chaperones of the droves of high school students who descend on the nation's capital each spring, without a political purpose.

Robertson was clearly uncomfortable with the overtly political agenda of the National Affairs Briefing in Dallas in August 1980. Shortly thereafter he quietly resigned from the Roundtable, the organization that had sponsored the gathering, and canceled an appearance at a meeting of the National Religious Broadcasters when of the three presidential candidates only Ronald Reagan agreed to appear.

His efforts to withdraw from politics notwithstanding, Robertson cares deeply about the direction in which this nation is moving economically, socially, and politically. He tells his audiences that the best thing they can do about the nation's problems is to pray. Indeed, he proclaims that prayer is the only thing that can be done, but almost in the same breath he encourages his listeners to write their congressmen. It is by no means certain that God will not one day tap Pat Robertson, the son of a once powerful United States senator, on the shoulder for a more overtly political assignment.

Paul Crouch

Jim Bakker started the "Praise the Lord" show for Paul Crouch's Trinity Broadcasting Network after Jim left Pat Robertson. When

Jim and Paul agreed to disagree, Jim took at least the initials *PTL* to North Carolina.

But Paul and Jan Crouch have made their show peculiarly California. No three-piece suits here; more sport shirts and bright California breeziness. The breezes do blow in a bit of religious ecstasy now and then, but mostly Paul and Jan do a lot of stand-up chatting (and kneel-down praying), with the usual run of guests and musical numbers.

The Trinity Broadcasting Network is trying hard to expand and take its place alongside CBN and PTL. In addition to the base station in Los Angeles, TBN owns stations in Phoenix, Oklahoma City, and Miami.

It all makes Jan shriek and cry for joy. When she announced that Paul had gone to Miami to close the purchase of Channel 45, she called Miami's large Jewish population "Little Israel" and exulted, "God has given us twenty-four-hour-a-day Christian television to reach the little Jewish people!"

THE ENTERTAINERS

A healthy slice of the electronic church seems to reflect the maxim "If you can't beat 'em, join 'em." The entertainment formats of television's secular offerings have been copied in many ways. One of the most obvious copies is the musical variety show. But the musical entertainment shows of religious broadcasting draw not only from Hollywood formats; they have successfully wed Hollywood—or Nashville—to the rousing styles of tent-meeting revival singers. Mainliners who are accustomed to stately hymns and choral anthems can find lots of new religious musical styles on TV today.

Jimmy Swaggart

Jimmy Swaggart, cousin of rock musician Jerry Lee Lewis and country-western guru Mickey Gilley, puts on a rollicking, if not rocking, musical show. Jimmy belts out good-time, hand-clapping gospel songs at the piano and sings with great feeling. He is backed up by a Nashville-style band, and even a skeptical viewer is likely to get caught up in the infectious rhythms.

Music has been good to Jimmy. Gold records, symbols of recording success, adorn his office walls, and the sale of Jimmy

Swaggart records and tapes accounts for a good chunk of the Jimmy Swaggart Evangelistic Association's income. He is the only evangelist we encountered with a vigorous sales as well as solicitation program. He pitches his records, tapes, Bibles, and study course with seriousness and aplomb. Viewers who get on the Swaggart mailing list are asked to contribute to a variety of causes—feeding children in India, buying TV time, building churches in Africa, and so forth. They also get the chance to buy eight-track tapes or cassettes of "Jimmy Swaggart's Greatest Hits."

Swaggart is a Louisiana moonshiner's son and a high school dropout. But the Assemblies of God are more impressed by commitment than education, and Jimmy is an ordained minister of that church. He supposedly has been speaking in tongues since the age of nine. He does not do so on his program, but he vigorously defends this "baptism of the Holy Spirit" and has lashed out at those who criticize the practice, particularly mainline churches, saying that some of them are dead because they don't have the gift.

Jimmy is an old-fashioned camp-meeting preacher. His sermons are impassioned. He patrols the platform restlessly while speaking, and his intensity may lead him to shout one moment and whisper pleadingly the next. He is urgent because he believes Jesus is coming soon and we may have little time in which to get ready.

His organization owns eight radio stations, and he buys time for his radio program on several hundred more. His TV show is syndicated on 222 TV stations, as well as on many cable systems.

He believes in at least a certain amount of financial disclosure. He claims that his organization was the first, even before Billy Graham's, to offer an audited financial statement to anyone who requests it.

"Gospel Singing Jubilee"

"Gospel Singing Jubilee" has nothing to sell you and won't put you on a mailing list. The program, which is sponsored by advertisers, is just another expression of the huge commercial gospel music market—and that is a big, big market. The million-sellers of gospel music don't get much attention in the secular press, but gospel music devotees amount to nothing less than a major subcultural market in the United States. *Christian Bookseller* magazine regularly publishes a Christian version of *Billboard*'s top forty songs.

"Gospel Singing Jubilee" is purely and simply an entertainment program for the gospel-loving subculture—albeit with an occasional light testimony thrown in.

Ross Bagley

Religious television has even spawned a televised deejay show. Plump and smiling Ross Bagley is the host. Between musical selections Ross relates anecdotes but always moves rapidly to the next number. Apparently, gospel recording artists furnish him with videotapes of their latest releases. A steady parade of tuxedoed, coiffed, and gowned entertainers lip-synch their way through their hottest-selling songs, in appearances and styles barely distinguishable from those of secular performers—except for the lyrics they sing. Commercial minutes in the Ross Bagley show are available to advertisers.

THE TEACHERS

Some religious broadcasters prefer teaching to preaching. Most who go this route sit quietly on sets, living-room style, and teach Bible lessons or discuss how one may live the religious life. There is some entertainment, but usually not much more than a couple of musical numbers by a bright-eyed group of young people, just to warm up the audience for the lesson that follows.

Richard De Haan and Paul Van Gorder

"Day of Discovery" is a direct descendant of one of radio's oldest continuous religious programs, "The Radio Bible Class." Pioneer evangelical broadcaster M. R. De Haan taught daily on "The Radio Bible Class" for many years. When the program went to television in 1968, it became "Day of Discovery." Richard De Haan, son of the founder, is one of the two principal teacher-speakers. Paul Van Gorder is the other.

The program opens with a musical number or two by the "Day of Discovery" singers, usually videotaped in Florida's colorful Cypress Gardens, and then Richard or Paul gets down to the quiet, serious business of teaching a Bible lesson. The atmosphere is friendly and dignified. There is no promotion except for the free offer of a copy of the day's lesson. "Day of Discovery" has Bible courses available if you want to do serious study, but money is never solicited on the air. Still, voluntary contributions from the show's serious viewers keep the program going, despite the low-key solicitation.

Frank Pollard

Frank Pollard is the teacher on the Southern Baptist study program "At Home with the Bible." As with others in this genre, entertainment is limited to a musical number or two. The set looks like a living room, and the cast has the casual appearance of a family. It's low-key, informal education, designed to appeal to the surprisingly large number of Americans who have a serious interest in Bible study. The Baptists don't buy time for the program; it is seen on sustaining or free time. Nor do they solicit funds on the air. As for "Day of Discovery," if you write for their Bible study materials, you'll receive them free of charge, and the appeal for financial contributions is low-key. A typical appeal, at the conclusion of a letter that makes no mention of money, reads as follows: "Please keep praying for us and for the support that makes our ministry possible." Of course, a pre-addressed envelope is enclosed in case you want to do more than pray.

THE RISING STARS

Styles change in television, and stars come and go. The electronic church can hardly be exempt from this fact of TV life, but since the programs are not so directly dependent on audience size as secular entertainment programs, the stars who fade away probably will do so in the Lawrence Welk style of gradual attrition. But for all who may be in decline or nearing retirement, there are others waiting in the wings for their period of stardom. There are three televangelists who are positioned to make a run for the big time. To succeed, they have to raise the money to pay for their telecasts, *and* they have to find time that can be purchased on an already crowded schedule. Since the way they pay for time is to get on the air and raise the money, this could prove to be a real

Catch-22; at least it is not likely to be easy unless one of the majors stubs a toe. The alternative, which Kenneth Copeland and Jack Van Impe are pioneering, is to buy time outside the normal slots for religious telecasts—Sunday evenings, Saturdays, even weeknights after prime time.

James Robison

Robison is one of God's angry men. He thunders from the pulpit against all manner of immorality, sinfulness, vice, un-Americanism, and secular humanism. The thirty-seven-year-old Robison has been an evangelist for eighteen years and has been on television since 1970. He is a truly dynamic preacher of seemingly inexhaustible energy. His dynamism reminds some of Billy Graham when he was younger. Although Robison's television ministry has not grown as rapidly as others, he stands on the threshold of becoming a major television preacher. His program, "James Robison, Man with a Message," is syndicated on sixty-four U.S. television stations.

Robison is the product of a broken home. His alcoholic father deserted his mother before James (never Jim) was born in a charity ward in Houston. His mother placed a newspaper advertisement offering her infant to whoever would give him a home. A minister and his wife responded, and James grew up with them. Later attempts at reunions with his father and mother had unhappy results. Saved at age fifteen, Robison attended school briefly at East Texas Baptist College in Marshall. By age nineteen he had received hundreds of invitations to conduct revival meetings. This heavy schedule of evangelism interfered with completion of a formal education.

One of Robison's several crusades is against homosexuality, and one of his attacks on gays got his program canceled by a Dallas TV station. When the Dallas Gay Political Caucus asked for equal time under the FCC's Fairness Doctrine, station WFAA decided that Robison's program was simply too much trouble. But when Robison drew 10,000 people to a "freedom rally" and retained Houston attorney Richard "Racehorse" Haynes to press a hearing before the FCC, the television station decided to reinstate his program.

Robison calls things the way he sees them, and there are few

Father Charles F. Coughlin addressing an outdoor rally in Worcester, Massachusetts, in the late 1920s. *Courtesy Wide World Photos*.

Aimee Semple McPherson, the fiery female evangelist, in Seattle, Washington, on the last leg of a world tour in 1935. *Courtesy Wide World Photos*.

The man who gave preachers all over America a fever for television: Roman Catholic Archbishop Fulton J. Sheen. When he received an Emmy in the 1950s, he quipped, ''I'd like to thank my writers—Matthew, Mark, Luke, and John.'' *Courtesy Wide World Photos.*

Evangelist Billy Graham has spoken to more than 90 million persons *face to face* in thirty-three years of preaching. Above, a younger Graham addresses 50,000 people gathered in the Rose Bowl in Pasadena, California, in September 1950. Below, thirty years later, Graham is pictured in his North Carolina home. His preaching still draws crowds—both in person and watching his televised specials. *Photos courtesy Wide World Photos.*

Oral Roberts in the 1950s (above) and the 1970s (below). His spellbinding preaching style and faith-healing reputation have made him a colorful figure in the evangelistic movement for more than thirty-five years. *Courtesy Wide World Photos (above) and Religious News Service (below).*

Jim Bakker, host of "The PTL Club." "My specific calling from God," he says, "is to be a television talk-show host."

On the set of "The PTL Club," Bakker's daily variety-talk show. Broadcast from a multiacre Charlotte, North Carolina, complex, the show is distributed by satellite to TV stations and cable systems all over the country. *Courtesy Religious News Service.*

James Robison, one of God's angry young men. At thirty-seven, he has been an evangelist for almost half his life and on television for over a decade.

Robison's move into politics has been decisive. He is vice-president of the Roundtable, which sponsored the August 1980 National Affairs Briefing in Dallas. He wants Americans to dislodge the ungodly people who he claims are holding the country hostage.

Cousin to rock musician Jerry Lee Lewis, Jimmy Swaggart is an old-fashioned camp meeting preacher with a Nashville flair for music. He has earned several gold records. *Courtesy Jimmy Swaggart Evangelistic Association.*

The Jimmy Swaggart Evangelistic Association was the first of the tele-vangelists' organizations to disclose a financial statement. The association owns 8 radio stations and produces a television program that is syndicated to 222 stations. *Courtesy Religious News Service.*

Robert Schuller is the only "mainliner" among the prime-time preachers. Shown with him in his original Garden Grove Community Church are three born-again witnesses: Watergate conspirator Charles Colson, left; Corrie ten Boom, Nazi concentration camp survivor; and, far right, Eldridge Cleaver, former Black Panther. The Garden Grove church has since been replaced by the spectacular Crystal Cathedral. *Courtesy Religious News Service.*

Opposite: Rex Humbard (top) preaches from the 5,000-seat Cathedral of Tomorrow, the first church ever designed specifically for television broadcasting. (Bottom) Rex and his wife, Maud Aimee (named for female evangelist Aimee Semple McPherson), pose with the Humbard family in front of the White House. All the Humbards are musically inclined and perform on Rex's show. *Photos Courtesy Rex Humbard.*

The Thomas Road Baptist Church, home of Jerry Falwell's "Old-Time Gospel Hour," started with thirty-five members in an abandoned Donald Duck soft-drink bottling plant. Today it has 17,000 members and encompasses a sprawl of several buildings. Below, the inside of the church, equipped with television cameras. *Photos by Les Schofer, courtesy "The Old-Time Gospel Hour."*

shades of gray in his world. He is a staunch defender of freedom of the press and blames his run-in with WFAA-TV on government intimidation of the press. He still believes homosexuality is a perversion (the word that got him into hot water), but he says he respects homosexuals' right to express their views. He appeared on a Dallas talk show with the homosexual responsible for pressing the complaint that resulted in cancellation of his program. Later Robison invited the same person to express his point of view in his monthly magazine, *Life's Answer*.

He is vice-president of the Roundtable, which sponsored the National Affairs Briefing held in Dallas during August 1980. During the summer of that election year, Robison aired a television special entitled "Wake Up, America: We're All Hostages!" Robison thinks that the government has been taken over by ungodly people and that the moral people of America are being held hostage by ungodliness, secular humanism, immorality, and other un-American attributes. Appearing on the special to help spell out those ills were many figures associated with the ultraright of U.S. politics.

Some of Robison's closest associates feel his overt move into politics could hurt rather than help his chances for achieving national prominence. But Robison is anything but timid. He believes the country is in trouble, and he intends to spend every ounce of energy he has spreading God's saving grace as the answer to godless humanism.

Kenneth Copeland

Kenneth Copeland is fun to watch. He enjoys preaching. He paces up and down the stage when speaking, and he loves to make his audience laugh. His audiences get into the fun-filled spirit of it all—they chuckle, roar, whistle, and applaud. Copeland loves it, and he pours on his special brand of Spirit-filled, good-humored gospel in response. But he is not good-humored about the dead, dry churches of the respectable mainline and the safe, sane gospel they preach. He likes churches and people who believe in healing, speaking in tongues, expecting miracles, and letting it all hang out for Jesus, homespun and high-powered. He made his television ministry debut in 1979, and he is already seen on thirty-eight stations, with more being added as fast as time can be bought. He is a zestful pilot and motorcyclist and probably will keep on moving as fast as he can in television, too.

Jack Van Impe

If you were watching Jack Van Impe during the summer of 1980, he would have offered to send you a free book, *Everything You Always Wanted to Know about Prophecy, but Didn't Know Who to Ask!* He, of course, is whom you should ask. And you'd better get your questions answered soon, because these days are the "end time" just before Jesus comes again. Until that actually happens, however, all Americans must be on guard against the menace of satanic communism in our midst.

Van Impe is the latest rising star of the electronic church. In less than a year he has managed to buy time on eighty-one stations, a truly phenomenal accomplishment. Van Impe appeals to those who are fascinated with biblical prophecy. Judging from the success of such books as Hal Lindsey's *Late Great Planet Earth,* there are large numbers of such people. Other religious programs have attempted to appeal to this audience, but Van Impe's is the first that meets the high standards of quality production. He uses fast-moving canned film for the opening of his show. The audience is usually entertained by his wife, Rexella, who then interviews her husband on some pressing issue. Van Impe then gives a sermon on the imminent threat of the holocaust.

If you write for whatever free book Van Impe is offering, you can expect to receive it more quickly than you receive the gifts offered on any other religious program. You'll also receive his magazine entitled *Perhaps Today.* Van Impe aspires to reach every TV market in the United States as soon as possible. After all, time is running out.

THE UNCONVENTIONAL

Ernest Angley

Ernest Angley has been called the "lunatic fringe" of religious broadcasting. He sees demons leaving the bodies of those he heals. He sees angels, too, standing by his side in healing services. And he sees God, who he says looks more or less like the pictures of Him.

Angley had his first visitation from God when he was only seven years old. It occurred while he lay in bed in the family farmhouse in North Carolina. God showed him millions of stars and told him that was how many souls he would win for Christ.

A typical program, videotaped in Angley's flashy Akron, Ohio, Grace Cathedral, features musical selections from the Grace Cathedral Singing Men, an Angley sermon, and a few healings videotaped at one of Angley's "Miracle and Salvation" crusades. If you can't get to a crusade, Angley may hold his hand up to the camera and invite you to put your hand on your TV screen. He then commands the demons to come out of you and yells, "Heal! *Heal!* HEEEEEAL-aaa!"

The visibility and success of the stars of the electronic church have caused a lot of preachers to want to emulate them. Every city that has a television station also has preachers who dream of becoming televangelists.

Some who have already made it onto local television are starting to branch out. It is a simple matter to ship video cassettes of a telecast to cable systems, and it is not difficult to find a time slot for program tapes on one of the religious satellite networks—PTL, CBN, and Trinity. With just a little financial support from network viewers, a TV preacher can think about negotiating for local station time and syndicating.

A recent issue of *Religious Broadcasting* contained full-page ads for two newcomers. Charles Stanley, pastor of Atlanta's First Baptist Church, has secured time on CBN and PTL and placed his program "In Touch" in several large markets. His advertisement sought additional stations for it. G. L. Johnson's "People's Church Worship Hour," which originates in California, was similarly being offered.

For each preacher who has successfully syndicated a program and achieved national recognition, there are many who would like to try. Some will do so; a few will succeed.

The Electronic
Communicants

FRANK PATRICK: *Jim Bakker is like a member of the family, or we are members of his family. He is full of empathy, sympathy, understanding, and we love Jim Bakker.*
DEIRDRE PATRICK: *We feel we know him intimately. He's a real person in our lives.*
FRANK PATRICK: *He's more than just somebody who appears on TV.*

During the winter and spring of 1980, Jerry Falwell proclaimed widely that 25 million people watched "The Old-Time Gospel Hour" every week. Then, in the middle of July, at the Republican National Convention in Detroit, while Falwell was engaged in some heavy politicking over the platform and the vice-presidential choice, the word slipped out from one of his associates that "OTGH" really had an audience of *50 million viewers!* How did Jerry Falwell get a viewing audience of 50 million? The same way he got 25 million: by proclamation. The truth is, fewer than 1½ million people tune in Jerry Falwell each week. One and a half million. That's 3 percent of the audience Falwell's man claimed in Detroit in the summer of 1980.

Falwell isn't the only TV preacher to get carried away estimating the size of his audience. Virtually all of them do. E. J. Daniels hosts a program called "Christ for the World," and in his ministry magazine for February 1980 he allowed as how, doggone it, he just didn't know *how many million* (emphasis added) listened to his show. Professional audience estimates for that same month indicate he had a total audience of 135,000.

Period. Even allowing for a margin of error, or for closet Christian viewers, it's a long haul from 135,000 to millions.

Virtually all the televangelists exaggerate their audience size. Many of them sincerely believe that they do reach literally millions. How do they come up with their estimates? Not all of them join Falwell in the fine art of proclamation. Some confuse potential audience with real audience. They seem not to grasp the fact that only a fraction of all television sets in a given viewing area are turned on at one time, and of those, only a very small percentage are tuned to their show.

Many have formulas they believe to be reasonable yardsticks for estimating audiences. The most common formula pivots on some ratio between letters received and number of viewers. Don Hull, who formerly headed James Robison's audience response division, told a group of Southern Baptist broadcasters that he estimated 3,000 viewers for each letter. By that formula, 1,000 letters would mean 3 million viewers. Some organizations believe the ratio of letters to viewers is as high as 7,000 to one. The major broadcasters measure their volume of mail in the tens of thousands of pieces per week. Applying the audience-to-mail ratio could produce some pretty phenomenal audience sizes for the majors, dwarfing even Jerry Falwell's proclamations.

Jerry Falwell uses the phrase *ministerially speaking* to joke about his exaggerations of audience size and other numbers. It's as if the preacher's cloak gives him license to embellish in the name of the Lord. Yea, for the glory of the Lord. Bigger is better, even in religion.

All of this truth stretching may seem pretty harmless, hardly different from the weekend fisherman who says you should have seen the one that got away. The difference is that when he tells you about the one that got away, you nod your head and smile, but you know that he's fibbing. It's all a game, and you're willing to go along with him because nobody gets hurt—nobody's really fooling anybody.

Television preachers, on the other hand, have succeeded in fooling almost everybody. The vast majority of press reports on TV religion in 1980 highlighted audience figures that, although not always as preposterous as the exaggerated claim of 50 million for Jerry Falwell, were nonetheless inaccurate. The

October 1980 issue of *Playboy* magazine ran a cynical, sarcastic article about the prime-time preachers. It chastised Ernest Angley for his amateurish toupee. It questioned the money doings of Rex, Oral, and Jim Bakker. It ridiculed fundamentalist beliefs and preaching styles all in one breath. But there at the bottom of the spread were capsule descriptions of the superstars and their shows—with audience figures easily three and four times the actual size.

Why is it that the same press that hounds these ministers on their every statement and move has simply accepted as truth the data they give out concerning their audiences? Is it holdover reverence for men of the cloth? Are they so busy hunting for the forest that they can't see the trees? Whatever the reason, this is one case where the country boys have taken the city slickers for a ride.

The TV preachers certainly aren't the first in the broadcasting industry to exaggerate the size of their audiences. TV and radio advertising rates have always been geared to audience size, just as print journalism advertising rates are a function of circulation. Thus, both radio and television broadcasters are prone to make exaggerated claims whenever they can get away with it. The mental gymnastics some go through to justify those claims can make the proverbial used-car salesman seem like Honest Abe Lincoln himself. Independent audience measurement organizations like the A. C. Nielsen and Arbitron companies emerged because they offered an invaluable service that permits advertisers to keep the radio and television industries honest.

But the prime-time preachers don't sell advertising. What tangible benefit could they derive from stretching the truth? The television ministries do not carry commercial advertising, but they do implicitly make advertising appeals in their solicitation of funds. Christians are charged with the responsibility of spreading the gospel message into all the world. When the electronic ministries solicit funds, they remind their audiences—either explicitly or implicitly—that a gift to the ministry is a contribution to the fulfillment of that great commission.

In a sense, these appeals for contributions are also advertisements for the ministries. The greater the success a ministry can claim, the more worthy it is of a viewer's support: it *is* spreading the gospel, it *is* fulfilling the great commission. To this the preacher can add that God obviously is using this particular ministry to fulfill His plan for the world. How, therefore, can the viewer decline the invitation to join in God's own triumphant march to victory? The belief that Christ is returning soon provides a theological rationale for the urgency of the task.

So it isn't surprising that the electronic preachers engage in a little hyperbole when it comes to estimating audience size. Viewers are much more likely to contribute to a thriving, significant ministry than to one that is struggling along, reaching only a few viewers.

Just how many people do tune in the prime-time preachers? During an average week in early 1980, Arbitron estimated the total number of persons viewing all sixty-six syndicated religious programs to be 20,500,000—less than the weekly audience size claimed by Jerry Falwell alone. Such huge discrepancies are the stuff of which controversy arises. Generally, the people of the electronic church claim their audiences are larger—some insist they are much larger. The critics of the electronic churches, wanting to downplay their importance, claim this figure is inflated. There are arguments to be made for both sides, but when the dust settles, the arguments pretty much cancel each other out.

Arbitron and A. C. Nielsen are two companies that have their fingers on the pulse of American television-viewing habits. Their continuous research into which programs get what share of a viewing audience, and how large it is, can literally spell the life or death of a program. And what they learn about the age and sex composition of audiences helps determine advertising rates.

Their clients pay handsomely for this information, which except in very broad terms remains a closely guarded trade secret. Like yesterday's newspaper, however, last month's Arbitron or Nielsen ratings are generally considered obsolete. How many people watched the Beatles on "The Ed Sullivan Show" in 1964 is of interest to few people. And who could possibly care how many watched "M*A*S*H" in the second week of November 1979, and whether that audience was larger or smaller than the previous week's or previous year's? Much of the information Arbitron or Nielsen so meticulously gathers is self-evident as far as most people are concerned. Everybody knows that kids watch cartoons, men watch sports, and women watch soap operas, right? And only television executives and advertising agents could possibly care about how many people watch each.

When something like the electronic church captures the interest of the American public, however, as it has during the past couple of years, that otherwise dull information becomes both interesting and important. And when the television preachers themselves make claims about the size, geographical distribution, and other features of their audiences, a systematic and objective approach to those statistics becomes essential. Until now, little factual information has been available to the public.

According to data for February 1980 supplied us by Arbitron, the following are the top ten religious television shows and their estimated audience sizes:

RANK	SHOW	PREACHER	AUDIENCE SIZE
1	"Oral Roberts and You"	Oral Roberts	2,719,250
2	"Rex Humbard"	Rex Humbard	2,409,960
3	"Hour of Power"	Robert Schuller	2,069,210
4	"Jimmy Swaggart, Evangelist"	Jimmy Swaggart	1,986,000
5	"Day of Discovery"	Richard De Haan and Paul Van Gorder	1,519,400
6	"The Old-Time Gospel Hour"	Jerry Falwell	1,455,720
7	"Gospel Singing Jubilee"		939,200
8	"Davey and Goliath"		672,000
9	"The PTL Club"	Jim Bakker	668,170
10	"Insight"		497,920

These shows, which include two mainline programs ("Davey and Goliath" is a children's program produced by the Lutheran Church of America, and "Insight," a Catholic drama show, is produced by the Paulist Fathers; both programs appear on donated time and neither solicits contributions over the air), represent almost 15 million viewers, nearly three-quarters of the total religious viewing audience. And six of those shows net 12 million people. That doesn't leave much of the pie for the other sixty syndicated programs.

Let's look at these figures—and a few others supplied by Arbitron—a little more closely. One of the most striking revelations from these data is that Jerry Falwell is in sixth place. Given his penchant for self-promotion and his incredible visibility throughout the 1980 election season, one wouldn't have expected him to be eclipsed by Rex, Oral, and the others. But Oral Roberts and Rex Humbard, both of whom have been involved in paid religious telecasting since the mid-1950s, have held their respective number one and two slots for the past decade. And although Roberts's crown may be somewhat in jeopardy of late, he still commands almost double the audience Falwell does.

The other surprising thing is the absence of "The 700 Club" from this top ten chart. The flagship show of Pat Robertson's Christian Broadcasting Network is one of the most sophisticated and slickest religious programs offered on TV today. A blend of "The Tonight Show," "Today," and the annual Jerry Lewis telethon, "The 700 Club" is the cornerstone of Robertson's $50-million-a-year enterprise. Yet its audience, according to Arbitron, is a mere 380,460, ranking it thirteenth in the religious roster. Aware of the need to attract a broader audience, Robertson began in the fall of 1980 to transform "The 700 Club" into a magazine-type format. Guest interviews have been shortened, and film clips about the guest or the topic of conversation are now often used to introduce guests and break up interviews. Investigative reporting, from a Christian perspective, has become a regular feature of the program, and there are "departments" that provide such things as cooking and consumer hints. All in all, the objective is to give the program more variety and a more upbeat, fast-moving pace.

James Robison, the fiery evangelist who gained national visibility during the 1980 political campaign because of his outspoken views, draws 464,800 loyal followers. Ernest Angley, the short, stubby Pentecostal healer who wears white suits and dark shirts, speaks in a twang reminiscent of Gomer Pyle, and performs miracles before a galaxy of stars on a deep blue background, commands an audience estimated at 314,600. Kenneth Copeland, another healer, at times lapses into what seems to be a comedian's caricature of an evangelist, a style that captures the attention of an audience of 237,140. Jack Van Impe is another veteran evangelist who has only recently moved into television. His message of the "final holocaust" being just around the corner reaches an estimated 175,150 viewers.

As we said earlier, there are those on both sides of the fence who would question all these figures. Perhaps the most persuasive argument comes from those who point out that the numbers include repeat viewers. If you were to turn on your television set one Sunday morning and watch five consecutive religious programs, you would be counted five times; total audience size isn't synonymous with the number of different people. It's like a football team reporting how many people attend its games in a given season—a season ticker holder gets counted once for every home game, not just once, period. Taking this factor into account, Ben Armstrong, who heads the evangelical religious broadcasters trade association, estimates the average weekly *unduplicated* audience to be 14 million. William Fore of the National Council of Churches, however, a natural "adversary," says 10 million is a more likely estimate. Nobody, of course, can know for sure.

On the other hand, there is an equally strong argument which suggests that the Arbitron numbers are too low: the relative absence of cable systems from Arbitron's input. At mid-1980 there were 4,200 operating cable systems in the United States with approximately 15 million subscribers, representing about 20 percent of all households in the country. Many cable systems are in markets that can receive television without cable, but in other communities cable is the only reliable source of TV reception. Arbitron measures some cable viewing but overlooks an indeterminate proportion. It is more likely to measure cable viewing in communities where virtually everyone receives television by cable than in communities where it is an option, and the optional subscription services are more likely to include an expanded number of specialized channels, including sports, news, *and* religion. The electronic church representatives who study their audiences feel that they are picking up a significant audience there that is unlikely to be measured by Arbitron or Nielsen. One argument they use in making this claim is that in-house studies of financial contributions reveal a disproportionate number of contributors who receive their programs on cable.

So there are arguments that would alter the Arbitron estimates in both directions, but given the methods of estimating, and even allowing for a small margin of error, we find it unlikely that Arbitron's data are very far off the mark. And those data add up to a very different picture of the electronic churches from that portrayed by the mass media, which have uncritically accepted the exaggerated proclamations of the television preachers. Furthermore, the Arbitron data are very close in order and magnitude to those published by Nielsen.

Still, the audience sizes are not insignificant. Virtually all the televangelists make enough money from their viewers to sustain their broadcasting. In addition, they conduct a variety of important outreach activities. But they need to be seen in perspective. Their combined efforts reach only a minority of the American population, a minority, even, of the evangelical community. Economically speaking, they are not a Fortune 500 enterprise. Compared with prime-time evening television, they are minor-leaguers. "M*A*S*H," a situation comedy with strong moral messages, commands a weekly audience a little larger than the combined audiences of the electronic churches. So does "The Muppets." And "Donahue," which leads the variety talk shows, has an audience three times larger than Oral Roberts's. The audience size the electronics reach, thus, is not insignificant, but it is not especially impressive by comparison with other audiences.

What about another claim the prime-timers make: that they are growing by leaps and bounds, saving more and more souls every day for Jesus? Is there evidence to prove that they are, in fact, a growth industry? This claim is implicit in their talk about expanding onto additional stations and cable systems, broadcasting overseas by satellite, and so forth. So also do their financial figures suggest rapid growth. Financial data released by several electronic church organizations indicate annual budget growth of

20 to 25 percent, and even higher, for the past several years. We have no evidence to dispute these figures; what we have seen suggests that they are probably accurate. But the fact is that *this very significant expansion in budget operations has not been accompanied by significant increases in total audience size.*

The great period of growth in the electronic church ministries occurred between 1970 and 1975, when their combined audiences more than doubled from just under 10 million to just under 21 million. Since 1975, however, the overall audience size has fluctuated within a fairly narrow range. The following table shows the audience size, as measured by Arbitron, for 1970 and for each year from 1975 on. Also shown is the number of syndicated religious programs, which has also fluctuated within a fairly narrow range since 1975.

YEAR	NO. OF SYNDICATED PROGRAMS	COMBINED AUDIENCE SIZE
1970	38	9,803,000
1975	65	20,806,000
1976	68	22,812,000
1977	62	21,998,000
1978	72	22,538,000
1979	66	21,477,000
1980	66	20,538,000

Source: The Arbitron Company

Although it is too early to call it a trend, the total audience size actually declined form 1978 to 1979 and from 1979 to 1980, with a net loss of 2 million viewers.

These overall figures, of course, are for syndicated programs only. In addition to these, many of the major television figures do occasional "specials" on evening prime time, which no doubt attract significantly larger audiences simply because more people watch television at that time. Special programs, however, aren't monitored for audience size. There are also scores, perhaps hundreds, of religious telecasts that are aired locally, mostly broadcasts of local church services. Many are poorly produced, but others have the technical sophistication of the better syndicated programs. Much of this production sophistication has been added within the past five years or so. Hence, it is at least possible that the total audience for religious programs is increasing through local programming. But like the overall audience size, that figure, if known, would probably not be very large.

The rapid growth of syndicated religious programming in the early 1970s corresponded with significant reductions in video production costs. As this happened, the major programs that were already on the air commercially expanded their markets rapidly. They included Oral Roberts, Rex Humbard, and Richard De Haan's "Day of Discovery." Among the commercial television programs that survive today, those of Jerry Falwell, Jimmy Swaggart, James Robison, and Robert Schuller have undergone major expansion.

Other programs were built up during that period which, for a variety of reasons, either did not survive or now command only small audiences. Garner Ted Armstrong, for example, built the television program of the Worldwide Church of God, "World of Tomorrow," to the point where it had an audience in excess of three-quarters of a million. Herbert W. Armstrong continued a television program after he excommunicated his son, Garner Ted, in 1978, but the program is but a remnant of what it was. Katherine Kuhlman, the only female televangelist, was attracting approximately three-quarters of a million viewers when she died in 1976.

While paid religious programming grew phenomenally during the first half of the 1970s, there was attrition among religious programs produced by mainline church groups which were aired on free or sustaining time as it is called in the industry. One program that lost ground was a religious drama, "This Is the Life," produced by the Lutheran Church—Missouri Synod. At one time this program had an audience in excess of 1½ million. The program survives, but despite the high quality of the production, it appears on only less than half as many stations, at basically undesirable times, and commands only about one-fifth of the audience it once had. "Insight," the drama program with religious messages produced by the Paulist Fathers, has managed to retain approximately the same audience size it had ten years ago, but it appears on half as many stations. Other programs disappeared altogether.

The two developments, of course, are related. The mainliners' programs that were aired on gratis time were pushed off the air as a direct result of the evangelicals' coming along and offering to pay for that time. One can much more easily appreciate the deep anger of mainline Protestant and Catholic broadcasters when one has examined the simultaneous growth curve of paid religious television and the sharply declining curve of sustaining-time audiences.

The airwaves, of course, are considered to be owned by the people; the government licenses and regulates their use in the public interest. From the perspective of mainline church leaders, part of that public trust involves the responsibility to make available free public service time for religious programming. When the evangelicals moved in and offered to buy the time, and the television stations accepted, that public trust, in the eyes of the mainliners, was violated. To be unaware of this, or to forget it, is to miss one of the important sources of tension between mainliners and evangelicals.

Oral Roberts's loss of audience is by far the most serious. His audience peaked in 1977 with an estimated 4,356,000 viewers. His February 1980 audience was measured at 2,720,000, a net loss of more than 1½ million, or 38 percent, in just three years. He lost almost an additional 400,000 in the May 1980 ratings. Part of that can be explained as seasonal adjustment, but his audience is off by a greater percentage than the average seasonal loss.

There are three general explanations for the Roberts audience decline. First, its beginning corresponds roughly to his change-over from a format with a heavy component of entertainment, featuring big-name stars, to a format that is more like a regular worship service. Second, Roberts has faced problems with the city of Tulsa, the state of Oklahoma, and the federal government over his medical center. From each level he has received complaints that the project is not needed, and there have been several political and legal maneuvers to block it. Third, he has been the subject of personal bad publicity. The divorce of his son, Richard, didn't help the public image of the Oral Roberts

Evangelistic Association. Then, in 1979, Jerry Sholes, a former employee and former brother-in-law of one of the top people in the organization, published an attack on the life-style and integrity of Roberts and others in the organization as well as a sweeping indictment of their fund-raising techniques. About the time the television newsmagazine "60 Minutes" went to Tulsa to do a story on Oral Roberts's operations, Sholes was beaten up. He was cautious not to accuse anyone associated with Roberts, but that implication seemed apparent in the "60 Minutes" story.

Roberts tried to handle the matter by pretending it didn't exist. He refused to talk to reporters. One of his top spokesmen also refused our repeated requests to visit the Oral Roberts Evangelistic Association headquarters and speak with officials about the ministry's operations. Other persons formerly associated with the Oral Roberts organization have told us that Sholes's exposé only "scratched the surface." Some of what upset Sholes, and some of what upsets other former associates, may be matters of taste. Still, Roberts's refusal to address serious charges that have been leveled against him, and his refusal to permit legitimate investigators to talk to his personnel, creates at least the appearance that he has something to hide. Evidence that people within the Roberts organization were responsible for derogatory rumors about Sholes added further doubts in our minds about the integrity of the Roberts operation.

As a result of diminishing audiences and rising financial liabilities associated with the medical complex, Roberts's appeals for contributions have appeared to become more and more desperate. In the fall of 1980 he claimed that he personally encountered and conversed with a 900-foot image of Jesus who instructed him to seek help in building the medical center. This caused the Reverend Carl McIntire, a right-wing radio evangelist, to comment, "Oral Roberts, I'm afraid, has gone berserk on these visions of his."

Oral Roberts's downfall, if that is indeed what is happening, may be substantially of his own making. Roberts is a man who speaks about and encourages his audiences to expect miracles in their lives. It may take one to get him out of the pinch he currently appears to be in.

Let's look at one more claim the televangelists make—that they are no longer a southern phenomenon. People have long associated fundamentalist-evangelical religion with the Bible Belt, which is more or less synonymous with the South. That isn't so anymore, say the prime-time preachers. "There's a Bible cloak in America that covers the whole blooming republic," Jerry Falwell told his audience at the National Affairs Briefing in Dallas in 1980. Here's what he told that same group in support of his contention that the Bible Belt exists no more: "The number-one city in America in our ministry in the number of persons and financial support is Los Angeles. Number two is Philadelphia. Number three is Boston. Number four is New York. Number five is Chicago. You come down to number sixteen before you get to a southern city, and that's Greenville, South Carolina."

We don't know what kind of formula Falwell used to mix people and dollars and come up with these figures. But here's what the February 1980 Arbitron figures show about his audience:

RANK	CITY	AUDIENCE SIZE
1	Los Angeles	63,000
2	Roanoke-Lynchburg	42,000
3	Philadelphia	27,000
4	Washington, D.C.	27,000
5	Knoxville	25,000

At least Falwell was right about Los Angeles being his top market. And if we were to grant him that it's not fair to count his hometown audience, then Philadelphia would be second. But Boston, which he said was his third-biggest market, didn't appear in the top twenty. And New York, which he said was fourth, was actually tied with Atlanta, Kansas City, and Monroe, Louisiana—El Dorado, Arkansas, for the eighth spot. And as for his claim that you don't find a southern city until position sixteen, we counted eight before we got to the sixteenth position. As for his top five markets, we've always thought Roanoke and Knoxville were in the South, and although many southerners don't want to claim it, so is Washington, D.C., for all kinds of official government purposes including the census.

The incredible aspect of Falwell's hyperbole, however, is that he was presumably comparing his total audience size in metropolitan areas like New York, with 20 million people, and metropolitan Los Angeles, with a population in excess of 10 million, with the audience size in southern cities. On the basis of audience size as a percentage of total population, of course, Falwell has scarcely penetrated major metropolitan areas.

Certainly, all the major religious television programs appear on stations in every region and metropolitan area in the United States. But when you examine the distribution of their audiences in comparison with the distribution of the U.S. population, it is immediately obvious that the electronic church is still heavily a Bible Belt phenomenon, as the accompanying table demonstrates. Whereas the eastern region of the United States contains 22.5 percent of the total population, most of the electronic churches fail to draw even half that proportion, or approximately 11 percent. Robert Schuller, the only mainline Protestant preacher in the group, is the exception to the generalization. In the Midwest, the home base of his own denomination, the Reformed Church in America, Schuller also does well.

All the television preachers except Schuller draw a disproportionate percentage of their audiences from the South. The South now has nearly one-third of the U.S. population (32.4 percent), and Oral Roberts draws almost 54 percent of his audience from there. Jimmy Swaggart also draws just over half of his audience from the South (51.3 percent). Rex Humbard, Jerry Falwell, and

Percent of Audiences by Region

	EAST	MIDWEST	SOUTH	WEST
Oral Roberts	10.3%	24.6%	53.9%	11.2%
Rex Humbard	14.7	23.8	46.5	15.0
Robert Schuller	24.0	33.2	30.1	12.7
Jimmy Swaggart	11.5	23.0	51.3	14.2
"Day of Discovery"	10.8	28.3	43.8	17.1
Jerry Falwell	12.9	26.9	44.9	15.2
% U.S. population in region	**22.5**	**26.7**	**32.4**	**18.4**

Source: The Arbitron Company, February 1980

Richard De Haan draw 46.5, 44.9, and 43.8 percent respectively—all well above the percentage of the country's population located in this region. "Gospel Singing Jubilee," which ranks eighth with an audience of just under a million, draws 97 percent of its audience from the South.

All of the electronic preachers are underrepresented in the western region. Schuller, whose home base is near Los Angeles in Orange County, did worse in the West than anyone except Oral Roberts. If Los Angeles, and a few other pockets of heavy southern migration, were excluded, the western region would show even poorer penetration than the eastern region.

Jerry Falwell may have a point about the Bible cloak spreading across America, because people from the South have migrated to the Midwest and West, even as the rest of the country is finding its way into the Sun Belt. But there is still very little migratory flow from the South to New England, and this area has been extremely difficult for the electronic churches to penetrate.

For as long as sociologists have gathered statistics on religious behavior, it has been consistently observed that women attend church more than men. Also consistent is the pattern of greater church attendance among older people than among the young. In light of this, it should not come as a surprise to learn that women also watch religious programs on television more than men do and that older persons do so more than young people.

What we found surprising in the Arbitron data is the consistency of age and sex composition from one religious television program to the next. *Virtually all the syndicated programs have audiences of which two-thirds to three-quarters are fifty years of age or over.* Entertainment and drama programs tend to have somewhat younger audiences. Among the top ten programs, three (Swaggart, "PTL," and "Gospel Singing") have a substantial element of entertainment. Sixty-two percent of their audiences is fifty or over, compared to an average of 74 percent for the religious service format of the other top ten programs. No program, except the children's programs, attracts a substantially younger audience.

Audiences also tend to be disproportionately female. Among the top ten programs, the percentage of females in the audience ranges from a low of 60 percent for "Gospel Singing Jubilee" to a high of 73 percent for "The PTL Club." Thus, entertainment is apparently not the factor that accounts for the variation in sex composition.

Among those persons fifty and over who watch religious television programs, about two-thirds are female. The variation, program to program, is fairly narrow, but there are some notable exceptions. Jimmy Swaggart, for some reason, attracts as many males fifty and over as he does females. By contrast, both "The PTL Club" and "The 700 Club" attract more than 70 percent females among their over-fifty audience. This, no doubt, is because these programs tend to be aired early and late in the day. Older people are more likely to suffer insomnia and hence be up when the programs appear, and there are more older females than males.

The data, thus, do confirm the stereotype that audiences of the electronic churches are disproportionately older and, among that group, disproportionately female. Extreme caution must be exercised, however, in jumping to another widely held conclusion—namely, that it is necessarily an exploitative relationship that exists between the electronic churches and their elderly audiences. Let's examine what evidence there is that may shed light on this important issue.

First of all, virtually every indicator available points to the conclusion that people become more deeply involved in religion as they grow older. This deeper involvement includes both belief and practice. People over fifty attend church more frequently, and they are more likely to say that religion is important in their lives and that Sunday has a particular religious or spiritual meaning. Moreover, the elderly are more likely to express evangelical, as opposed to liberal or mainline, beliefs and practices. Thus, they are more likely to report that they have had a "born-again" experience, believe the Bible to be the literal word of God, and to have "witnessed" their faith to another.

In light of this evidence, it should not be surprising at all to find the elderly more deeply involved in the electronic church than younger age groups. They are simply more involved in all kinds of religious expression. Moreover, females are more involved than males for the simple reason that as a group they survive males by an average of 7.7 years.

There is another important reason to expect the elderly to be more deeply involved in the electronic church. As people grow older, they are more likely to experience illnesses, accidents, degenerative diseases, and other fates that restrict their mobility. In a society that has become age-segregated, we tend to forget this fact. One of the initial rationales for radio broadcasts of religious services was that they provided a way to reach the sick and elderly.

Whether there is a tendency for elderly people to find the electronic church an "easier" way to worship and have a sense of religious experience is not known for sure. We can speculate that the drift toward the electronic church as the primary or sole source of religious involvement is more likely to occur when elderly people fail to find a meaningful experience in their local congregations. Another factor that affects an elderly person's involvement in his or her local church is the degree to which that congregation makes an effort to care for and involve the elderly.

In July 1980 *TV Guide* published an article by William Fore entitled "There Is No Such Thing As a TV Pastor." Those who wrote the "Letters Department" disagreed overwhelmingly with this negative assessment of the pastoral possibilities of the electronic churches. Letter after letter extolled the virtues of this or that favorite TV pastor. But quite a few letter writers were also explicit in their disappointment, if not downright anger, with the failure of their local church to meet their needs. One expressed what is no doubt the experience of many of the elderly in the United States: "My own church, which I support as much as I am able financially, has really failed me. Now that I have recovered from an illness due to a successful operation, I want to go to church and mix with fellow Christians. Although I called the church office and explained I had no transportation and also told the pastor, nothing was done. No one ever offered to take me, although I offered to pay for gas. Where else can I turn but the electronic church?" Clearly, there are many churches that would never knowingly permit this kind of neglect of elderly members. But just as certainly, there are others that lack a sense of community and caring for their members, young and old alike.

John Gilman spent twelve years with Pat Robertson and played an important role in building the Christian Broadcasting Network into the giant communications operation that it is today. He left CBN, in part, because he was troubled by some of the electronic communications practices common to all religious broadcasting. In particular, he was bothered by the fund-raising techniques that are necessary to keep these enterprises afloat. But he is also critical of the local church for creating the vacuum the electronic church stepped in to fill. To those Christians critical of the electronic church Gilman says: "You've created this electric church. You've created these superego, high-powered evangelistic types of people. . . . You're part of it. You've got debts you didn't pay in your own church. You didn't go and visit the sick like you should have. You didn't minister to the people that you had. These people flocked to their television sets, and they hunted down anybody that had anything to say that you weren't giving them. And that's why God created this [the electronic church] in the first place. Pat and Jim, Oral, all these people that have these programs . . . they've met an incredible need in this country."

Whatever else may be said about the electronic churches, it does seem evident that they fill an important need of older people. Our society has too long neglected the elderly, so those who do address their needs are certain to find a following. Although we have no doubt that most members of the electronic churches serve out of sincerity and devotion to their ministerial callings, the relationship between serving and the extraction of tithes from their followers needs to be examined. The electronic churches minister to their elderly followers. In return, the elderly contribute significantly to financing the multimillion-dollar empires of the stars of the cathode church, most of whom, to date, have been extremely reluctant to reveal any financial details. The question of the stewardship of the electronic preachers will be treated in Chapter 6.

The question about the electronic communicants that remains, however, is motivation. What is there in the psychological makeup of the televangelists' audience that draws them to this method of worship—not just draws them, but encourages the bonds they feel, bonds that include substantial donations? Frank and Deirdre Patrick, the couple whose comments open this chapter, are retired and live in a suburb of Boston. He is an invalid, and neither gets out much these days. Like many TV religion fans, they have a study filled with books, pamphlets, records, and cassette tapes from religious programs. They admit that they use 30 percent of their income for the television ministries.

Are the Patricks particularly susceptible? If they are, there are an awful lot of people out there who are potentially just as susceptible. Or are we overlooking the unique "psychological makeup" of television that helps cement the bond between viewer and broadcaster?

"One of the most striking characteristics of the new mass media," wrote Donald Horton and R. Richard Wohl in *Psychiatry* a quarter of a century ago, "is that they give the illusion of face-to-face relationship with the performer." Theater, at its best, draws members of an audience into feeling intimate with what is happening onstage. But the relationship ends when the play ends, and we usually identify with a character or a role, not with an actor. In movies, people identify with individual actors independent of the roles they play. In its early days Hollywood exploited this by creating fan clubs, and actors and actresses tended to get stereotyped in roles that were already proven box office successes.

But modern methods of mass communication, especially television, can create a continuing face-to-face relationship, and over time the performer becomes familiar to the audience. The audience, in turn, feels a certain intimacy with the performer, an intimacy that breeds trust, caring, and dependency. (Remember the reaction when the producers of "M*A*S*H" had McLean Stevenson killed on his way back to Bloomington, Illinois, from the 4077th? Viewers were outraged that their beloved Colonel Blake didn't survive the war.) "In time," wrote Horton and Wohl, "the devotee—the 'fan'—comes to believe that he 'knows' the persona more intimately and profoundly than others do; that he 'understands' his character and appreciates his values and motives. . . . The persona may be considered by his audience as a friend, counselor, comforter, and model."

Horton and Wohl gave the term *parasocial interaction* to this rather widespread phenomenon in mass culture. Before television, radio developed many illusions with which various age groups in the audience could identify. Buck Rogers, Captain Midnight, the Green Hornet, and Superman were real in the imaginations of millions of youngsters in the 1940s. Real also were characters who were not "bigger than life," but ordinary people like Dagwood Bumstead and Fibber McGee, characters who reminded us of our own capacity to bumble and sometimes be abused by others.

Television greatly expanded the capacity of performers and their producers to let the audience participate. In drama this is accomplished by creating characters who are real, rather than celebrities who can be viewed only from afar. The phenomenal success of Norman Lear's "All in the Family" and all its spin-offs in the 1970s can substantially be attributed to the creation of characters that were true to life as a significant segment of the viewing audience knew and experienced it.

In nondramatic programming, a variety of techniques or strategies may be used to create and sustain the illusion of intimacy between performer and audience. The first is to make the performance as casual as possible in a setting that appears appropriate for informal face-to-face social intercourse. Second, members of the supporting cast are treated as intimates. Using first names or nicknames as well as sharing off-camera experiences gives credibility to the appearance of intimacy among performers. Another way to sustain the illusion of intimacy between performer and audience is to use live audiences and to blur the distinction between the audience and the stage set. Perhaps no show has ever done this as successfully as the Phil Donahue show, where the audience *is* the set. Still another way that television has created the illusion of intimacy is through what television pioneer Dave Garroway called the "subjective camera." The camera goes down the ramp from the football stadium and follows the players to the dressing room. The camera, situated backstage, follows the orchestra conductor as he leaves the stage and moves with him to his dressing room. A camera fixed to a roller coaster can do more than create the visual experience of a roller-coaster ride; it can create the physiological sensations for the viewer as well. It's as though the viewer weren't really confined to his or her living-room chair.

The audience, of course, has to be a willing participant in this illusion of intimacy, but that isn't hard once rapport has been established between the performer and the audience. But being there can be more than a state of mind. Early television programs were broadcast with an audience in the studio, and even today the major networks film many shows in front of an audience. Tickets for the taping of television shows and tours of television studios are in high demand. And for those who have thus participated, the illusion of intimacy created on a cathode screen and the reality of anonymous parasocial interaction can become quite fuzzy. The same is true of the prime-timers. Tens of thousands of loyal followers of each of the major TV ministries have made pilgrimages to the sites where the programs are broadcast.

The electronic churches have moved beyond parasocial interaction to *parapersonal communication*. Television is only one component of the religious broadcaster's parapersonal network, however. The producers of religious programming have added the capacity of the computer to produce all those thousands of direct-mail letters that begin by addressing the recipient by name. There are a lot of people who believe that their favorite televangelist really does answer his mail personally. And there are many, many more who may know better but choose to incorporate the illusion of personally answered mail into their generalized identification with and belief in the stars of the electronic churches. Still others are conscious of the fact that the TV preachers cannot personally respond, but they view their helpers as extensions of a family of persons who love and care.

The members of the audience are thus transformed into communicants—loyal members of the television ministry's family. Alone in the privacy of their living rooms, the electronic communicants are able to transcend their sense of loneliness and little worth. As financial partners and emotional participants in the television ministries, they become part of God's plan to fulfill the great commission.

4

The Evolution
of a Revolution

*It is not without significance that the first voice
broadcast was a Christian religious celebration.*
J. Howard Ellens,
Models of Religious Broadcasting

Religious diversity has always been a characteristic of American society. Each colony on the eastern seaboard attracted a different group of people who found there a congenial religious climate. The Pilgrims had made New England a land comfortable for Congregationalists. British Baptists fit into the middle colonies. Scottish and Irish Presbyterians found Pennsylvania and the Carolinas to their liking. Methodism was exported from England to all parts of the country. There were religious enclaves—and occasional persecutions—but for the most part diversity and tolerance became American principles, and after a while just about any religious group could be found anywhere in the states of the new republic.

The Presbyterians and Episcopalians tried to keep up with the expansion of the frontier, but their insistence on a properly educated ministry left them undermanned for frontier work. They sent learned and literate preachers wherever they could, but the unlearned settlers on the frontier sometimes found them too highfalutin.

The Baptists, already a substantial part of the population, had no such hang-ups about education. Godly men who had the call to preach were ordained as needed. The Baptists suffered few staffing problems and kept right up with the westward and southward expansion of the young nation. Besides, they found revivalism congenial, and they grew rapidly during the Great Awakening (religious revivals) of the eighteenth century. Methodism, born as a pietistic movement within the Church of England, came to America and threw itself into the expanding frontier. After its split from the "head" religion of Anglicanism, the "heart" religion of Methodism was downright suspicious of theological education until the end of the nineteenth century. A Methodist preacher's theological library had to fit into his saddlebags.

The Methodists, Baptists, and others who considered theology subordinate to religious experience succeeded on the frontier where the intellectuals failed. On the edges of civilization, the ability to call sinners to repentance was inspired by God, not inculcated by education.

Those early evangelists gave the United States two important religious traditions. The first was that educational preparation is not prerequisite to preaching. The second was that warmhearted religious experience is the right and due of true believers, and that, if necessary, they ought even to separate themselves from the establishment churches to get it.

If a man (rarely a woman) felt called to preach, who could deny the calling? On the frontier, anyone who got the call got his chance. If he seemed to his hearers to "divide the Word rightly," his calling was confirmed. He could be ordained as a pastor by a congregation or a bishop, or he could travel from town to town as an evangelist.

Not only on the frontier, but in the grubby cities as well, life was hard and diversions were few. Religious services, not always held on a regular schedule, offered a respite from the rigors of life, a chance to sit, to hear a man describe the fiery punishments of hell and the beauty of heavenly streets paved with gold. The traveling evangelists, in the absence of a church, might construct a "brush arbor," a rude shelter offering protection from the sun. Families brought lunches in their wagons. On occasion they might stay for several days and sleep in the wagons. In the cities the evangelists preached wherever they could—in churches, in halls, in homes, or in the open air. If a man could preach at all, he was assured of hearers. For the poor, there was little else to do except go to a tavern.

Religious revivals swept whole regions of the country periodically during the eighteenth and nineteenth centuries. Mainliners experienced revivals, too, and establishment preachers often earned fame with the power and eloquence of their oratory.

By the latter part of the nineteenth century, there was no more frontier. America had been settled. But the evangelists kept right on moving. They pastored churches in some cases; but they maintained tradition by holding periodic revival meetings in those churches. Some continued to travel and still do today. Jim Bakker, of "The PTL Club," was such a traveling evangelist. So were Oral Roberts and Rex Humbard. Many of the lesser lights of the electronic church today are still itinerant preachers on the stump who go wherever an evangelistic meeting can be organized. They are the modern-day gypsies of the gospel. And the pastors of the churches in which they preach are fellow heirs of their common evangelical tradition.

Whether in a rural brush arbor or a city church, every evangelist sought to draw a crowd and preach to it. The larger the crowd, the more opportunities there were to convert sinners. Most evangelists were sincere in wanting to bring the comforts of Christ to the unconverted. There were occasional charlatans, but not many. Elmer Gantry was the creation of a twentieth-century novelist, not a realistic depiction of the evangelical movement. Most evangelists beat the drum for offerings only as a matter of economic survival—of course, some were more accomplished drum beaters than others.

The evangelical tradition placed a heavy emphasis on preaching. Platform oratory was the measure by which the assembled crowd determined whether a preacher was "mightily used of God." Evangelical religion was felt in the heart, not exercised in the intellect. The preacher's job was to call sinners to repentance through graphic descriptions of what would happen to them if they didn't heed the word. But the preacher also had to comfort the converted with glowing descriptions of what awaited the redeemed.

Although many preached in fiery fashion against Demon Rum

and other evils of the flesh, there was little effort to connect the teachings of the Bible to any larger social concerns. Indeed, the Bible was used often to justify what was going on in society. Preachers of the frontier and of the established churches had no difficulty finding texts to support the institution of slavery, for example. The purely subjective, personalistic nature of the evangelical religion of the period is reflected in its hymns, a type still popular among the followers of the tradition. Modern church musicians call them the "I-Me-My" hymns because they are filled with first-person pronouns describing an individual relationship to God. There is also a heavy emphasis on the cross and Jesus' blood, by which the believer is transported into the blessedness of salvation.

Protestantism always has had a tradition of lusty congregational singing, encouraged by the early reformers as one means of transferring worship from altar to pew. Charles Wesley wrote several thousand hymns, many using popular tavern tunes of the day. The easy rhythms, catchy tunes, and subjective joy of such music became an important part of revivalist services. Song leaders, introduced to ensure that singing was enthusiastic, became part of the evangelistic traveling team, a tradition continued today and exemplified by Cliff Barrows, Billy Graham's song leader.

Relationships between revivalist religionists and establishment churchmen were never good. The revivalists tended to be scornful of the rational establishment approach to religion. The establishment felt the same way about the unrestrained emotionalism of the revivalists. But deeper issues underlay the hostility between the two groups. The establishment churchmen were beginning to toy with new ideas of science, historical studies concerning the writing of the Bible, and a blasphemous new theory called evolution. The evangelists rejected all these things out of hand and began swearing eternal enmity against all persons and ideas not in accord with a plain, literal reading of the Bible. This theological division gathered steam in the late 1800s and erupted into open warfare after the turn of the twentieth century. Thus battle lines were drawn when radio was introduced in the early 1920s. The history of religious broadcasting in the United States is in part the history of the fight between evangelical fundamentalism and the more liberal establishment churches. Radio—and today, television—became the battleground of a religious war.

Credit for launching the first nonexperimental regular radio broadcasting service goes to Westinghouse Electric and Manufacturing Company for KDKA in Pittsburgh. The station went on the air on November 2, 1920, to broadcast the Harding-Cox election returns, followed on succeeding days by regular evening broadcasts of musical programs.

Westinghouse wanted to stimulate audience growth so that it could sell more radios. It was decided to broadcast a church service. Although the U.S. Signal Corps had broadcast a service from the Trinity Church of Washington, D.C., on August 24, 1919, such a program would be a first for private broadcasting. A Westinghouse engineer was a member of the choir at Calvary Episcopal Church of Pittsburgh. The rector, the Reverend Edwin Van Etten, agreed to the experiment. On Sunday, January 2, 1921, with three microphones installed in the church, two Westinghouse engineers donned choir robes and put the church's evening vesper service on the air. The rector had previously arranged for his associate, the Reverend Louis B. Whittemore, to conduct the service. He thus unwittingly accorded to Whittemore the distinction of being the first man to preach on a radio station.

Van Etten said of the occasion, "The whole thing was an experiment, and I remember distinctly my own feeling that after all no harm could be done! It never occurred to me that the little black box was really going to carry out the service to the outside world. I knew there was such a thing as wireless, but somehow I thought there would be some fluke in the connection, and that the whole thing would be a fizzle! The opportunity had come to us rather suddenly and in this dazed sort of mood we did not prepare any special service or sermon for the occasion."

Within a few months, many more radio stations followed KDKA on the air. The success of the KDKA church broadcasts was noted and widely emulated by new stations all over the country. In the beginning there were few regulations, anyone could have a station license just by asking for it, and a station could be built for a few hundred dollars by any talented radio experimenter. *Popular Radio* magazine said in January 1925 that of 600 stations on the air, 63 were owned by churches and other religious groups. Those stations came and went with dizzying suddenness. The shortest duration on record for church owner- ship was for WHBQ in Memphis, which the Men's Fellowship Class of the Methodist Episcopal Church South owned for one month in 1925. Other periods of ownership lasted from six months to a few years. Religion was destined from the inception of radio to be an important part of broadcasting. The Department of Commerce had noted in 1922 that the wavelength of 360 meters (approximately 830 kilocycles) was assigned for the transmission of "important news items, entertainment, lectures, sermons and similar matter."

If getting into radio was easy, staying in it was much more difficult. Today, just eight of the ninety-five noncommercial educational and religious stations licensed in the 1920s are still in noncommercial hands. There are several reasons why the churches were not able to maintain their early foothold in broadcasting.

Commercial broadcasters, who had established stations in the beginning either for public relations purposes or to promote the sale of radio receivers, discovered the business of selling time in 1924. Now the newspaper or department store which had established a radio station merely to publicize its own name had a new source of revenue that promised to be a gold mine. The commercial broadcasters exerted heavy pressure to get rid of the noncommercials with which they had to share time. In many cases they succeeded in capturing legally all the air time and forcing the noncommercials off the frequencies. In other cases they simply bought out the noncommercials, a practice that increased rapidly in 1930 after churches and educational institu- tions began to feel the financial crunch of the depression.

But if the experiments in church ownership ended in failure, there were other visions of religion on radio that did not. If one could not successfully operate a radio station, why not simply preach over someone else's station?

Chicago's mayor, William Hale "Big Bill" Thompson, set up a radio station on top of the Chicago City Hall in 1922. Lacking program material, Mayor Thompson issued a general call for volunteers. He hoped that professional entertainers would respond, but they were suspicious of radio and refused. Among those who did respond was evangelist Paul Rader, who brought along his musicians and reproduced a typical evangelistic service on the air. Rader, a Chicago pastor, was typical of the fundamentalist evangelists of the day whose styles had evolved from the itinerant preachers of the nineteenth century. Evangelical broadcasters were thoroughly and almost universally imbued with the evangelistic meeting concept, which attempted to draw the largest possible crowd to hear the word. Revivalists saw radio as a way to reach even greater numbers of people.

The revivalists and the churches that first used radio for religious broadcasting saw it as a way to extend what took place in the meeting or the church to people who could not or would not attend. But even this altruistic and seemingly benign utilization of the airwaves met with some criticism. Some churchmen wondered aloud whether the practice would entice people to stay home from church and listen to the radio services instead. This question is the oldest one in religious broadcasting, and it is still being asked by critics of the electronic church.

The controversy heated up even more when some preachers actually used the airwaves to invite people to come to their churches. And indignation rose to new heights when some radio preachers asked for donations to help them pay for their broadcasts.

Although Ben Armstrong is credited with coining the term *electric church* (*electronic* is now generally used), he was not the first person in religious broadcasting to think of the concept of a church existing over the airwaves. According to Armstrong himself, pioneer Omaha evangelical R. R. Brown may have been the first to envision the radio audience as a new form of congregation. Listeners to Brown's "Radio Chapel Service" in the 1920s were invited to join the World Radio Congregation, which issued official membership cards. The notion of an electronic church was also prefigured in the early broadcasting efforts of Herbert W. Armstrong, head of the Worldwide Church of God, who launched his movement in 1934 as the Radio Church of God.

California's legendary Aimee Semple McPherson, who established a radio station in her Angelus Temple of the International

Church of the Foursquare Gospel in Los Angeles, even took in members through a combination of radio broadcasting and telephone conversation. McPherson's disciples set up tents in cities around Los Angeles, where crowds listened to her broadcasts and converts responded to her by telephone, thus being received into membership. McPherson applied for a television license in 1944, but she died that same year. It is interesting to speculate whether, if she had lived, she might have speeded up the development of the electronic church.

For the most part, only the names of the successful and controversial have survived to be entered in the history books. But in every city and town in the country with a radio station, there were preachers who wanted to broadcast. Many did. Ministers of mainline churches usually contented themselves with broadcasting their Sunday worship services or devotional programs, usually presented by the stations and not by the preachers invited to appear on them. As is true today, however, for every one of those mainline types there were a dozen evangelicals.

Local religious broadcasting was, by the end of the 1920s, in a troubled state. In 1927 *Christian Century* magazine headlined an article "Should Churches Be Shut Off the Air?"

A friend of ours spent a night not so long ago near Los Angeles. He kept a record of the religious services which were on the air, and of the subjects with which these services dealt. Located where he was, the loudest station proved to be one carrying a Christian Science service of that church. From a wave-length close on the dial came the voice of a Presbyterian minister, launched into a vicious tirade against Roman Catholicism. From her own broadcasting station the dramatic voice of Mrs. Aimee Semple McPherson expounded her special brand of Four-square gospel. A Bible institute had a station of its own and was using it to present an ultra-conservative type of prophetic interpretation to any who might care to listen. The calm, cultured and persuasive voice of some Unitarian came on the wave-length assigned to one of the commercial stations. At the same hour it happened that a Baptist was trying to make plain the fallacies underlying Christian Science. A Church of Christ evangelist specialized in the Old Jerusalem gospel, while another evangelist, connected with the Church of the Nazarenes, was also on the air. And from the new station of his Methodist Church, the Rev. "Fighting Bob" Shuler was making a desperate effort—via radio—to clean up Hollywood. All this at one time, and from within a radius of twenty-five miles.

. . . there is serious question whether religion, as now carried on the air, is a community friend or a community nuisance.

If the radio is to be rightly used, church federations in the centers where broadcasting stations are located will have to give the method by which this is to be done much more attention than they have in the past.

The unfettered and troublesome development of religious broadcasting in the first few years of radio did not go unnoticed by those who were thinking seriously about the future development of the medium. NBC, the first radio network, was determined to avoid some of the problems. The network did not want to be bothered by requests for time from many different sectarian broadcasters and denominations. Its solution to the problem in 1928 had a permanent and profound effect on the development of religious broadcasting in the United States.

NBC asked the Federal Council of Churches (predecessor of today's National Council of Churches) to take responsibility for all Protestant religious broadcasting on NBC. The Federal Council, then representing twenty-five Protestant denominations, agreed. NBC subsequently made similar arrangements with the National Council of Catholic Men and the Jewish Theological Seminary of America, but those groups lacked the organization by which they could move as far and as fast as the Protestants.

Charles F. McFarland, general secretary of the Federal Council, was a member of the NBC Advisory Committee on Religious Activities which shaped the following policy: (1) Religious groups should receive free broadcast time but pay for program production costs. (2) Religious broadcasting should be nondenominational. (3) Network broadcasts should use one speaker for continuity. (4) Broadcasts should use a preaching format, "avoiding matters of doctrine and controversial subjects."

But the Advisory Committee policy that caused the greatest strife and led directly to the present-day mainline-evangelical division was the committee's first principle: "The National Broadcasting Company will serve only the central national agencies of great religious faiths, as for example, the Roman Catholics, the Protestants, and the Jews as distinguished from individual churches or small group movements where the national membership is comparatively small."

Some of the influence of the NBC—Federal Council partnership was moderated by the formation of the CBS radio network in 1927. But CBS also adopted a policy in 1931 of refusing to sell time for religion.

The Mutual Broadcasting System network, formed in the mid-1930s, followed a policy of providing *only* purchased time to religious broadcasters for a few years. Charles E. Fuller of "The Old-Fashioned Revival Hour" was Mutual's biggest customer in the early 1940s, when more than 25 percent of the network's revenue came from religious accounts. But in 1944 Mutual shifted all religious broadcasting to Sunday morning, cut down program length and—most important—forbade the solicitation of funds on the air. Mutual's religious billings plummeted.

The ABC network, which was originally one of the two networks operated by NBC, followed NBC's lead in refusing to sell time for religious broadcasting and giving time only to the mainline faith groups. The network stance was adopted widely by local station managers. The explanation seems simple enough. Evangelical broadcasters were both multitudinous and troublesome. Their programs and sermons often were hotly sectarian. All things considered, it was simply a lot easier to give the time to the mainline groups that were certain to be inoffensive. It also is obvious that the network officials and local station managers felt a much greater degree of personal identification with the mainliners than with the evangelicals. The broadcasting executives *were* mainliners, if they had any religious inclinations at all. William J. DuBourdieu, a scholar who classified Protestant broadcasting into "conventional," "fundamentalist," and "irregular," said in 1932, "The Conventional Protestant group is the one which has been chosen by radio stations and chains [networks] to be their agent in supplying religion to the Protestant section of the nation."

The future course of nonmainline religious broadcasting in the United States was set: it would of necessity be entrepreneurial. Fundamentalists would have to buy time, and their audiences would have to furnish the money. This was their only avenue to radio, and they would fight to keep it open.

That the Federal Council of Churches encouraged local and state councils of churches to produce better-quality religious broadcasting around the country is unquestionably true. That they went much further than that, as evangelicals alleged, and tried to drive evangelicals off the air cannot be proved. Eugene R. Bertermann, longtime president of the evangelical National Religious Broadcasters, claimed at a Senate hearing in 1947 that the Federal Council did so in 1929, sending a representative on a tour of the country to sign up stations "with ironclad contracts obliging them to use the Federal Council's religious programs and none other. . . ." Lowell Saunders, an evangelical who sympathizes with the NRB, searched unsuccessfully for documentation of this charge. Rather, he found a good deal of testimony and evidence that the charge was *not* true: "From the vantage point of today, such charges against the Federal Council can only be considered hearsay." He also concluded that if Federal Council pressures ever were exerted to stop the sale of time to evangelicals, they certainly did not work. Saunders found, instead, a high correlation between the economic health of the broadcasting industry and the willingness of stations to sell time to evangelicals. When stations and networks needed evangelical money, they sold time to evangelicals.

Ralph Jennings, media watchdog for the United Church of Christ, who studied religious broadcasting during the same period, said that "there is no evidence that the Federal Council of Churches was guilty of any overt acts against any religious programs." Jennings, however, who is very much a mainliner, has stated that the Federal Council's policy of requesting time for itself alone as the central representative of Protestantism was unfair to some evangelical groups, notably the Southern Baptists and Missouri Synod Lutherans.

What matters most is that many evangelicals *believed* there was a conspiracy against them. Most realized that they would never have significant access to free time, and they gradually arrived at a position of constant vigilance against what they perceived as threats to their right to buy time. Evangelical literature and pronouncements from the period suggest high levels of paranoia.

Broadcasting stations, under the Communications Act of 1934, are not common carriers; they are not obliged to sell time just because someone wants to buy it. As radio stations grew prosperous, many adopted policies of refusing to sell time for religion and giving it only to ecumenical groups. Unfortunately, many evangelicals saw in each instance of this the hand of the hated Federal Council of Churches.

Since the turn of the century, American fundamentalists have been involved in a holy war against liberalism. That the liberals have seldom noticed the war against them, or bothered to retaliate, has not taken the fun out of the fight for the fundamentalists. To most of them, the worst features of liberalism were collected and embodied in the Federal (now National) Council of Churches. The Council has served as a convenient focus for evangelical militancy for decades. The development of religious broadcasting in the first twenty years of radio played no small part in intensifying that focus.

The National Association of Evangelicals was organized in 1942 specifically, in part, to counter Federal Council activities and influence. The NAE's organizational purposes include the words ". . . to raise up a witness against the apostasy of groups claiming to represent Protestant Christianity without such loyalty to the historic Gospel of the Lord Jesus Christ." The list of the NAE's "fields of endeavor" included radio, and the new organization quickly passed a resolution calling for the establishment of a Radio Committee "in order to help in securing a fair and equal opportunity for the use of radio facilities by evangelical groups or individuals."

When the NAE was unable to devote time and resources to radio, it invited evangelical broadcasters to form a separate association under its wing. The National Religious Broadcasters (NRB) was born in 1944. Although it was officially separate and independent, it remained subservient to the NAE for many years. As Lowell Saunders puts it, "It remained captive, for fifteen years, to the idea that its main purpose was to combat the Federal Council and later the National Council of Churches." Gradually, the NRB outgrew its obsession with the Federal/National Council. It discovered its own agenda, which was still largely protectionistic, but came to see that the liberals actually had very little power in the media.

At the same time, evangelicals were beginning to achieve power of a different sort through buying and building their own stations. The modern religious stations, unlike the church-owned stations of the early days, were strictly commercial ventures, organized to make a profit. A new generation of religious broadcasters had emerged—men who understood that the fundamentalist gospel had to be undergirded by capital investment and business management. The NRB had only 104 members in 1968. In 1980 it had about 900. Members of the NRB produce at least 70 percent of all the religious broadcasts in the United States.

The growth of the NRB parallels the growth of fundamentalist entrepreneurial religious broadcasting which occurred explosively in the 1970s. That growth could not have taken place without a massive evangelical move into television. Television did for the movement what radio never could do.

Television is one of the most powerful social forces in human history. Radio was a marvel, but television is a miracle. Radio was a table of mental snacks; television is force feeding for the brain.

The first religious telecasts took place on Easter Sunday, 1940. The Protestant telecast was presented in cooperation with the Federal Council of Churches and the Catholic program, presumably, in cooperation with the National Council of Catholic Men. A Jewish service for Passover, most likely under the aegis of the Jewish Theological Seminary of America, was presented a month later.

By 1948 video was established and more than forty stations were on the air. TV sets began to come off the assembly lines by the millions. TV stations were springing up all over the country, and by 1950 coaxial cable links were completed which made possible nationwide TV networks. An estimated 10 million receivers had been sold by 1950, and by 1958 the number of TV sets roughly equaled the number of households in America.

The man who gave preachers all over the country a fever for television was a Roman Catholic bishop. He was baptized Peter John Sheen but renamed himself Fulton J. Sheen. He went before the cameras for the first time as the speaker on that historic Easter Sunday, 1940, Roman Catholic religious telecast. When he returned to television in 1952, he astounded the world of religious broadcasting with his audience ratings.

Sheen was no stranger to religious broadcasting. He was the first speaker on "The Catholic Hour," presented by NBC radio in cooperation with the National Council of Catholic Men, in 1930. He remained the speaker on that program until he went on television in 1952. He was the most outstanding public speaker of the Catholic Church in the United States.

Sheen's program, called "Life Is Worth Living," originated from the Adelphi Theater in New York before a live audience (everything in television was live in those days). Sheen was consciously and clearly Catholic, but his messages were designed for people of all faiths or of no faith. He spoke about common human problems and aspirations—and millions watched his prime-time presentations.

Sheen began in 1952 on the old DuMont television network, and the first telecast was carried by seventeen stations. DuMont began receiving more than 10,000 letters a week, and Milton Berle's ratings dropped about ten points. Realizing that it had a winner, Sheen's sponsor, the Admiral Corporation, quickly moved the program to ABC (NBC and CBS turned it down), where Sheen immediately attracted an audience of millions.

Sheen was not a young man at the time. He had become a priest in 1919, a monsignor in 1934, and an auxiliary bishop (under New York's Francis Cardinal Spellman) in 1951. He was fifty-seven years old when he went on the DuMont network.

But Sheen was a spellbinding speaker and a master showman. He was visually impressive. On television he wore a black cassock with a wide red sash, a red skullcap, and a flowing, floor-length red cape. His stage setting was austere, consisting of little more than a Bible and a blackboard.

He was well educated and had been practicing public speaking all his life. His voice was resonant, and his diction was perfect. He opened his program with a courtly bow and a word of thanks "for letting me come into your home again." His voice could lull like gentle waves or crash like breakers. His eyes were underlighted in order to emphasize his piercing gaze. Sheen was made for television, and television was made for him. When he received an Emmy Award on the same night as Bob Hope, he quipped, "I'd like to thank my writers—Matthew, Mark, Luke, and John."

Under pressure from Cardinal Spellman, with whom he carried on a running feud for years, Sheen left television in 1957. He returned in 1959 to produce two more series which aired in the early 1960s, but he could not recapture the magic of the early years. Sheen was appointed archbishop of Rochester, New York, in 1966, but served only three unhappy years there before retiring.

Sheen's success in television probably was the single most important factor in persuading evangelicals that television—far more than radio—was the medium best suited to their purposes. TV could bring back the evangelistic face-to-face meeting in which a powerful and charismatic preacher could sway audiences and enlist followers. It probably was for intuitive reasons— certainly not because of his theology—that Sheen's appearance at the 1977 convention of the National Religious Broadcasters was greeted with thunderous applause.

5

The Sermon
from the Satellite

*I believe that God has raised up this powerful
technology of radio and television expressly to reach
every man, woman, boy, and girl on earth with the
even more powerful message of the gospel.*
Ben Armstrong, *The Electric Church*

The electronic church has created a new counterculture in the
United States, one that is grimly determined to halt the spread of
liberal, laissez-faire attitudes and policies in society, culture, and
government. Whereas the counterculture movements of the 1960s
pushed America toward the left, the *counter*-counterculture of the
electronic church is pushing equally hard—in its own way—to
the right.

Its goals are restorative: To restore morality to America. To
restore dignity to the family. To restore fear of God and Jesus'
Second Coming to all sinners. As such it is an aggressive
morality that dictates monitoring the sins of others as closely as
one's own. You can't be saved unless you know you're a sinner.
The prime-time preachers feel a responsibility (and a genuine
one) for the salvation of individual souls.

This salvation will come only when America is rid of its many
ills, ills that the prime-time preachers are fond of classifying as
secular humanism. Tim LaHaye, a Californian who serves on the
governing board of Moral Majority, is credited with identifying
secular humanism as the archenemy of the New Christian Right.
Shunning broader historical meanings of humanism, LaHaye
conceived of secular humanism as "man's attempts to solve his
problems independently of God." He and other fundamentalists

85

place responsibility for the rising crime rate, rebellious youth, identity crises, high divorce rates, coddled criminals, drug addiction, situational ethics, a deteriorating educational system, and a whole host of other social blights squarely on the shoulders of the humanists. In an interview with the Wittenberg Door LaHaye said: "We have been led to Sodom and Gomorrah by a hard-core group of committed humanists who set out over a hundred years ago to control the masses. They have us in a stranglehold. There are only 275,000 of them, but they control everything—the mass media, government, and even the Supreme Court." The politically active LaHaye also stated in the introduction to his book, *The Battle for the Mind,* "We must remove all humanists from public office and replace them with pro-moral political leaders."

LaHaye's thesis is that secular humanists control state and national governments, news networks, the radio and TV industries, newspapers, magazines, public education, colleges and universities, textbooks, and such organizations as the ACLU, NOW, and the Ford Foundation. Secular humanism is thus a rather broad category that would appear to include just about everything religious conservatives don't like.

In 1979 many fundamentalists had not even heard of secular humanism. It was not mentioned in sermons and writings. But by the end of 1980 nearly all had adopted it as their enemy. All social movements need enemies, and the fighting fundamentalists recognize this. Jerry Falwell said in a speech at the National Affairs Briefing, "A man from whom I took great inspiration used to say, 'Fellows, if you're going to be successful, keep a fight going all the time. You do pretty well at that.' " The New Christian Right found a good enemy when it latched onto secular humanism.

Edward John Carnell, past president of Fuller Theological Seminary, an evangelical school of some repute (named for Charles E. Fuller, the evangelical radio broadcaster), has said, in effect, that fundamentalism's distinctiveness is found in its attempt to maintain its own house by the negation of others. When fundamentalism started dwelling on the negative, according to Carnell, it changed from a religious movement to a religious mentality. It never developed an affirmative world view and made no effort to connect its convictions to the wider problems of society. Said Carnell: "Fundamentalism is a lonely position. It has cut itself off from the general stream of culture, philosophy, and ecclesiastical tradition. This accounts, in part, for its robust pride. Since it is no longer in union with the wisdom of the ages, it has no standard by which to judge its own religious pretense. It dismisses non-fundamentalistic efforts as empty, futile, or apostate. Its tests for Christian .fellowship become so severe that divisions in the Church are considered a sign of virtue. And when there are no modernists from which to withdraw, fundamentalists compensate by withdrawing from one another."

When fundamentalism changed from religious movement to religious mentality, it did so at the expense of its vitality. Mentalities do not affect the world the way movements do. Access to television has given fundamentalism a power it never had before. It has once again become a social movement, and its vitality is now being restored.

Martin Luther, John Calvin, and other leaders of the Protestant Reformation established firmly in Protestantism the doctrine of *sola scriptura*—the Bible, not the church, was the sole guide to authentic religion. The Bible had been inspired verbally by the Holy Spirit, almost by dictation, and therefore was without error. Furthermore, anybody who could read could understand it, because it could be interpreted by a literal reading of its words. Nobody in either the Catholic or the Protestant church questioned the literal truth of anything in the Bible. Indeed, to do so could get one burned at the stake by either side.

In the seventeenth and eighteenth centuries, rationalism questioned such absolutism. Rationalists considered human intelligence to be as God-given as the Bible and sought to reconcile religious belief and reason. The process led to the allegorizing, if not to the rejection, of certain scriptural passages. With time, subjective religious experience was joined to reason as another way of validating or establishing scriptural meanings.

Most of the rationalists and the experientialists were in universities, however, not churches, and they had little effect on religion in the pews. But in the nineteenth century came the discovery of very old biblical manuscripts that differed from modern versions. Bible scholars began to face the fact that if the original Scriptures had been dictated by God, they had not been copied all that faithfully. The sciences of biblical "lower" and "higher" criticism emerged. Lower criticism, in a process still going on today, seeks to penetrate history to find the oldest and presumably most reliable manuscripts and the best translation of them. Higher criticism studies those manuscripts in the light of history to try to determine the meaning biblical writers originally intended in their own times.

In the mid-nineteenth century there were few religious people on earth who questioned a literal reading of the Bible. The questions of rationalism, experientialism, and biblical criticism were known only to scholars. Darwin's theory of evolution had not been popularized, astronomy was little more than a fuzzy hobby, and geology was largely interpreted in the light of Noah and the Flood. But the gradual intrusion of these matters into the consciousness of Christendom in the late nineteenth century began to threaten—at least in some minds—the popular religious understanding based on an inerrant Bible. To accept what science was saying would have been to doubt the Bible and shatter a world view that had been shaped by it.

The term *fundamentalist* entered the American lexicon shortly after World War I. It was drawn from the name of a series of volumes called *The Fundamentals*. Lyman and Milton Steward, wealthy Los Angeles businessmen, financed the printing and free distribution of more than 3 million copies of these books, beginning in 1910. Each volume set out certain tenets of the orthodox Christian faith with the objective of defending them against any erosion from religious modernism. Fundamentalism was a reaction against what the fundamentalists perceived as assaults on the true, revealed Christian religion of biblical purity. By the advent of radio, the issue facing the theological conservatives, the fundamentalists, had become clear: Is the Bible to be believed? For most TV preachers decades later, that issue has remained central.

It would be impossible to describe a complete set of specific beliefs that characterize the electronic church today. Some of its practitioners were educated in mainline theological seminaries.

Others were self-taught and self-ordained. A few are blatantly political, although most are not. Some are charismatics who speak in tongues and hold healing services, whereas some others would be very uncomfortable in the presence of such activities. But it is fair to say that most are fundamentalist in theology and thus rely on the Bible for both general guidance and answers to specific issues.

The fundamentalists' attitude toward evolution is a prime example of their unswerving commitment to what they consider the plain meaning of a book that is utterly sacred to them. Most fundamentalists would subscribe readily to this statement of the International Council of Biblical Inerrancy: "Being wholly and verbally God-given, Scripture is without error or fault in all its teaching, no less in what it states about God's act in creation, about the events of world history, and about its own literary origins under God, than in its witness to God's saving grace in individual lives."

Fundamentalists today still fight the teaching of evolution in the public schools, and everywhere else. In 1978 the Smithsonian Institution assembled an exhibit on the evolutionary "Emergence of Man" in its Museum of Natural History. Two groups, the National Foundation for Fairness in Education and National Bible Knowledge, Inc., brought suit in federal court, claiming that the Smithsonian, as a government institution, had violated the First Amendment guarantee of the separation of church and state. The groups sought an order requiring the Smithsonian to allocate equal sums to explaining Creation in terms of the biblical account. The suit was unsuccessful.

The Bible also instructs fundamentalists that a rationale for life apart from God cannot exist. Nothing in life is an accident; rather, all is a part of God's plan. Bad things happen as God's chastisement of us or as God's way of closing doors on mere human plans. Good things are the blessings of God. God is always good, but His goodness is sometimes rather terrible.

The terrible goodness of God as experienced by some fundamentalists was described by reporter Joel Saiatin in a 1980 Associated Press story: "God didn't like it when they broke their promises, Carroll Baggett and his wife, Edna, feel. As children, each made commitments to the Lord and didn't keep them.

Cumulatively, they went through two divorces, two children who died in a car wreck, a son born deaf and retarded, a nervous breakdown, the loss of three fingers, and paralysis. But now they're honoring those promises. . . . They say God took them through death, disease, divorce and distress before they surrendered.'' The surrender the Baggetts made was to give up performing country music to start singing gospel.

Fundamentalists cannot think or speak of their history, their present, or their future apart from God as *deus ex machina* who makes all things happen. God thus is credited, without anger, for accident, human waywardness, and natural disaster. On balance, however, God is to be thanked for all happy occurrences, the results of industriousness, good fortune, and the as yet unknowable benefits that will come out of what only appears to be misfortune.

Fundamentalists, who see God as relating one on one with all human beings, cannot find an explanation for catastrophes that overtake whole regions, races, and tribes. Indeed, they rarely think about the cause of large-scale disasters or misfortunes except, perhaps, as signs and wonders signaling the approaching end of the world. Fundamentalists thus feel little or no responsibility for those not of their own tribe because whatever has happened is God's doing.

To evangelicals, one of the most important messages in the Bible is in Mark 16:15: ''Go ye into all the world and preach the gospel.'' The word *evangelical* itself is from the Greek verb *euangelizo,* meaning ''to announce the good news'' and generally translated in English Bibles as ''to preach the gospel.'' Evangelicals take this biblical message seriously and feel a distinct obligation to evangelize. Matthew's Gospel too refers to this ''great commission'': ''Go therefore and make disciples of all nations, baptizing them in the name of the Father and of the Son and of the Holy Spirit, teaching them to observe all that I have commanded you, and lo, I am with you always, to the close of the age'' (Matthew 28:19,20). These verses, together with other, similar instructions from the four Gospels and the Pauline letters, form the keystone of more than 1,900 years of Christian missionary and evangelistic activity. The missionary impulse to make converts is the raison d'être of all Christian religious broadcasting, and most especially of evangelical broadcasting.

Evangelism is understood to mean proclaiming the gospel of Jesus Christ and thereby evoking decisions or commitments to him. To "be saved" is to accept Jesus Christ as Savior and Lord, the Son of God. One's sins are canceled through this act of faith; Jesus comes into one's heart, and a new life begins. This is called being "born again." The phrase is found only in the Gospel according to John: "Jesus answered, and said unto him, Verily, verily, I say unto thee, Except a man be born again, he cannot see the kingdom of God" (John 3:3). Being born again means to have the life-changing experience of turning one's life over to Jesus.

The term *born again* began to be popularized during the first presidential campaign of Jimmy Carter. In the past five years it has moved from being an evangelical phrase describing spiritual regeneration to a secular term used to describe all kinds of evangelical activities and involvements—as in *born-again politics*. Billy Graham used the phrase throughout his preaching career, but in late 1980 he announced that it had been so much abused that he was dropping it. Henceforth he would speak of "being born from above."

This conversion, or second-birth experience, is essential to salvation. Through it, one is saved from everlasting punishment in hell, which is the fate of unrepentant sinners. But one is saved also from personal futility and meaninglessness. Here are the words of a "700 Club" volunteer worker who had the experience: "My life had come to a place that I couldn't handle it anymore. Being a military wife, I had turned to alcohol and Valium, so I came to the place within my own mind, within my own will, that I said, 'Lord, I can't handle my life anymore. And I take hands off my life and I let you take control of it.' And in my den, in Virginia Beach, we sat—and the Lord moved in and baptized me in His Holy Spirit. The whole den lit up, with a *Shekinah* glory, and I had a tremendous release of happiness and joy and laughing and crying that day. I even know what day—in the morning, you know—that it happened!"

Shekinah is a Hebrew word meaning "the glory, radiance, or presence of God." It is the Old Testament equivalent of being "filled with the Spirit." The phrase means to have an ecstatic experience of the nearness of God and sometimes is used to refer to a special quality of life that follows the born-again experience.

Persons who are filled with the Holy Spirit often are heard to say things they would not normally say, or to "prophesy." Jim Bakker, in a fund-raising letter, described the experience of his daughter: "Under the power of the Holy Spirit, Tammy Sue began to speak: 'Jesus is coming very soon. . . . We will all be in heaven with Jesus soon. . . . He is coming. . . . He is coming. . . .' Can you imagine the joy in my heart, and Tammy's [Bakker's wife, Tammy Fay], as we listened to these prophetic words pour out of the lips of our ten-year-old? And as we listened, she began to say things far beyond her knowledge and years."

As ideally characterized on the TV programs, the evangelical religious experience is warmly emotional and joyous, and it confers a sense of spiritual and social community or belonging. Much of the conversation on the programs proceeds in a kind of evangelical code, with liberal sprinklings of words and phrases in praise of God.

Being "baptized by the Holy Spirit" is a euphemism for the charismatic religious experience of "speaking in tongues." "Unknown tongues" or ecstatic utterances (*glossolalia* is the correct term) are foreign and frightening to all but a handful of charismatic evangelicals. Several televangelists practice glossolalia in private, but only occasionally does it burst forth on the air. Generally, even conversation about it is downplayed, and one cannot detect references to it unless one is familiar with the code words.

The same is true of "divine healing." Many of the televangelists believe in supernatural healing, and a few engage in the "laying on of hands" as a part of the healing ritual. They talk about healing a good bit on their broadcasts, but only a few engage in the act on television. Ernest Angley is the only figure with any following who makes healing a significant feature of his program.

Oral Roberts began his television career with healing services filmed in the "world's largest gospel tent." When he adopted a new television entertainment format (plus the credentials of the Methodist Church), he dropped healing from his act—at least on the air. He still practices it in crusade meetings around the country. The July 1980 issue of Oral's magazine, *Abundant Life* (formerly *Healing Waters*), featured nine pages, filled with color photographs, of an Oral Roberts healing service in Norfolk, Virginia. According to the magazine, the lame were made to walk, the deaf to hear, the blind to see, and cancer was cured.

Oral has always made much of the healing power of God flowing through his right hand as a "point of contact." "My hand tingled all over with a hot feeling from my wrist through my fingers when the presence of God would move through it," Oral said. As a fund-raising ploy, he has even sent to contributors the imprint of his hand on a piece of cloth. In the Norfolk service, however, he discovered a new device that was less limiting than having to touch everybody with his right-hand "point of contact." Now he simply speaks "the word of power" over the whole audience. He reported in *Abundant Life* that "it was wonderful not to be confined so much by His presence in my right hand." Another issue of *Abundant Life* reported recently that Oral's son, Richard, also now has the gift of healing.

Ernest Angley is the most flamboyant of the healers. His television program features "healings" videotaped during "Ernest Angley Miracle and Salvation" crusade meetings. *Atlanta Constitution* reporter Jim Auchmutey described one such meeting: "For the next three hours, Ernest Angley 'healed,' squealed and ranted in the name of God. A line of the afflicted formed at one side of the stage, and the faith healer attended to them, usually one at a time, laying hands upon their foreheads, casting out 'foul demons' and 'loosing' them from Satan. Many were so overcome by Angley's cathartic commands that they collapsed to the floor, 'slain in the spirit,' and rose stunned, sometimes murmuring gibberish—'speaking in tongues.' The multitude applauded frequently, urged on by Angley: 'Give God a big hand, everybody!' " Auchmutey also reported that a North Carolina woman died of a heart attack moments after receiving Angley's healing touch for her weak heart.

Evangelist Kenneth Copeland takes the power of healing through the laying on of hands very seriously. He told, in one of his sermons, of deciding to buy a used airplane: "I walked all the way around it, putting my hands on it. I'm talking to this airplane, and I said, 'I'm speaking to you in the name of Jesus.

And I demand any kind of corrosion or malfunction to get out of you right now—in the name of Jesus—you're not going to have that!' ''

Among faith-healing fundamentalists, much of life's misfortune, tragedy, and even illness is caused by Satan and his minions. Satan is seen as a personal enemy of the Lord and thus of the Lord's people on earth. Copeland also described on one of his television programs how he had marched around his home ordering Satan to leave the premises and to "keep off!" Since that time, said Copeland, "our doctor bills have been zero."

A belief in the Devil and in the demons and evil spirits who serve him is widespread among evangelicals and nearly universal among fundamentalists. The Devil is Lucifer, the fallen angel, the personal, active enemy of those who would find and serve God.

Oral Roberts regularly blames his financial problems on the Devil. His fund-raising letters include such statements as: "The Devil has launched an all-out attack to stop this ministry." "The Devil has tried everything to stop us. Now he is trying to stop us financially." "The Devil is pushing harder and harder to keep us from obeying God." "We can't let the Devil win in this emergency." Roberts also is careful to explain on his programs and in his letters that Satan is working in his viewers' lives as well. But Oral promises to help: "I will command the Devil, in the Name of Jesus and in the authority of His name, to stop stealing your HEALTH from you, . . . your FINANCES and WORK . . . your PEACE OF MIND . . . the WELL-BEING of your loved ones. Then when I feel peace about it, I will KNOW the Devil will be STOPPED in your behalf."

To fundamentalists, the world is one giant battleground for the struggle between good and evil, which rages in all realms: moral, religious, social, spiritual, and political. There is no room in fundamentalism for differing social perspectives or political systems. Compromise is sin. This outlook informs their view of U.S. national defense and foreign policy. Many of them fully expect a final apocalyptic war between the United States and the Soviet Union—and they support this expectation with what they regard as specific prophecies in the Bible.

Not all the TV preachers believe and say the same things about the coming "end time." Some (notably Robert Schuller, who is not a fundamentalist) would disassociate themselves completely from any such speculation. Many of the major TV preachers, however—Falwell, Robertson, Robison, Bakker, Swaggart, and most of the lesser lights of gospel broadcasting—do believe in some form of millennialism.

The "millennium" is a prophesied thousand-year period of events on the earth surrounding the Second Coming of Jesus. Premillennialists believe Jesus will come before the millennium, to reign for a thousand years, finally defeat all the forces of evil, and claim the world for God. Postmillennialists believe that Jesus will come to reign after the thousand-year period of seeing the gospel finally conquer the world. Most TV preachers are premillennialists.

But before the millennium begins (some say seven years before), the last trumpet will sound and all the saved will be caught up instantly into heaven. This event is called the rapture, a belief that has given rise to bumper stickers that say, "Warning! In case of the rapture, driver will disappear." Charles R. Taylor, speaker of "Today in Bible Prophecy," has written in *World War III and the Destiny of America:* "Millions of people will suddenly disappear from the face of the earth, including infant children. From all walks of life there will be people missing. The freeways, subways, airports and streets will be a shambles as many engineers, pilots, busdrivers, and a multitude of private car owners shall suddenly be caught up out of this world."

In the classic view of these events (which has many modern permutations), the seven-year tribulation after the sudden rapture of the saints will be filled with two major happenings. The gospel of the kingdom will be preached (by believing Jews, it seems, since all Christians have departed), and Israel will be converted. The second major event is the rise of the Anti-Christ, who will attack Israel. After the defeat of the Anti-Christ, Jesus will come down to establish his earthly throne at Jerusalem.

It is a complicated doctrine, and many of the TV preachers have their own variations on it. What makes these millennialist beliefs important to analysts is their connection to the U.S.S.R. and Israel in the modern world. Evangelical political support for Israel has been noted widely. Support of Israel, to the fundamentalist preachers, simply is cooperation with God in the fulfillment of biblical prophecy. A Christian America cannot do otherwise.

Many of the seekers after prophecy identify the Soviet Union with the hordes that will come "out of the uttermost parts of the north" (Ezekiel 39) to fight against Israel. The fundamentalists have noted that the Soviets side with the Arabs against Israel and refuse to let Jews emigrate to Israel. The conviction among many, if not most, TV evangelicals is that the U.S.S.R. is an implacable enemy of God, of the United States, and of Israel. If war is not inevitable, a lack of defense preparedness certainly invites it. Most of the fundamentalists therefore urge, on biblical grounds, a tough military line against all Communist countries—especially the Soviet Union, since it is Israel's enemy.

Pat Robertson of CBN has identified the European Common Market countries with the ten-nation confederacy mentioned in the prophetic vision of Daniel in the Old Testament (Daniel 7:24). According to Robertson, the entry of Greece into the European Common Market brings its membership up to ten countries and sets the stage for the rise of the Anti-Christ, a charismatic and winning person who is simply Satan in disguise, it appears. This person, Robertson says, will promise to lead the world out of the economic and social collapse toward which it is headed: "Undoubtedly, God's purpose is a world harvest. Nevertheless, He has set other forces in motion. Within five years there will undoubtedly be a currency collapse and world depression of alarming proportions. During the same period, Russia will probably invade the Middle East and strike at Israel, causing a major war. On top of that, some astronomers forecast unusual gravitational pull on our planet when all the planets line up in 1981—the so-called Jupiter effect. This planetary activity could trigger earthquakes, tidal waves, volcanic eruptions, and other widespread natural disasters. In short, we will soon be entering turbulent days and what is done in Jesus' name must be done quickly."

Not all fundamentalists analyze the fulfillment of prophecy as being so imminent, but the consensus is that the importance of the United States has never been greater. TV preachers believe without question that God caused the founding of America in order that this country might carry out His purposes in the world.

Their patriotism is unabashed in its expression and white-hot in its fervor. The United States was created by God to fight the Anti-Christ.

The fundamentalists often identify the Anti-Christ with communism. How communism will give birth to the person or spirit of the Anti-Christ is not clear to them just yet, but the preachers can hardly think of one without the other. They would have all Americans understand that communism is inextricably linked with atheism and thus is the enemy, not only of America, but of God. Jack Van Impe, for example, explains regularly why a person cannot be a Christian and a Communist at the same time. An America cleansed of all Communist influence and standing in opposition to such godlessness is, they are convinced, what God Himself desires.

The America the preachers have in mind, however, is idealized somewhere in the nation's past, the strength and glory of which must be resurrected. They do not see this country moving forward to greatness; rather, they see it falling from it. The decline has been caused by immorality of all kinds, socialism, communism, the welfare state, and a weak national defense system. The idealization of the American past is revealed in the evangelicals' insistence that this nation was founded with God in mind and in words which they use constantly as they speak of returning, rebuilding, restoring, and saving America. James Robison's words from *Save America* are typical: "America's star is sinking fast. If Christians don't begin immediately to assert their influence, it may be too late to save America from the destruction toward which it is plunging. And, since America now stands as the key base camp for missions around the globe, to fail to save America now would almost certainly be to miss its last opportunity to save the world."

TV religion, accordingly, has developed and refined a set of battle cries, an agenda for the 1980s to conquer the sins of society and restore to America the strength it needs to fight the Anti-Christ. If the millennium is approaching, the need to save as many souls as possible beforehand is crucial. And the urgency the prime-time preachers feel is genuine.

The first of these battle cries is against the threatened destruction of the family by the forces of ungodliness. TV preachers seem to have a heightened sense of the utility of "glad words" and "bad words." *Family* is a glad word, and to be pro-family is to be in favor of everything that is good and decent and commendable. According to the more political stream of TV religion, the family is under attack by the forces of secular humanism, ungodliness, homosexuality, and the Equal Rights Amendment.

To most fundamentalists, the traditional concept of the male-dominated nuclear family is sacrosanct. The family is, of course, the basic unit of society. That there could be any change in the traditional Western view of the family as a social unit in which women are subservient to men is simply unacceptable to the fundamentalist mind. This view is based on certain New Testament passages as well as on cultural conditioning. The notion that male supremacy accords to women an inferior status is incomprehensible to fundamentalists. They maintain fervently that they accord women *superior* status. Said Jerry Falwell: "I'm a Christian and all Christians believe that women are special and that God made men to take care of women, to protect them, to help them with their jackets and to make sure nobody else messes with them."

An equal rights amendment for women is anathema to the fundamentalists. The locus of their objections is that women might lose what the fundamentalists perceive as their preferred, protected status in society. They simply cannot see anything that women would gain from such an amendment, but much that women might lose. In a Moral Majority fund-raising letter, Jerry Falwell said, "Our women have a constitutional right to be treated like ladies, mothers, and wives under our family laws." That women might want to be anything else does not seem to be a topic of discussion among fundamentalists. Nor has any question arisen about the rightness of male dominance.

Fundamentalist fervor about certain issues is illustrated in the abortion question. The fundamentalists of television believe devoutly that abortion is murder. To them, the abortion of a fetus (except for pregnancies resulting from rape or incest) is simply and surely the killing of an unborn human. They hold this belief in common with nearly all Roman Catholics and millions of other nonfundamentalist Protestants, and they are quite willing to join with them in the struggle for laws that would outlaw abortion. They cannot by any means be said to like Catholics or liberal Protestants, but on a single issue they are able to put aside all other differences and work diligently with them to achieve a common goal. Jerry Falwell often has chided his audiences, saying, "For far too long we left the Roman Catholics to fight the abortion battle alone. Now we've got to join with them in this fight."

The issue that most quickly enrages fundamentalists is homosexual rights. They consider that homosexuals have no right to practice a deviant life-style. The issue is clear to the preachers: homosexuality is an ungodly perversion that is specifically condemned by the Bible. In a Moral Majority fund-raising letter, Jerry Falwell decried the laying of a wreath at the Tomb of the Unknown Soldier by homosexuals as turning that shrine into the "Tomb of the Unknown Sodomite." When Anita Bryant fought homosexual rights legislation in Florida, she received massive support from the TV preachers, who believed she was upholding the God-given order of heterosexuality. Praise from the pro-family partisans was universal.

Evangelist James Robison's attack on homosexuality as "despicable" and "perversion of the highest order" led to a challenge under the FCC's Fairness Doctrine. Dallas television station WFAA granted a gay group equal time—and canceled Robison's program, reinstating it only when he agreed to abide by the Fairness Doctrine. Throughout the episode, however, Robison expressed difficulty understanding why he should be penalized for preaching what he called the plain message of the Bible: "I did not attack an individual or any group, but rather a life-style condemned by the Bible." He believed his freedom of speech had been violated.

Pornography is another of TV religion's battle cries. The fundamentalist definition of smut is broad enough to include sex education in public schools as well as many popular TV programs. Jerry Falwell enclosed in a Moral Majority fund-raising letter a sealed envelope marked with the warning that it contained sexually explicit material. The contents of the envelope proved to be paragraphs from a sex-education curriculum. Although some of the ideas in a given sex-education course might be disturbing to some parents, the preachers of TV tend to view all sex education as an attempt by anti-family forces to corrupt youth and destroy American ideals of the family.

When civil liberties groups began to challenge the appropriateness of prayers in public schools, they found support for their position among some liberal Protestants who reasoned that in a pluralistic society religious instruction belongs in the home and the churches. Not so the fundamentalists. They believe this nation has a special relationship to God and that it was the intent of the founding fathers that we acknowledge His sovereignty over our affairs. Pushing prayer out of the schools is just one more case in which the secular humanists have gained an upper hand in American culture. God is displeased with this development, and it is the responsibility of Christians to fight to return prayer to the classroom.

Fundamentalist social and political views are products of fundamentalist theology. Fundamentalists are passionate about social and political matters precisely because they are passionate about theology. And they believe earnestly that their positions are totally biblical. They can quote biblical texts to prove every point. The notion that they could be reading meaning into those texts is incomprehensible to them.

The fundamentalist mind cannot accept the notion that a true "Bible believer" could interpret Scripture from the perspective of a social or political tradition. Fundamentalists believe that only liberals read the Bible that way. And if there is any conflict between their reading of the Bible and the rest of the world's, it is the rest of the world that is wrong.

The manner in which the televangelists sell their message must conform to the logic of television, whose stock-in-trade is an endless stream of easy answers to difficult questions. The most difficult human problems are brought to satisfactory resolution in one hour. Many require only a half hour. Many more are handled in just thirty seconds, the length of most television commercials. Christian broadcasters understand this lesson of the thirty-second solution. One commercial on the Christian Broadcasting Network shows a handsome young man in a red roadster winding confidently down a mountain road. As he floors the gas pedal and passes other cars, a voice-over begins addressing the man and his accomplishments. "You're smart, you're confident, you're on top of the world," the deep bass says. The scene shifts occasionally and we see the same young man dancing with an equally lovely young woman, lunching with the boss, playing tennis. "You're attractive, you're the boss's favorite, you've got the best backhand in the club." Suddenly the scene shifts back to the roadster, and we see the car take a tailspin onto a beach. When the car comes to rest, the young man has his head in his hands and the voice says, "But you're not happy." Fade to clouds and sky, out of which emerges a Bible. "Read the Bible," the voice admonishes, "and you will be."

TV preachers must say what they have to say quickly and simply, and it must be entertaining and supportive of viewers' values and sense of self-worth. These requirements result in three basic themes that run through their messages.

The first is that the world and the self are to be understood in unambiguous terms. God has a message and a plan. Believe in Him. Trust in Him. A successful TV preacher must relieve viewers of ambiguity in spiritual, ethical, and moral matters. He must communicate the impression of absolute certainty.

Most mass communications research has shown that television is inefficient as a way of changing people's minds. What it does best is reinforce the opinions and beliefs that viewers already hold, and thus the TV preachers who do not challenge viewers' beliefs are the most successful. They accomplish this, in part, by offering only the bare rudiments of faith, leaving aside complex theological issues about which people might disagree. In addition, they emphasize an active sense of the demonic to relieve guilt; Jesus washes away all sins and the Devil is responsible for all backsliding.

A second theme in the messages of the electronic preachers is the enormous benefit to be derived from taking a positive approach to life. In one sense this appears to be little more than a warmed-over rendition of Norman Vincent Peale's "power of positive thinking." Robert Schuller clearly conveys this message in its most pristine form. Acknowledging his indebtedness to Peale, he calls his brand *possibility thinking:* "Every person is either a possibility thinker or an impossibility thinker." Schuller takes serious exception to the criticism that he preaches "mere" psychology. It is the principles of psychology, rather, that are grounded in firm theology. There is nothing wrong with self-confidence, Schuller believes, and "finding and following God's plan for your life is the soundest, surest way to self-confidence."

If Schuller's version of positive thinking is the most easily discernible, the same message is pretty pervasive in the sermons, songs, and testimonies of almost all electronic church programming. If you would just let God be in command of your life, everything would be super A-OK. Only the Devil can mess up God's glorious plan for your life. But the Devil cannot win, and his daily encroachment on Christians' lives can be checked if they would just stick together.

The third message of the electronic preachers is that it's all right to look out for yourself; human selfishness, properly viewed, is not a sin. Few have ever flaunted this theme quite as blatantly as Reverend Ike. "You can't lose with the stuff I use," he tells his audiences. You can have money, health, happiness, love, and just about anything else your heart desires if you join his "God's Success and Prosperity Club." This takes a little long green, but the benefits are yours "as fast as you want God to start blessing you"—that is, as soon as Reverend Ike has your money.

Among the major preachers on television, Oral Roberts comes closest to equating personal desires with God's will and the success of his ministry. "God wants to bless you with blessings—good measure, pressed down, shaken together, and running over!" reads the banner headline on the cover of a recent issue of Roberts's *Abundant Life* magazine. Rex Humbard offers a book to his viewers, *Your Key to God's Bank,* whose subtitle is *How to Cash Your Check for Spiritual Power, Physical Healing, Financial Success.*

As a medium that fuses message with method, television is the perfect forum for the fundamentalists, for theirs is a simple message—the old, old story, passed through the ages in unchanging form. That access to the airwaves is largely controlled by a free-enterprise market system is no real problem to them, for this economic philosophy is compatible with their world view. They believe in free enterprise, *and* they have something to sell—the Good News of Christ's atonement for the sins of mankind.

This Business
of TV Religion

Dear Thomas,

Last week I knelt at the prayer altar to pray for every member in the Prayer Key Family Book, and I wanted to pray for you . . . but your name was not there. . . .

Rex Humbard

The Prayer Key Family Book is Rex Humbard's directory of sinners for whom Rex and his family will pray. You get listed there by contributing to his TV ministry. Once you're in the good book, Rex is pretty patient with you. He'll keep right on praying and sending you letters—more opportunities to contribute—for quite a spell before he sends you the whammy letter quoted above.

Rex never quite says you'll go to hell without his prayers. The letter just goes on to tell how prayers are answered, homes put back together, bodies healed, and failures overcome. All these good things can come to you, and the Devil be defeated, if you get your name back in the good book so that Rex can stand up for you the way he wants to do. A few dollars in the envelope isn't much to pay for all that, just to be dead certain that the Lord does what you want Him to do for you in your daily struggles right here on earth, not to mention the hereafter.

This basic pitch, embellished differently by the various tele-vangelists with offers of freebies and hints of togetherness, finances most prime-time preaching. The fundamentalists prosper on TV precisely because they're not afraid to make the sales pitch so blunt. Liberals mumble around, never quite willing to claim that they've got God's own cleansing power right there in their hands, but television's evangelicals have tested every form of promise, semi-firm and yours-for-the-asking. Not since Vatican officials sold papal indulgences—written protection from the wages of sin—has there been such a public marketing of Christian favors. And never, surely, has any religion found a mass market like TV's many-channeled auction block.

Peter Cartwright, the legendary circuit rider, must be in heaven turning green with envy. He wore his bottom down to solid bone and callus taking Methodism to the frontier, singlehandedly churching up the roughnecks in the Northwest Territory. But in all his life Cartwright never reached a tenth of the folks that Rex Humbard talks to on just one television broadcast.

Both Rex and Peter mastered the blunt sales pitch, and they never got so smug in their intellect as to put too much distance between the altar and the snake-oil wagon. Both had hard-sell competitors to keep them down to earth where the sinners live. Both understood the lonely soul's need for the sure cure and for a guaranteed reservation in the heavenly motel at the end of this earthly haul. And so today's televiewers are tapping directly into the lusty tradition of frontier Protestantism with hellfires burning hot just down the hill. Jesus loves me . . . just as I am. The foot-stomping, gut-busting hymns that the choirmasters and theologians just about censored out of the Cokesbury Hymnal have come thundering back full bass in the biggest revival tent ever, prime time.

For all the talk about television, however, the tube makes up less than half the technology that supports the new social movement of fundamentalism. The other half comes in the form of the ubiquitous computer. Like an invisible spirit, the computer allows the prime-time preacher to come down out of the television and listen to you alone, or seem to, and to pray with you, or seem to, and to call you by name when he holds out the collection plate. From the broadcast image in the studio, the preacher comes down to the narrow-cast of the junk-mail letter that is designed to go directly to your heart, as you've divulged it in mail or on the phone, and to let you know that Brother Jim or Brother Rex knows all about you. For one thing, he knows something that many a pulpit preacher would give his stained-glass voice to know: who has, and (more important) who has not, put green paper into the plate. "Your name was not there," Humbard writes to the delinquent sinner in need of prayer. Then he quits wasting stamps and paper on a prospect who never pays.

While driving through the mountains of Tennessee with the radio tuned to a local religious broadcast, it is not uncommon to hear the preacher mention by name persons he "hasn't heard from for some time." That's a polite way of saying, "You haven't sent me any money recently." Chances are that the preacher can identify by name virtually everyone who has contributed to his radio ministry for the previous five years.

The mailing lists of contributors and potential contributors of the major electronic church operations number quite literally in the millions. Like the contributors to the radio ministry of the Reverend Mr. Smith in the back ways of Tennessee, the potential contributors to the electronic church ministries have to be lured and then periodically prodded if they are to be reliable sources of revenue.

The computer provides a sort of technological equivalent of the Book of Judgment. It lets the preacher divide the sheep from the goats, those who offer golden fleece from the stubborn goats who don't grow any or won't share it. Its practical value is that it allows the preachers to mount a giant direct-mail campaign, sending out millions of fund-raising letters as if passing one huge collection plate. And it allows the preachers to run economical direct-mail systems by concentrating on the names and addresses that pay off well enough to support their multimillion-dollar programming costs.

The future of the computer in its service to religion may best be suggested by the computer-written letters that drop a listener's name into the body of the text once or twice. Whole paragraphs of advice respond to troubles that someone has asked the preacher to pray about, either in calls to the free in-WATS, the 800 lines, or in a letter asking for a free gift. The preacher writes standard paragraphs that his assistants can drop into any letter with a push of the computer's efficient buttons. Out of the pleas for help, prime-time preachers are building monumental data banks on the most intimate personal problems mentioned by the millions who phone in.

In the specialized trade of direct mail, promoters constantly test different sales pitches, different words and themes, to sell anything from coins and sexy lingerie to pottery and magazines. The pros gather once a year to hand out Golden Mailbox awards to the most successful marketers. They can compare one sales pitch with another down to a thousandth of a percentage point of response. If the preachers recognized the precision of such testing, it would open a whole new frontier for them to talk about the highly personal concerns of target audiences.

As of now, the preachers have not pushed the uses of the computer's cheap memory much beyond the standard ones. But this is beginning to change as *parapersonal communication* techniques are perfected. As preachers, the televangelists can go more directly into personal matters, and their theology lets them assume considerable power to influence people's lives. In the summer of 1980, for instance, uncertainty was running high. Unemployment had hit 7.8 percent, but economists were nervously guessing that the recession had bottomed out. Oral Roberts was into reruns, so he was airing the most profitable of his previous shows. His guest one morning was a former Miss America, Cheryl Prewitt, the charismatic who believes that her crushed leg was healed by a miracle. As the time came for the invitation to write or call in, Oral asked Cheryl to pray for all those in the viewing audience in need of a miracle.

Then on the television screen appeared a young mechanic who was being laid off work. His boss was apologetic. The young man assured him that he understood times were tough. He went home and was met at the door by a consoling wife. This scene was followed by a pitch for a free copy of Oral Roberts's book *Don't Give Up.* Then the camera returned to the young man who was again being greeted, this time by a seemingly jubilant wife. No words were spoken, but the implication was that the man had found another job. And the obvious message was to trust in God in time of financial need.

Then Oral Roberts returned to the camera with the following message: "If you have something on your heart, if you're hurting, if you're ill, if you have a great need, or a little need, if you just need to write to someone, I'll be so glad to hear from you. I'll pray with you and write you back. And I'll expect a miracle of God to happen in your life. My address is Oral Roberts, Tulsa, Oklahoma. God bless you.'' People do write Oral Roberts. Wayne A. Robinson, a onetime associate of the Oral Roberts Evangelistic Association, claims that Oral was receiving in excess of 6 million letters annually by the mid-1970s and that immediately after a prime-time special the postal service would deliver 100,000 a day. Other prime-time preachers receive mail in proportion to their audience size. Billy Graham claims to receive 40,000 to 50,000 pieces of mail a week, but immediately after his prime-time crusades it is not unusual for him to get that much in a single day. Who reads all this mail? Oral Roberts gives his viewers every indication that he does, but even working a fourteen-hour day, which he claims to do, Oral would have to read twenty-four letters a minute just to get through his mail— and that doesn't leave any time for him to respond. Instead, it is the thinking machine that plugs in names, thanks Martha or Ray for the $10 contribution, tells John that the Lord will see him through unemployment, and asks Jim one more time if he won't make a special sacrifice for the glory of God.

On television, one of the most common cries that brings in the mail is that the foreclosing banker is on the doorstep. Many are the times that the stars of the cathode church have stood in front of the cameras and made urgent pleas to their audiences to bail them out before they have to cut back on the number of stations on which they are seen. And most of the majors have, on more than one occasion, quite literally been on the brink of financial insolvency. But each time this has happened, to date, their faithful followers have heard their pleas, and their empires have been snatched from the threat of oblivion.

If their operations have frequently lacked a sound set of business principles for planned growth, their faith and hard work have thus far gotten them through adversity. From their perspective, this deliverance is abundant evidence of God's providential involvement in their ministry as well as a sign that the Lord expects yet bigger and better projects for the glory of His name. And this is all the encouragement they need to launch even more ambitious projects that seem destined to put them out on a limb yet another time.

The logic of the evangelical success formula demands reaching as many people as possible, a requirement that many critics attack as a principal cause of corrupt acts. In order to pay for the increased production costs of reaching larger audiences, one needs—an even larger audience. It's a fiscal Catch-22. The compulsion this predicament creates translates into getting on a lot of stations, at the most desirable time slot possible, and with a program that catches and holds a large audience. Each of these requirements brings its own special agonies. In the final analysis, all the TV ministers have to ask themselves whether the contributions received from a particular market and market area are equal to or greater than the costs of broadcasting to that market.

This necessity of examining the profit and loss columns, market by market, creates a dilemma of conscience. On the one hand, the raison d'être of the ministries is to reach out and spread the gospel message. On the other hand, they can't carry a ministry in a market very long if they don't attract an audience of sufficient size to cover the costs. Presumably those areas where it is most difficult to cover costs are also those most in need of the gospel. Those that easily pay their own way, in contrast, can probably be judged to be less in need of the gospel message. Since few markets are exceptionally profitable and, thus, most are running somewhere close to the break-even point, there is constant pressure to drop unprofitable markets and replace them with markets where the televangelists might fare better.

The syndicated television ministries compete with one another, first of all, just to get on the air. But inasmuch as audience size and revenues are dependent, in considerable measure, on the time in which a program appears, the competitive pressure can become pretty fierce. In a word, this competition has triggered a fundamental free-enterprise principle of supply and demand. The greater the demand for air time during a particular time period, the greater the price tag it can demand.

Getting on the air at the right time is critical to developing an audience of significant size, but the right time slot is insufficient if the program itself does not hold the audience—thus the final compulsion to produce a show that can compete on commercial television's terms. Mike Nason, executive producer of Robert Schuller's "Hour of Power," strongly asserts that the quality of religious television is paramount. "What are they asking us to do?'' he asks. "Get black and white, adjust our glasses before we read a Scripture, shuffle up to the camera? By that time we've lost our viewer. He's gone to watch Bugs Bunny."

And this, of course, brings us back to that old nemesis, money.

By almost any standards, the ability of the electronic churches to raise money is impressive. The top four programs on television collectively took in over a quarter of a billion dollars in 1980. The next five largest took in more than $100 million. That's a lot of money. Even more impressive is the fact that most of it comes in $5, $10, and $15 contributions.

There is no question that raising this money is costly. Most of the major TV ministries eventually turn to direct-mail fund-raising organizations. Many fund raisers do not work on the principle of how many cents out of each dollar must be used for fund raising. Rather, they sell clients on the idea of investment for the purpose of acquiring a donor base, just as one would lay down capital to build a store. They may begin with the notion of a break-even acquisition—you spend a dollar to get a dollar back.

Suppose you invest $100,000 to acquire 5,000 donors who give an average of $20 each. That's a break-even acquisition. But once you have the donors, you can expect a fairly large proportion of them to be repeaters. So the second year, the cost of obtaining a contribution from those who have already given once is much lower. Assume that an organization retains 3,000 of the 5,000 donors, or 60 percent, for the second year. Amortizing in this way, it takes ten years for the list of 5,000 donors to diminish to a mere 500. But each year the average gift goes up a little—say, an average of 5 percent—and each year the cost of raising that money declines.

Let's look at how fund raising works in the concrete context of a religious television program. Let's assume you wrote in for a free book, which you read and thought was pretty interesting. You have also become a fairly regular viewer of the program. Along about the third or fourth time you receive a letter appealing for money to support the ministry, you decide that the religious telecast really is worthwhile and that you ought to be doing your share to support it.

Once you have become a donor, the organization pursues

several techniques to retain you as well as to upgrade the level of your giving. Many organizations attempt, even as they try to get you to make a first contribution, to retain you as a regular contributor by getting you to join their organization of regulars. Rex Humbard has his Prayer Key Family members, Pat Robertson his 700 Club members, Oral Roberts his Faith Partners, and so forth. These memberships, at once, create a sense of belonging as well as an obligation to contribute. Some require a specific amount per month; others, only the expectation that you will make a regular contribution commensurate with your capacity to give. So the goal of all these organizations is not simply to get a one-time contribution from you, but to capture your ongoing commitment.

Once they can count on you as a regular contributor, they endeavor to increase your contribution. This may be done in a variety of ways. For one, you can simply be asked to contribute more than you did the last time. Computers can keep better track of that sort of thing than individuals, so subsequent appeals often include a reminder of the amount of your last contribution. Or you might be reminded that inflation is driving the cost of everything up, including religious broadcasting, thus implying that if you are to remain even with your level of giving, you should give more.

In addition to regularizing and upgrading, almost all television ministries make special add-on appeals. They may ask you to respond to a specific financial crisis, which may or may not be real. Or they may ask for a seasonal sacrifice or a contribution to some special project or event. At least one reason almost all television ministries have building projects is that they have learned that people like to contribute to bricks and mortar—to something vaguely immortal.

At the heart of a successful direct-mail operation, of course, is the appearance of highly personalized communications, those friendly computer mentions of your name in letters. (If you look closely, you'll probably find that all that first-naming is done on the first page; it's cheaper to personalize one page and duplicate the rest.) The reader may also find mention of his or her hometown or state in the body of the letter. To the unsophisticated, the letter has every appearance of having been written especially for them. It is, of course, computer-produced, using technology unavailable until only a few years ago.

As the organization acquires more information about you, that information may be stored in computers and automatically re-called to be scattered through future communications in the same manner as name and residence may be inserted in initial com-munications. How much you gave the last time, when that was, and whether it might have been for some special cause are all easily retrievable facts that can be blocked into form letters that are going out to thousands of others who share with you the fact that they are contributors.

One of the functions of telephone counseling services and prayer request calls is that future mass mailings can recall your requests along with the expression of hope or trust that prayers have been answered. Furthermore, if you've called to request special prayers, let us say, for someone who is about to die, you are likely to receive a pamphlet or sermon about dealing with bereavement. Or you may receive a letter in which appropriate paragraphs have been selected from hundreds in storage for use in dealing with a particular problem.

Many people take a highly cynical view of this kind of high-technology response to real people with real problems. But as Jim Bakker has admitted, there is just no way that he and all the other television ministers can respond personally. In one sense the practice is highly deceptive. On the other hand, the system is set up so that many people get responses to problems that trouble them. And to the best of their abilities, the direct-mail organizations are trying to respond as Rex or Oral or Jim would respond *if* there were enough hours in the day for them to do so. Again, the paradox of technology: the greater the skill of the organization in promoting parapersonal communication, the more likely it is to establish rapport with its followers, and, in turn, the more likely these people are to become even bigger contributors to the ministry.

A small proportion of the television audiences become genuine communicants of particular ministries. They give a great deal, some beyond their means, and they communicate frequently both in writing and on the phone. Not unlike charitable organizations, the electronic church organizations are on the lookout for these types of people and do go after them personally for bequests. They have trust departments that can arrange for deferred giving, life insurance policies, guaranteed income if someone wills his or her estate to the organization. Personally, we find this more distasteful than any other aspect of the electronic churches' fund-raising practices. But it would be less than fair to the TV ministries that engage in such practices to fail to note that almost every organization in our society that seeks charitable contributions uses essentially the same techniques.

A few programs never solicit funds on the air. Some feel that the mood of the religious program should not be interrupted by solicitation. On the other hand, others have a more practical reason for this policy: they say that indirect techniques are more effective. "Day of Discovery," for example, offers Bible study materials to its viewers with the assurance that if you write for the free offering, your name will not end up on "another mailing list." And this pledge is honored. When the offer comes, you receive a card that you can check and return *if* you want to continue to receive materials. If you return the card, you will receive Bible study and daily devotional materials, along with the opportunity to contribute to the ministry. But there is no hard pressure to do so.

At the other end of the continuum, a few ministries devote a significant proportion of their air time to solicitation. Often there is a direct correlation between the amount of time spent appealing for money and the current cash-flow troubles of the ministry. Oral Roberts normally rattles the cup for only a few minutes during each telecast, but his overextension with the City of Faith medical complex has forced him to lengthen his solicitation talks. In late September 1980 he mailed to everyone on his mailing lists "Special Announcement" postcards that said to be sure and watch on October 5. The message in Oral's handwriting read, "This may be the most important news I've ever announced on national television." On that morning the television cameras were moved outside, and for a significant portion of the program Roberts stood in the midst of his unfinished City of Faith, pleading for money.

Oral Roberts's solicitation pivots on the concept of "seed faith." "You Sow It, Then God Will Grow It" is the title of an article by Oral in a recent issue of his *Abundant Life* magazine. His approach is always that giving to God, through the Oral Roberts Evangelistic Association, will earn you personal rewards. It's for your own good that you contribute.

Most television preachers push the self-interest idea, but some pursue giving as a matter of duty. Dr. Eugene Scott, a Pentecostal preacher with a doctorate from Stanford University, presides over a program called "Festival of Faith" on the Faith Broadcasting Network which broadcasts in Los Angeles, San Francisco, and Hartford, Connecticut. When it's time to raise money, he goes after his loyal followers with a righteous fervor, a fervor in defense of a preacher's duty to solicit funds:

There is no higher worship expression than giving. . . . I don't believe in solicitation. I don't like the word. We don't solicit. That's begging. We feel religious giving is the Christian frame, which is a sacrificial expression of worship and it is axiomatic. If you don't know the worth of God, the worth of God's word, the worth of eternal things, you will not invest in them. But if you truly know the worth of God, the worth of God's word, the worth of eternal things, you will invest in them in the place where you are taught those things.

That's self-evident Christianity. Now why don't you get on with it? Don't make me sit here and wait. I'm talking to the people who understand value. . . . It's sacrificially giving to God. Only those who know it are going to respond. But you who know it, get on with the responding now. Get on that telephone. Let me see them jam up for a change.

Following a videotape of a singing group that appears regularly on "Festival of Faith," Scott comes back on camera and says he doesn't know whether to be glad or sad. He counts the pledge slips, announces that he still needs another $2,800, and enjoins his viewers to "get on with it while they sing again." The same tape is played again, Scott comes back on camera and preaches some more about giving as worship, then he orders the control studio to "track that up again." And to the audience he says, "You got six minutes."

All of this, mind you, is a videotape filmed at some earlier date and perhaps rerun several times. The daily talk shows, "The 700 Club" and "The PTL Club," utilize a modified telethon format to raise money. In their own way they can be nearly as heavy-handed as the Reverend Dr. Scott, although neither Pat Robertson nor Jim Bakker would see his techniques in that light.

As in all telethons, the appeal to make a pledge is more or less continuous and not infrequently nauseous. What differentiates the religious from the secular pledge is the holding out of the promise of healing, miracles, special personal blessings from God, claiming the whole earth for Jesus, and so forth. The tel-evangelists go for the heartstrings in a pretty obvious way. And the 800 toll-free number makes it easy for the viewer to call in a pledge.

On the night the 700 Club concept was conceived, Jim Bakker, who had joined Robertson's organization only a few weeks earlier, appeared on camera just before the scheduled sign-off and told the audience: "Our entire purpose has been to serve the Lord Jesus Christ through radio and television. But we've fallen short. We need $10,000 a month to stay on the air, and we're far short of that. Frankly, we're on the verge of bankruptcy and just don't have the money to pay our bills." Robertson recalls in his autobiography, *Shout It from the Housetops,* that Bakker's voice broke and that he cried. He continues: "The cameraman in the studio held steady, his camera focused on Jim's face as the tears rolled down and splattered on the concrete floor. . . . Im-mediately the phones in the studio started ringing until all ten lines were jammed. Those tears had touched the hearts of the people all over the state. People called in weeping. . . . By 2:30 A.M. we had raised $105,000."

Beyond any shadow of doubt, Robertson and Bakker believe that this was God's way of delivering their budding television station from bankruptcy. Their critics might doubt that the tears flow at God's behest, but on that evening Bakker clearly found a winning formula that made contact between people's hearts and pocketbooks on the one end, and the religious broadcasters' telephone lines on the other. Many people who are old enough to remember that "The Tonight Show" has not always been hosted by Johnny Carson refer to Bakker as the Jack Paar of the religious networks. But whereas Paar's bawling on the air contributed to his demise as a talk-show host, tears are possibly Bakker's greatest asset. They show him to be human, someone who is moved by the things that move other people, a person worthy of trust and support. Some of Bakker's financial scrapes are enough to make any man cry, but when he does it on camera, it's like money in the bank.

Bakker carefully shed a token tear at the end of his January 1981 interview with President-Elect Ronald Reagan, then brushed it away. "Let's keep those pledges coming in," he said briskly while the call-in numbers blazed across the screen under his picture: "Pledges 1-800-331-1702, Prayers 1-704-554-6000." With the phone-answering forces lined up on camera, Reagan paid back his campaign debts fast in money raised for PTL.

No matter how emotional the appeal, some people just don't get sucked into impulse giving. So the televangelists use a variety of other methods to raise the cash they need to sustain air time. Besides direct appeal on the air, there are three other categories: the offering of gifts; the sale of books, records, tape recordings, religious art, and other items; and prayer and counseling services. Many of the programs utilize all these techniques to some degree, but there are distinct differences in their approaches to fund raising. As we have seen, direct appeal on the air can vary from the straightforward pitch to the emotional plea to a duty/obligation rap. Perhaps the most widely used technique for getting names and addresses for the solicitation lists, however, is the offering of gifts. The staples of this approach are printed matter and inexpensive but attractively presented jewelry. But all sorts of other things are offered as well—cassette recordings of sermons, records, prayer cloths, decals, bumper stickers, and even samples of earth from the Holy Land.

The printed materials come in all sizes, shapes, and quality, ranging from basement mimeograph machine products to four-color commercially printed jobs. They include sermons, monthly Bible study and devotional materials, pamphlets, magazines, and books (both hard- and soft-cover). Magazines have been around for quite a while, but high-quality four-color magazines have only recently exploded on the TV religion scene. One is reminded of the sudden appearance of airline magazines; once they existed, every airline had to have its own.

Lapel buttons and necklaces are the most frequently offered types of jewelry. Often the jewelry identifies the program, with logos such as "PTL" and "700 Club," but necklaces in the shape of stars, crosses, and brief messages are among the repertoire of offerings. Medallions with inscribed messages are also popular. Robert Schuller preached a sermon entitled "Turn Your Scars into Stars" and offered a five-pointed-star necklace on which that message was inscribed.

During the summer of 1980, James Robison offered a "Vote" lapel pin with the letter *T* enlarged and in the shape of a cross. If you wrote or called, you also received a bumper sticker with the same word and a message from Robison extolling the virtues of Christian citizenship.

Two principles underlie the offering of free materials. The first is the principle of reciprocity. Although there is indeed no contractual obligation in accepting the gift, the psychological theory of reciprocity holds that when someone does something for you, it is proper that you respond by doing something in return. We don't feel comfortable being in the debt of others. Giving to someone who has given to us restores the balance of interpersonal relations. This, of course, is paradoxical to the urge to get something for nothing, but the human psyche is complex and sometimes contradictory.

Charities have understood this principle of reciprocal giving for a long time, but perhaps it has not been so fully exploited as in recent years by the electronic church ministries. As early as the 1940s, the Easter Seal organization sent out those beautiful stamps, knowing people would be tempted to affix them to their mail. But to do so would conjure up a bit of guilt unless one had contributed to the charity. And for years veterans' organizations sent out miniature license plates, imprinted with the individual's own license number, which were designed to fit on a key ring. They came with the request to return them if you didn't want them, but obviously one's own license number was of no value to anyone else. So in order not to feel guilty about sticking the little license on the key ring, millions of people stuffed a dollar or two in the return envelope that came with the gift.

Most of the gifts sent out by the electronic churches are inexpensive, usually costing less per unit than the handling and postage. Ideally, the total cost, including handling, is less than the monies received, and the net gain goes to pay for television program production costs and the purchase of air time.

In reality, a lot of people accept the gifts but do not reciprocate as the theory of reciprocity says they should. This leads to the second principle underlying the offering of gifts. The names of persons who take the time to write a note or call a toll-free number to get a gift automatically go onto the computer list for direct-mail solicitation. Such people are more likely to contribute than people on a random list. They have watched the program and are apparently not negative in their attitudes or they likely would have turned off the program before the offer was made. The task is to transform these interested parties into contributors to the ministry—preferably regular contributors.

The offering of gifts has become the most successful way of attracting people to the television ministries. "You can't just preach the gospel and wait for the money to come in," Carl Wallace, director of administration of Robert Schuller's "Hour of Power," told us. "It doesn't happen that way. You've got to offer some incentive for people to communicate with you. The minute we stop offering gifts, our revenues go down dramatically." The money Schuller's program raises is a lot less than that of the other major religious programs, perhaps just because he uses a less aggressive approach to fund raising. That revenues fall when he stops handing out the freebies is as good as any indication of how important the hard sell is.

The offering of religious items for sale—rather than giving them away—is another important way in which both radio and television ministries support their operations. This is done both over the air and through the mail once an individual is on a mailing list. Actually, the items are usually not identified as being for sale but are made available for a donation of a specified amount. There are two basic strategies in this approach. The first implicitly acknowledges that although the item being offered does have some real monetary value, it is not equal to the price for which it is offered. It is rather a gift sent in exchange for a donation. For example, Jerry Falwell recently offered a boxed set of the seven books that had most influenced his life in exchange for a gift of $100 to Liberty Baptist College. They were paperback books that were obviously worth only a fraction of the offering price, but the contributor knows that he or she is making a donation, not purchasing an item of great value. The items are intended to be an inducement to give. Jim Bakker's PTL Masters' Art Collection is a clear case in point. In the promotional material Bakker writes that the painting of Jesus as a baby is so moving that "Tammy cannot look at it . . . without crying."

A different strategy is to offer items at what is, generally speaking, a fair market value. Because the radio or television ministry produces the items itself, or buys them in bulk, there is a net profit in each transaction. Jimmy Swaggart, more than any of the other television ministers, uses the hawking of religious merchandise as a mainstay of his fund raising. Swaggart is a successful gospel recording artist as well as a television evangelist, and his records are one of his most important offers.

Those who get on Jimmy Swaggart's mailing list receive a monthly magazine entitled the *Evangelist*. The September 1980 issue consisted of forty-four pages, twenty-eight of which were devoted to "advertising" things one could receive for a donation of a specified amount. More than forty record albums were offered, which were also available on eight-track or cassette tapes. In addition, there were cassette recordings of Swaggart's sermons, Bibles, books, photo albums, calendars, Christmas cards, song books, and "Jesus Saves" pen sets.

In effect, this is a mail-order catalog business in which items are offered for a fixed donation, which makes it a tax-deductible transaction. In itself, the mail-order business is inadequate to cover the costs of putting Jimmy Swaggart on more than 200 television stations, but it does help pay the bills. A lot of radio and television ministries have utilized this technique of fund raising, but the hard-selling Swaggart has done so more extensively and successfully than any of the others.

Another fund-raising technique that is utilized by even some of the smaller radio and television ministries is the promotion of travel. Trips to the Holy Land, of course, are the most popular. That September 1980 issue of the *Evangelist* promoted a trip with Jimmy and Frances Swaggart to Israel, with stopovers in Jordan and Egypt, for $1,449. But Swaggart apparently found another lucrative travel route. Readers of the *Evangelist* were invited to join him for the Second Annual Hawaiian Crusade in the dead of winter. They reserved the best rooms in the "exquisite" Hilton in Honolulu, and the promotional copy claimed that "thousands will be coming." The advertisement then went on to say: "The warmth of Hawaii will strengthen you physically and the spiritual experience will be priceless." If the spiritual experience itself was priceless, the base price tag for surf and salvation in the sun was $999 from Dallas, per person, double occupancy. If, indeed, thousands of Jimmy's followers did follow him to the land of aloha, the travel agent's commissions to the Jimmy Swaggart Evangelistic Association were considerable.

All of these operations are, of course, quite legitimate ways of raising money. Professional organizations, alumni associations, automotive clubs, and other groups promote travel packages as a means of bolstering revenues, and there are very few sacred shrines in America where a gift shop for the hawking of religious merchandise doesn't exist.

It's hard to draw the line between the fair and the shoddy. For example, some radio ministries have offered items of real value at less than the going retail price. One Texas radio preacher offered video-cassette recorders for about $200 less than retail. The giver, thus, not only got a bargain, but also received the bonus of a nice tax deduction for a charitable contribution. And the minister, because he had purchased the recorders at wholesale discount rates, netted a profit on each transaction. Critics, however, might object to such discount retailing under God's banner.

Soliciting prayer requests and offering religious counseling is the fourth way the television programs draw people into their ministries. Oral Roberts and Rex Humbard encourage people to write, but they also offer telephones for the receipt of prayer requests. Both "The 700 Club" and "The PTL Club" strongly encourage the use of the telephone and prominently display their phone counselors on the air. The new CBN facilities are equipped with fifty-four incoming telephone lines for twenty-four-hour counseling. In addition, CBN has seventy telephone counseling services in metropolitan areas around the country. Fifty of those centers have paid staff members, and telephones are manned by a total of 10,000 volunteers. "The 700 Club" broadcasts intermittently flash the telephone numbers of both the local and the national centers on the screen, and during the broadcast viewers are repeatedly encouraged to call.

The rationale for "The 700 Club" telephone ministry is grounded in Scripture. Matthew 18:19 reads, ". . . if two of you shall agree on earth as touching any thing that they shall ask, it shall be done for them of my Father which is in heaven." Telephone counseling, thus, is a way of yoking volunteers to persons in need of a prayer partner. If two shall agree, God will answer their prayers. Counselors at both "The 700 Club" and "The PTL Club" are mostly charismatic Christians. Their sense of God's personal, intimate involvement in life is quite foreign to most mainline Protestant and Catholic traditions.

But the prime-timers are sensitive to the thin line between counseling and the use of the prayer lines to build their mailing lists. A television documentary on the electronic church entitled "The Gospel According to TV" filmed a PTL counselor receiving a phone call from a person who needed a house with three bedrooms and a fenced-in yard for not more than $200 a month. Without any hesitation the counselor said, "OK, let's go to the Lord in prayer." The counselor prayed that the caller would be led to the right realtor, that guardian angels would protect the house until he could claim it, and Satan was commanded not to interfere in the transaction. We asked PTL personnel about this film clip. Did they find it offensive and feel that it was intended by the producer of the documentary as a put-down? They did not object to anything—except the fact that the sequence included the counselor taking down information about the caller.

This scene, of course, strikes at the heart of the paradox and dilemmas of evangelism, servitude and solicitation. In 1979 "The 700 Club" and its local counseling affiliates received 1,397,000 telephone calls. According to Pat Robertson, 75,000 of those persons made a "decision for Christ" and were referred to a local church. How could you pass their names and addresses along if you didn't write them down? And as long as you've got them down, how can you pass up the opportunity to merge them into your direct-mail list?

In addition to the prayer requests and spiritual decisions, every month produces tens of thousands of calls from people with emotional problems, family problems, drug and alcohol problems, and so on. ''700 Club'' counselors deal with more than 250 suicide calls and a whole catalog of other personal troubles per month.

The nature of the counseling offered by the various electronic church organizations varies, but the total volume is considerable. There is plenty of room for those with different training and values to question the adequacy and appropriateness of all or most of the counseling that occurs. The burden of proving the assertion that these people are doing more harm than good, however, rests with the accusers. There is solid research that suggests that sensitive laymen can help anxiety cases more than Ph.D. psychologists.

For whatever reason a person may call, counselors obtain sufficient information to get that caller on the organization's mailing list—if he or she is not already there. The one exception we found to this was the telephone counseling service affiliated with Robert Schuller's ''Hour of Power.'' People who call NEW-HOPE do not get cycled into the mailing list unless they explicitly request to have their names placed there. Other organizations told us they would honor a caller's request *not* to be placed on a list.

People don't normally call an anonymous counselor unless they experience loneliness, anxiety, or hurt that cannot be relieved by family or friends. For many callers, the opportunity to become involved in a television ministry is exactly the kind of support they need to deal with a problem. In many cases, this involvement does lead them to a local church. In others, the transformation of counseling into an opportunity for solicitation is a betrayal of a trusting relationship and the epitome of a religious hucksterism.

However an individual becomes known to a TV ministry, his or her name goes onto a computerized list for direct-mail solicitation. How long a name remains on the list, and what the person can expect to receive, varies from organization to organization. Generally speaking, a name remains on a list longer if some financial contribution has been made than if the individual has only requested a gift.

In December 1979 those on Jim Bakker's direct-mail list received a letter describing the importance of the PTL phone lines over the Christmas holidays, which for many people is a time of loneliness and despair. The previous December, 20,000 people had called. The letter stated that there was an average of sixteen suicide calls a day. A gift to PTL, thus, could help save lives. Later that same month, a letter described the 1980 PTL Club Devotional Guide, filled with photos, testimonial materials of PTL guests, and 366 pages designed to bless and help the reader grow closer to the Lord each day of the year—yours "when you send a gift of $15 or more to help support the PTL Club and all its programs." January brought an offer of a collection of religious art. February informed the potential giver that a contribution could help keep "The PTL Club" on the air in his or her city. March provided the opportunity to contribute to the building of the Heritage USA "Barn."

And so it goes each month, or with each mailing. If you're not attracted to contribute for one reason, perhaps another pitch will appeal to you. Jerry Falwell may ask you to give to a special project, the Liberty Missionary Society one month, Liberty Baptist College the next, and to join in cleaning up "smut" in America the following.

A few of the TV preachers, usually those of the minor league, effectively hang out "Givers Only" signs. One of our inquiries resulted in a straightforward message: "If you can't give to our ministry, you won't receive anything from us"—except, we were promised at the conclusion of the letter, the prayers of the TV minister. In another case we were informed that the free book that had been offered was out of print. We followed up with a request for the same book using a different name and enclosing a contribution; the book was promptly mailed. Most television ministries deny that contributors and noncontributors receive different treatment in the processing of requests, but our research revealed that this simply is not always the case.

Some organizations, however, send the same materials to contributors and noncontributors alike. This is likely to include magazines, newsletters, devotional materials, as well as letters of solicitation. Others hold out the promise of these things *if* you become a contributor. Letters of solicitation may be spaced as far apart as every three months or arrive as frequently as every ten days. Some organizations drop a name after only a few attempts if no contributions are forthcoming, but others seem never to clean their mailing lists.

One thing that is fairly standard in direct-mail solicitations is the fact that they are systematically varied. Key codes hidden on the response cards let the junk-mail experts compute the exact level of response from each pitch they test.

To date, the government has been reluctant to become involved in the regulation of financial matters of religious organizations, and religious organizations have not been very eager to open their books for inspection. By the end of 1976, only 13 percent of the fifty-five most inquired about religious organizations had provided audited financial information to the Better Business Bureau. Two years later, that figure had nearly doubled to 24 percent, but that still leaves three-quarters who offer no financial accountability.

In 1977 Senator Mark Hatfield informed a group of evangelical leaders that if they did not assume responsibility for regulating themselves there was every likelihood that legislation would be required. In fact, Congressman Charles Wilson of Texas had already introduced a bill that would have required disclosure "at the point of solicitation." In December 1977 representatives of thirty-two evangelical groups met in Chicago to discuss cooperative efforts. Thomas Getman, chief legislative assistant to Senator Hatfield, told the group, "Legislation is not important; disclosure is." Getman encouraged "a voluntary disclosure program . . . that will preclude the necessity of federal intervention into the philanthropic and religious sector."

Almost two years later Dr. Stanley Mooneyham, president of World Vision, acknowledged, "There is no denying that this threat of governmental action was one of the stimuli" that produced the December meeting and the subsequent activities which led to the founding of the Evangelical Council for Financial Accountability.

In early 1980 the ECFA listed 115 charter members, but the television ministries were conspicuous by their general absence. Jerry Falwell's Thomas Road Baptist Church and Related Ministries was the only charter member among the regular syndicated TV ministries. Also among the charter members were the Billy Graham Evangelistic Association, which broadcasts specials rather than weekly programs; Mooneyham's World Vision, which produces telethons to raise money for its international ministries; and Bill Bright's Campus Crusade for Christ.

It is still too early to determine whether the ECFA will provide the kind of self-regulation that Senator Hatfield and others hope for. Our own efforts to gain information that would permit us to evaluate the financial status of these organizations left us with doubts, although we concede that it may be a matter of their getting organized and clarifying policies. In addition, the apparent reluctance of all but one of the major television ministries to join the ECFA can only raise concern about their financial operations.

Born-Again Politics

For too long, Christians have been so busy with the paramount work of making individuals right with God that they have let others do the business of politics and of government. . . . It's time today for Christians to move from their churches to the halls of Congress to bring about a change in the direction of this nation. For too long, Christians have seemed to think that politics was too dirty and messy for them to be involved in. I say that to the extent that politics is dirty and messy, the answer isn't to turn your back on it and walk away. It's to go out and get yourself a bar of soap and roll up your sleeves and make politics clean again. I think it's a Christian's duty to get involved in the political process. I think the big difference between America today and the America of our founding fathers is not the lack of goodness in our people, but back then good Christian people were the ones who were doing the voting and the electing and the serving. Christians for many decades have sort of taken a sabbatical. It's time for them to get back and get involved . . . [and] . . . change the direction that America is traveling.

Congressman Guy Vander Jagt
addressing the National Affairs
Briefing in Dallas, August 1980

Pollster George Gallup declared 1976 the "Year of the Evangelical." It was really the year that the press discovered the millions of evangelicals in this country, estimates of whose numbers vary from 30 to 85 million. Jimmy Carter's public profession that he was a "born-again" Christian had much to do with the discovery. And when the votes were counted and the analysts had finished their scrutiny of voting patterns, it seemed probable that Jimmy Carter's margin of victory on his improbable march to the White House may well have been provided by evangelicals.

Most analysts, however, either missed or underplayed the importance of this group as a potentially powerful voting bloc in future elections. There was a tendency to see Carter's candidacy and victory as an aberration. He ran primarily *against Washington* in the fallout of Watergate. His opponent was an accidental president who was prone to accidents. Television cameras frequently caught President Ford stumbling down steps and bumping his head on helicopter doors, and when he played golf he sometimes bumped other people's heads. And no one could ever forget those immortal words, attributed to Lyndon Johnson, about Jerry Ford's being too dumb to walk and chew gum at the same time. In many people's minds, Jimmy Carter was also a kind of accidental president. Thus, there was no real need to assess seriously the significance of the "evangelical vote." All that changed in 1980.

George Gallup didn't get a chance to declare 1980 the "Year of Born-Again Politics." The evangelicals beat him to it.

Seldom in modern history has the emergence of an interest group attracted so much attention so swiftly as this group of conservative Christians who have been labeled the New Christian Right, headed by Jerry Falwell's political arm, the Moral Majority. It is not particularly difficult to understand why. The high visibility that a few of its leaders received immediately after a symposium they organized, the National Affairs Briefing, in Dallas in August 1980, led many Americans to perceive them as a threat. The 1980 elections resulted in greater losses in liberal leadership in government than in any election since the emergence of Roosevelt's New Deal in 1932, thus seeming to confirm that the perceived threat was real. Furthermore, the election of Ronald Reagan as commander-in-chief shattered an old folk wisdom that Americans don't elect extremists. Ultraconservative Barry Goldwater had been overwhelmingly rejected in 1964, and the very liberal George McGovern suffered the same fate in 1972. What was happening to America?

The attribution of cause is a social and political process. The events that occur in the world around us are screened through our value presuppositions. We interpret things as good or bad, right or wrong, by subconsciously calling on our religious beliefs, political ideologies, and other systems of meaning that are a part of our consciousness. But we experience directly only a tiny fraction of the events of the modern world that require explanation or understanding. They come to us through the medium of mass communication—newspapers, magazines, radio, and television. However diligently the media may try to transmit messages without bias, there are all sorts of biases that affect what is brought to our attention and how. The most powerful of these biases affects the selection of what is newsworthy.

During the summer and fall of 1980, the attention the media gave to the New Christian Right's involvement in the election was out of proportion to any objective measure of their political strength, thus heightening their visibility and, hence, their influence. But media coverage occurred because all sorts of groups, having heard about the New Christian Right and listened to them boast of their objectives, took them seriously. Each time some group or influential person spoke out against some New Christian Right group or its leader, the born-again politicians were made more viable.

The first major political happening of the electronic preachers was a prayer gathering called Washington for Jesus. Organized by a group incorporated under the title One Nation Under God, WFJ was a two-day affair that took place on April 28 and 29, 1980. Scheduled activities included a twelve-hour marathon of singing, praying for the sins of the nation, and listening to seventy-five speakers and entertainment groups. The National Park Service estimated that 200,000 people showed up for the event. The organizers claimed there were 300,000 to 400,000 present. Whichever estimate one chooses to believe, the evangelicals fell far short of the *one million* participants they sought to organize by saturating Christian radio stations with promotional announcements.

The idea of gathering in Washington to pray and repent came from the Reverend John Gimenez, a Puerto Rican who grew up in New York City. His testimony includes sixteen years on drugs and four prison sentences before he was born again. Following his salvation he became a traveling evangelist and eventually settled down in the backyard of the Christian Broadcasting Network in Virginia Beach, Virginia.

Gimenez credits the idea for a gigantic prayer meeting on the

Mall to a vision sent from God. When he told his friend Pat Robertson about this, Robertson agreed to chair the program. From the beginning there were two rationales underlying the Washington for Jesus effort. The first was scriptural; 2 Chronicles 7:14 reads as follows: "If my people, which are called by my name, shall humble themselves, and pray, and seek my face, and turn from their wicked ways; then will I hear from heaven, and will forgive their sin, and will heal their land." This is an Old Testament promise God made to King Solomon to save the Kingdom of Judah. The organizers of WFJ believe that God will honor this promise again if this nation turns from its fallen ways. Washington for Jesus, thus, was conceived as a way of honoring God, confessing personal sin, and calling upon the nation to repent.

The second rationale for the rally was a historical precedent established by Abraham Lincoln in the midst of the Civil War. At the request of the Senate, Lincoln declared April 30, 1863, a national day of "humiliation, fasting, and prayer." In the eyes of the leaders of the modern rally, the multiple crises facing America today are similar in magnitude to those of the Civil War.

At a meeting in Arlington, Texas, in September 1979, Bill Bright, head of the Campus Crusade for Christ, told a group of people that he believed God was leading him to call a conference in 1980 at which 25,000 pastors would gather to pray and, in turn, to influence their constituencies of millions. Learning of this, John Gilman, national publicity coordinator of WFJ, approached Bright about lending his support to the rally in the nation's capital. Bright wasn't sure whether this scheduled gathering was one and the same as what God was laying on his heart, but he felt confident that it was of God, and he agreed to cochair the program with Robertson.

Bright's participation was important because he commands influence in different religious circles from Robertson and Gimenez. In fact, the Washington rally was to be the first time that charismatics, headed by Robertson, and evangelicals, headed by Bright, had ever cooperated on anything of significance. The roster of sponsors read like a *Who's Who* of the electronic church: Ben Armstrong, Jim Bakker, Bill Bright, Paul Crouch, Rex

Humbard, James Kennedy, W. Stanley Mooneyham, Pat Robertson, James Robison, and Robert Schuller. The only major figures missing were Oral Roberts, Jerry Falwell, and Billy Graham; Roberts is not a joiner, Falwell was busy organizing Moral Majority, and since getting caught out on a limb in support of Richard Nixon, Graham has been extremely shy of anything that looks even remotely political.

The organizers of the event called it nonpolitical, but it was hard for many to buy that. For one thing, there was a document entitled "A Christian Declaration," drafted on January 10, 1980, which was to have been a statement of purpose for the rally. It contained explicitly partisan political and economic views. Under heavy criticism the statement was withdrawn, but not until it had been fairly widely distributed. Then there was a letter to all senators and representatives from a congressional liaison for Washington for Jesus. It boldly invited the nation's legislators to contact the rally's representatives so that they could learn "how we want you to vote" on various issues.

These documents brought threats to investigate the tax-exempt status of One Nation Under God as well as of the ministries of the organization's leadership. Those threats, plus internal disagreement regarding the line between praying and politicking, resulted in a swift retreat from the overtly political activities. Still, on the day of the rally, delegations from every state swarmed Capitol Hill to call on congressmen, presumably to convey the message that the nation needed to pray.

The principals in the WFJ rally sincerely believe that what they went to Washington to do was nonpolitical. But you also have to believe that they are sincerely naive about the nature of the political process. To veteran Washington watchers, it is difficult to imagine that anything happens in the nation's capital without a political motive. One certainly doesn't assemble nearly a quarter of a million people on the Mall and dispatch representatives to visit Congress unless there is a message to be sent.

Perhaps the most amazing thing about the April gathering was that it received so little attention when, in fact, it was the third—possibly the second—largest group ever to assemble on the Mall. Oh, it was in the news all right, but not very prominently. The attention it got from both print and broadcast media was far less than has often been devoted to gatherings only a fraction that size.

Media awareness of the movement of conservative Christians into politics began to increase gradually through the spring and summer of 1980. Their consciousness increased severalfold when Jerry Falwell and his Moral Majority showed up in force at the Republican National Convention in Detroit. Some of the more conservative planks in the Republican party's platform were broadly credited to the Moral Majority. And on the day after the ''dream ticket'' of Reagan and Ford fell apart, Jerry Falwell and other representatives of the New Christian Right spent an hour with the governor trying to persuade him to select almost anyone as his running mate but the ''liberal'' George Bush. Immediately after the convention, Robert Billings, executive director of Moral Majority, joined Ronald Reagan's staff as liaison to the religious community. When Reagan prefaced his silent prayer at the conclusion of his acceptance speech with the comment that he was a little afraid to do so, but more afraid not to, the media knew that something important was happening in U.S. politics.

The National Affairs Briefing held in Dallas on August 21 and 22 and sponsored by another conservative Christian caucus, the Roundtable, was a masterfully planned and executed media event. Advance publicity described it as a forum for pastors to be briefed by national authorities on all sorts of topics vital to making informed and responsible decisions about the forthcoming election. The speakers included many figures from the ultraright in American politics: Senator Bill Armstrong, Congressman Philip M. Crane, Senator Jesse Helms, Major General George Keegan, Brigadier General Albion Knight, Tim LaHaye, Connie Marshner, Ed McAteer, Howard Phillips, Adrian Rogers, Ed Rowe, Phyllis Schlafly, and Paul Weyrich. Then there were several of the big TV preachers—Jerry Falwell, Pat Robertson, and James Robison—along with a supporting cast of many local and regional stars. Add to this Congressman Gay Vander Jagt, who three weeks earlier had ignited the Republican convention with his keynote oratory. And finally, the big catch: presidential candidate Ronald Reagan.

This time the press was ready; they showed up more than 250

strong. All the network radio and television stations were represented, as was every major newspaper and newsmagazine, and there were more than a dozen foreign correspondents. Another hundred or so media personnel showed up with Reagan for the closing ceremonies of the conference.

The National Affairs Briefing received news coverage on all the television networks as well as front-page coverage in major newspapers across the country. This was followed by scores more in-depth analyses of the movement of politically conservative evangelicals into the political arena. On September 15 Jerry Falwell made the cover of *Newsweek,* and that same week "Preachers and Politics" was the lead feature story in *U.S. News and World Report*. Born-again politics was clearly destined to be one of the big stories of the 1980 campaign.

Jimmy Carter was also invited to address the National Affairs Briefing, but he knew his relationship with that group of Christians was strained and chose not to risk an embarrassing scene. Carter's instincts were right. Of the sixty-some speakers who were crowded into the two-day schedule, only one uttered words of kindness for President Carter. And for his voice of moderation the speaker received a solid round of boos and hisses. There's an Old Testament story about Shadrach, Meshach, and Abednego, who were delivered by angels unsinged from the fiery furnace of the wrathful King Nebuchadnezzar. Schooled in the Bible and politics, Jimmy Carter correctly sensed that no angel could possibly deliver him unsinged from the Reunion Arena in Dallas. The irony of it all was that four years earlier, candidate Jimmy Carter had persuaded a lot of evangelical Christians that it was all right to get involved in politics.

It was 104 degrees outside the Reunion Arena on the day Ronald Reagan spoke to the National Affairs Briefing. He arrived promptly on schedule to deliver his address, but the preachers weren't ready for him. So the man who at that moment appeared destined to be the next president of the United States waited. Before he finally got his chance to speak, he got a taste of the hellfire-and-brimstone religion that was giving birth to a new way of doing politics.

He waited for Senator Jesse Helms, a dull orator but darling of the New Right, to complete his remarks. Then he waited to hear

James Kennedy, pastor of what has been called for fifteen years the fastest-growing church in the country, introduce James Robison, the fast-rising star of the electronic church. Then the governor listened as Robison demonstrated his skills as a pulpit-pounding, Bible-waving, crowd-rousing evangelist.

"Don't you commit yourself to some political party or politician," Robison commanded a crowd that belonged to him. *"You commit yourself to the principles of God and demand those parties and politicians align themselves with the eternal values in this word* [the Bible]!" As the crowd came to its feet, so did Reagan. For a moment, at least, he must have felt as though the preacher and all 15,000 members of the audience were speaking directly to him. The audience interrupted the fiery young TV evangelist fifteen times before he sat down.

But it was not yet Ronald Reagan's turn. Such an honored guest deserved two introductions. James Kennedy made his. Before W. A. Criswell, pastor of the 20,000-member First Baptist Church of Dallas, could rise and walk to the podium for the second introduction, however, Jerry Falwell cut him off. Like any good Baptist, Falwell realized that he could not let this crowd get away without taking an offering. So Reagan listened and watched for another ten minutes as Falwell displayed his rather considerable skill as a fund raiser. He announced that an offering of $100,000 was needed to meet the budget of the National Affairs Briefing. "And that's what it's going to be"—with a wry grin on his face—"because the doors are locked." After he worked his magic, which included asking a thousand persons who would pledge $100 to stand, he concluded by jesting, "We'll have it counted while the governor is speaking. If it isn't adequate, we'll take another." It wasn't a bad demonstration that Jerry Falwell put on for Reagan: $10,000 a minute!

Finally, an hour behind schedule, two motorcades and a 1,500-mile plane trip from home, it seemed it was the sixty-nine-year-old presidential candidate's turn to speak. But not quite yet. He had to wait still longer while Falwell heaped accolades of praise on W. A. Criswell. Falwell declared Criswell to be "the Protestant Pope of this generation," which brought another tremendous ovation. Criswell's introduction of Reagan was mercifully brief. "My assignment," Criswell said, "is to get out of the way.'' He did. In one long breath he welcomed Ronald Reagan, on behalf of the governor of the great State of Texas, the people of the Queen City of Dallas, and 30 million evangelicals, to *"one of the greatest assemblies of the twentieth century!"*

Had the governor been a Bible scholar, he might have wondered, as he watched and waited, if he too were in King Nebuchadnezzar's fiery furnace with Shadrach, Meshach, and Abednego. He thought it was to be a friendly crowd, but James Robison, the man who warmed up the crowd for him, had told those folks not to commit themselves to a candidate, and they loved it. And with all the introductions and offerings and other carryings-on, no one seemed the slightest bit interested in hearing Reagan. Certainly they didn't have any respect for his grueling schedule, his age, or his position.

But Ronald Reagan hadn't spent all those years as an actor for nothing. When he finally got his turn, he knew just how to handle it: ''A few days ago I addressed a group in Chicago and received their endorsement for my candidacy,'' he told the Christians. ''Now I know this is a nonpartisan gathering and so I know you can't endorse me, but I only brought that up because I want you to know that I endorse you and what you are doing.'' Those now famous words were not in the advance text, but they worked magic as 15,000 enthusiastic Christians came to their feet with wild applause and exuberant shouts of *"Amen!"* It was the governor's turn to collect his share of the cheering.

Who are these people, the New Christian Right? Why their seemingly sudden move into politics? What are their goals? What strategies do they employ? What resources do they command?

The New Christian Right is a coalition of a range of diverse and previously only loosely connected groups. Many, such as anti-abortion and anti-ERA organizations, are concerned with a single issue. The hallways of the Reunion Arena in Dallas were crowded with the exhibits and literature of two dozen groups, including Christian Voice, Pro-Family Forum, National Prayer Campaign, Eagle Forum, Right to Life Commission, Fund to Restore an Educated Electorate, and the Institute for Christian Economics. And there were several newspapers, like *Christian Inquirer* and *Christian Courier,* which have sought to be catalysts to bring together the diverse causes and interests represented in these groups.

Although they have diverse interests and goals, these groups are united by their anger, grounded in their evangelical faith, about what is happening in the United States today. American society has moved significantly in directions that seriously affront their personal moral beliefs. Explicit sex in print and the broadcast media is morally wrong, they feel, and there is a definite relationship between it and the soaring divorce rate, living together out of wedlock, casual sex, and other evils. Abortion is the taking of human life. To them, talk of the right of a woman to decide whether to carry a pregnancy merely disguises the fact that millions of unborn babies have been murdered.

But these issues represent only the tip of the iceberg. The anger and moral indignation of these conservative groups run deep and their resentment has been building for a long time. Perhaps what infuriates them most is the fact that they don't believe the rest of society, and the government in particular, has taken them seriously. They are tired of being treated as a lunatic fringe or just another interest group that isn't strong enough to be factored into political decisions. Partly because their own values have held politics to be dirty, and partly because the political process has discounted their importance, they have developed feelings of powerlessness and second-class citizenship.

From their vantage point, this nation has fallen from greatness because it has turned its back on God. Getting right with God requires repentance and eradicating a lot of individual and collective sin. Evangelicals have shared substantial segments of this belief system for many years. Billy Graham's crusades haven't strayed very far from those themes in a quarter of a century.

The new ingredient in the emerging coalition is the belief that it is the responsibility, indeed the *duty*, of Christians to engage in the political process as a means of bringing America back to God. And like the liberals of the 1950s and 1960s, they believe morality can be legislated. Therefore, it is important to get the right people elected to office.

The dynamos behind the thrust of born-again politics are the televangelists. Whether or not they directly advocate political involvement, most constantly remind their audiences of the collective sins of the nation and the need to repent.

Jerry Falwell's Moral Majority is by far the best organized and best known of the several organizations that collectively make up the New Christian Right. To understand them better, we need to know something of their beginnings.

Robert Billings was president of Hyles-Anderson College, a fundamentalist school in Hammond, Indiana, in the mid-1970s when he was invited to attend a seminar on government and politics in Washington sponsored by the Christian Freedom Foundation (now defunct, it was for twenty years the most influential of the "old" Christian right organizations). A onetime English professor, Billings now admits it was his ignorance about politics that brought him to Washington. "As a college president," he told us, "I thought I ought to know something." So turned on by the seminar was Billings that shortly thereafter he resigned his college presidency and ran for Congress. Unsuccessful in that effort in 1976, Billings moved to Washington anyway and in January 1977 founded a group called Christian School Action for the purpose of monitoring legislation that had implications for Christian schools. Two years later, in December 1978, the organization's name was changed to National Christian Action Coalition and its mission broadened to include lobbying.

Billings developed ties with New Right political groups and began envisioning ways to draw the potential clout of religious television into their common concerns. Jerry Falwell was a prime candidate to enlist. Billings first approached Falwell in 1977 about creating an organization very much like what Moral Majority was to be, but Falwell wasn't ready. When Billings approached Falwell again in 1979, he brought along most of the big guns of the New Right. The alliance was forged, and Billings became executive director of the Moral Majority, a post he held until he became Reagan's liaison to the religious community during the campaign.

Jerry Falwell's views about mixing religion and politics and his decision to create Moral Majority developed gradually over several years. When Billings first approached him, Falwell had already been engaged for nearly two years in holding patriotic rallies around the country. His message, timed to correspond to the celebration of the nation's bicentennial, was that we are a nation under God that is now violating *"His* principles and *His* heritage."* As Falwell traveled, ministers continually approached him and said, "We must do something."

"I think I was really hoping," Falwell told us, "that somebody else would do it." Finally, the pressure on him to spearhead a political organization built to the point that he consented to do so. The critical meeting took place in March 1979. But it wasn't until June 1979 that the lawyers were called in to draw up incorporation papers for Moral Majority. Then, in September, Falwell debuted his new organization with a rally on the steps of the Virginia State Capitol in Richmond. From there he set out with an entourage of clean-cut Liberty Baptist College singers to stage I Love America rallies in the capitals of all fifty states. Technically, the I Love America rallies were sponsored and paid for by "The Old-Time Gospel Hour," but on the same days rallies were held, pastors were invited to Moral Majority luncheons. So if a state chapter of Moral Majority had not yet been established, the luncheons provided an occasion to do so.

The original design called for rallies in all fifty states over a period of eighteen months. But patience is not high on Falwell's list of virtues. When he decides to do something, he moves. It took Falwell only about half that time to organize semiautonomous chapters of Moral Majority in all fifty states. In June 1980 he bought prime time on 215 television stations nationwide to air a special entitled "America You're Too Young to Die." This patriotic program featured extensive footage from the I Love America rallies, especially clips of U.S. senators and congressmen, governors, and other political celebrities. Immediately thereafter the program was repackaged, and three teams of Life Action Singers fanned out to present live entertainment along with multimedia sight and sound spectaculars to scores of audiences in large and small communities. Each stop was an occasion to pass out pledge cards, take a collection, and build a mailing list for Moral Majority.

In the meantime, Falwell lost no time in putting together other pieces of a mass communications political organization. In January 1980 he started a newspaper called *Moral Majority Report.* In April he began a five-day-a-week radio newscast, also called "Moral Majority Report," which the promotional material described as being "much like the Paul Harvey newscast." The program was offered to stations without cost. Viewed from the other side, Falwell was asking for free air time—and he got it. At the end of the first six months, he was on 260 stations, most of which were Christian radio stations. The newscast involved no direct solicitation, but listeners were offered a free subscription to the newspaper *Moral Majority Report*.

The I Love America rallies and the radio program provided the means to build a subscription list for the newspaper. The first edition of *Moral Majority Report* had a circulation of 77,000. In mid-October 1980, 482,000 copies were being printed, a sixfold increase from the beginning of the year and an increase of nearly 50,000 over the previous month. The newspaper, of course, serves an important educational function. But more important to the magic of building a financial base for this burgeoning political organization, each name on the subscription list is also a target for direct-mail solicitation. Following the same formula that was used to build a financial base for "The Old-Time Gospel Hour," the direct mail comes racing out of the computer with clockwork precision. Each month the letter addresses a different issue— homosexuality, pornography, ERA, and so on. And each letter bears a personal touch, including the addressee's name and/or home community in the body of the letter.

It's a formula that works. Moral Majority's vice-president, Dr. Ronald S. Godwin, told us that the organization raised a total of $3.2 million in calendar 1980—not a bad accomplishment for an organization in its first full year of operation. Godwin was unable to identify what proportion of this was raised by direct mail, but he conceded that it was probably the lion's share.

Moral Majority has gotten most of the publicity, but other organizations are also working diligently on the New Christian Right political agenda. Ed McAteer, founder of the Roundtable, is another person who stands with a foot in both the secular and religious political camps. He was with the Colgate-Palmolive Company for twenty-eight years, and when he resigned in 1976 to work full-time for the Christian Freedom Foundation, he was a district sales manager stationed in Memphis. Long interested in encouraging Christians to apply their faith to economics and politics, McAteer was a member of former Southern Baptist Convention President Adrian P. Rogers's Bellevue Baptist Church.

McAteer's job with the Christian Freedom Foundation was to travel around the country and promote the very point of view he has so long cherished. In fact, it was one of his seminars that ignited the political interest of Robert Billings. Later, McAteer went to work for Howard Phillips and the Conservative Caucus. With knowledge, experience, and friendships in Christian circles, it was McAteer more than anyone else who built the bridge between the New Right and the emerging New Christian Right. During the time Billings was encouraging Falwell to make a decisive move into the political arena, McAteer passed frequently through Lynchburg to make similar encouragements.

Then, in 1980, McAteer put together the Roundtable (the original name was the Religious Roundtable, but it was changed in a calculated move to broaden its appeal). In creating a Council of 56, McAteer spoke often of the signers of the Declaration of Independence: "The fifty-six signatures on that Declaration of Independence were kept secret for one half year because the gallant fifty-six who made that promise knew when they signed that they were risking everything. If they won the fight, the best they could expect would be years of hardship in a struggling new nation. And if they lost . . . they would face a hangman's rope as traitors. . . . If those fifty-six men were willing to risk everything in order to give birth to freedom, can we do any less to preserve it in our generation?"

Conscious of the need for media visibility in forging a political organization, McAteer recruited TV evangelist James Robison to be the Roundtable's vice-president. Dallas was probably chosen to be the site of the National Affairs Briefing, the first major Roundtable event, precisely because Robison could be counted on to attract a crowd. If McAteer had any doubts about the appropriateness of Robison as his media man, those doubts were put to rest during the two days of the Briefing when, on successive evenings, Robison repeatedly brought a wildly enthusiastic crowd to its feet.

With key personnel in place and some national visibility, the Roundtable is now prepared to go about the business of building

Moral Majority founder Jerry Falwell commutes to a meeting . . . but keeps in touch. *Courtesy ''The Old-Time Gospel Hour.''*

Jerry Falwell and the "Old-Time Gospel Hour" singers at the I Love America rally in Washington, D.C.

At the same rally Falwell and Phyllis Schlafly, head of the STOP ERA campaign, stand side by side during the singing of a patriotic song. *Courtesy Wide World Photos.*

More than 200,000 people turned out for a Washington for Jesus rally in April of 1980. Although organizers claimed it was a nonpolitical event, the agenda was to call the national leadership back to God. *Courtesy Wide World Photos.*

Many in attendance at the day-long rally on the Mall appeared the night before, and as the sun broke over the horizon the crowds joined in early morning prayers. *Courtesy Wide World Photos.*

Rain failed to dampen the spirits of singer Pat Boone and his wife, Shirley, as they opened the previous day's rally at Robert F. Kennedy Memorial Stadium. *Courtesy Wide World Photos.*

Jerry Falwell addresses a summit meeting of Moral Majority state chairmen in Lynchburg, Virginia, in October of 1980. *Photo by Les Schofer.*

Organized by the Roundtable, the National Affairs Briefing in Dallas brought 15,000 Christians—and Republican presidential candidate Ronald Reagan—together in August 1980.

James Robison, vice-president of the Roundtable, assumes a familiar pose in front of the National Affairs Briefing audience. The meeting galvanized the televangelists' political ambitions.

Jerry Falwell, Ronald Reagan, and Howard Phillips pose for the cameras during the 1980 presidential campaign. Phillips, national chairman of Conservative Caucus, was one of several New Right leaders who encouraged Falwell to form Moral Majority. *Photo by Les Schofer, courtesy "The Old-Time Gospel Hour."*

an organization. You used to have to build organizations the other way around—from the ground up—but modern communications technology has changed that too.

Christian Voice, Inc., is a nonprofit organization created for the explicit purpose of lobbying and expressing political viewpoints from a Christian moral position. It is the product of a "grass-roots" effort that began in California. Richard Zone, executive director of Christian Voice, relates that the organization began as a result of a threat from the IRS to challenge the tax-exempt status of his church in Glendale, California. He and members of his congregation were working for the defeat of Proposition 6, a referendum to give homosexuals equal protection under the law. "I realized," said Zone in an interview with *Christian Life,* "that this moral issue had been politicized and that our government was telling the moral conscience of the nation [the church] to stay out of the battle."

Organized in October 1978, but not officially launched until January 1979, Christian Voice claims to have 190,000 members, including 37,000 ministers. The organization has been built by the direct-mail route with few financial contributions of any size. What has most given Christian Voice visibility is its "Congressional Report Card." "Report Card" scores are a reflection of the number of times a member of Congress voted "correctly" on fourteen "key moral issues."

The "Report Card" probably would not have received such considerable attention save for the fact that Congressman Richard Kelly of Florida, convicted of accepting an ABSCAM bribe, and Congressman Robert Bauman of Maryland, a pet of the New Right who has confessed to "homosexual tendencies," scored 100, whereas the ordained clergymen on Capitol Hill failed to receive even passing grades. Catholic priest Father Robert Drinan of Massachusetts scored a big fat zero, and Robert Edgar, a Presbyterian minister from Pennsylvania, received a score of 8. In many people's minds, these seeming anomalies raised questions about the extent to which moral principles were the underpinning of the "Report Card."

Examination of the specific issues that constituted the votes revealed a significant equation of ultra-right-wing partisan views with morality. For example, voting for a resolution that would "guarantee the United States' commitment to defend Taiwan" was considered a moral vote. Opposition, by implication, was immoral. The issue was black and white and allowed no room for dealing with the complexities and ambiguities of the past twenty-five years of dealings with Taiwan and the Communist government of mainland China. So also was it immoral to vote against an amendment that would have eliminated $4 million from a National Science Foundation appropriation for biological, behavioral, and social science research. The authors of the "Report Card" were confident that "most of these funds are used to stack the ideological deck in favor of Godless behavioral humanist research. . . ."

Despite the obvious flaws in conception and content—and many would wish to add moral integrity—of the "Report Card," it is an effective political weapon. A summary statistic that rates the moral character of a congressman is a handy device for those who don't think and are willing to follow blindly anyone who claims to represent their views.

There is another sense in which the "Report Card" is effective. In an era in which we get most of our information in blips, congressmen know that they will not have the opportunity to go home to their constituencies and offer a penetrating, perceptive critique of the "Report Card." And there are few congressional districts left in the United States where a zero on the Christian Voice "Report Card" can be worn as a badge of courage and independence. Hence, many congressmen are going to be much more cautious about how they vote on all sorts of issues. That, itself, is not a bad idea. When the contemplation of how to vote becomes even subconsciously guided by fear of being targeted by Christian Voice as immoral, however, the integrity of individual conscience is no less compromised than when a congressman votes in a certain way because he has accepted a bribe or is beholden to a special-interest group for large financial contributions.

The fourth significant political group of the New Christian Right is National Christian Action Coalition. NCAC was organized in 1977 by Robert Billings as Christian School Action and at that time had a narrower objective of monitoring and lobbying on legislation pertaining to Christian schools. It has a full-time staff of three, headed by Billings's son, William, and it provides a variety of service functions for regional and single-issue groups of the Christian right. NCAC has produced and distributed a movie featuring Senator Jesse Helms which tells Christians how they can get involved in politics. Other materials on how to develop a political organization and legislative alerts are sent to approximately 1,200 churches and an undisclosed number of individuals. The group has also produced a "report card" of congressional voting on family issues which is distributed by their political action committee called the Christian Voters' Victory Fund.

There has been a great deal of confusion in the media about the New Right and the New Christian Right. Many have failed to understand that the concept of New Right does not refer to the resurgence of conservative forces in the United States, but rather to a fairly small group whose common bond is mastery of the uses of modern communications technology. Almost without our recognizing it, that technology has transformed politics from an art form into a science—an inexact science to be sure, but one in which the likely outcomes of alternative strategies can be estimated.

Consultants, advertising specialists, pollsters, and direct-mail experts are the new king makers of American politics, having replaced the political bosses in the smoke-filled rooms of another era. Ironically, it was the efforts of a liberal Congress to enact post-Watergate election reforms that gave great momentum to the New Right. When the reforms cut out the fat cats, those who were experts at direct-mail fund raising took on greatly enhanced importance in U.S. politics. Previously considered to be nickel-and-dime junk dealers by a lot of political pros, the direct-mail experts were able to demonstrate that if they zeroed in on the right audience, a lot of little contributions could add up to big bucks.

All the components of modern communications technology are now widely employed by Republicans and Democrats, conservatives and liberals alike. What has made the New Right such an important force is that it got a big jump in mastering the technology, which it has utilized effectively to tap discontents and frustrations of that sector of society which Spiro Agnew labeled the "silent majority" back in the early 1970s. The active participation of the New Right in the political sweepstakes dates roughly to that period.

The New Right stands largely outside the party structures and the inner circles of power in Washington. Howard Phillips, who heads Conservative Caucus, is an exception. He was the architect of Richard Nixon's "southern strategy" and the person Nixon tapped to dismantle Lyndon Johnson's "war on poverty" program. Whether he was the first among the New Right leadership to recognize the importance of drawing Christians into the conservative coalition, he certainly understood the importance of such an alliance. He has called the movement of conservative Christians into politics "the most significant development in American politics since organized labor discovered the ballot box."

The New Right sought to recruit television preachers for some time before it succeeded. Its leaders understood well the lessons of history. When you lock horns in social conflict, it's good to have God on your side; your people fight harder and the opposition wilts more easily. The liberals won the battle to define whose side God was on in the civil rights struggles of the 1960s. Staking out the territory of life, family, and country as theirs has given conservatives some pretty good ammunition for the ensuing battles of the 1980s. They frequently invoke the name of God as the progenitor of their cause, but they need highly visible religious leaders to sanctify the invocation. The TV preachers could serve them well as legitimizers of their cause, but they could also mobilize their own large conservative constituencies. So it happened that Jerry Falwell was sought out to create Moral Majority.

The New Christian Right, thus, obviously owes its genesis to the master plan of the New Right. The New Right needs the New Christian Right to broaden its base of support and to render legitimate its causes. For the present, the New Christian Right needs the New Right, because the leaders of the former are no more than novices at big-league politics. But they are fast learners, and the New Right can expect to equate its agendas with those of the New Christian Right only as long as the Christians agree. The one big carrot the New Right has to dangle before conservatives to induce them to join the club is a command of modern communications technology. But this won't get the New Right very far with the New Christian Right, which has pioneered in the field. The technology that the New Right is using to transform American politics is essentially the same technology that the televangelists are using to build their religious empires. If they choose to use it to develop political empires as well, there is nothing that can hold them to the New Right if they choose to go in other directions.

The National Affairs Briefing in Dallas provided crucial momentum for the emergence of the New Christian Right. The extensive news coverage of that event announced to the nation the emergence of a budding social movement. News coverage begets news coverage just as certainly as yeast leavens dough and television hits beget spin-offs and imitations. The media's discovery of the born-again politicians served also to legitimize their efforts to become politically active. Although the notion that religion and politics don't mix is historically a myth, it had guided the consciousness of most evangelicals in recent history. Separation of church and state was one of the chief rhetorical weapons that conservative churches used to oppose the entanglement of liberal churches in civil rights during the 1960s.

Undoing old beliefs is not always easy. People have to be assured and reassured that new beliefs or behavioral patterns are all right. Most of the evangelicals in the United States were not getting the message that involvement in politics is all right from watching religious programs on television, first, because only a few of the many television preachers delivered the message that Christians should involve themselves in the political process. More important, a lot of evangelicals, perhaps a majority, never or seldom watch the TV preachers.

News coverage of the National Affairs Briefing served, thus, to draw attention to the efforts of a minority within evangelical ranks to draw the majority into the political arena. Sheer awareness of the fact that kindred souls are doing something provides confirming evidence that it might be all right to do. When one's own pastor becomes bold about political issues, the awareness that the same thing is happening elsewhere may cause people to listen rather than question the wisdom of his mixing religion and politics. Even if they are not prepared to follow his invitation to become organizationally involved, the fact that they choose not to oppose his engagement is an important step in legitimizing born-again politics. The shift from a generally negative or neutral posture toward political activism, thus, is an important step in developing support for a broad-based movement.

The media coverage of those scorching hot August days in Dallas served another important function—it aroused the anxieties of those who view right-wing Christians as a potential threat to their interests. The mobilization of any group is certain to trigger the countermobilization of those who stand to lose something if the newly organized group gains power. It was only a matter of days before the New Christian Right knew it was in a dogfight as organized opposition began to appear from almost every sector of society.

The Establishment
Strikes Back

*Such Christians gave us the Crusades, the Spanish
Inquisition and the Salem witchcraft trials. When
you're convinced you're doing God's work, it's only
a short step to becoming convinced that everything
you do is justified. The Christian Voice people are
fond of quoting this line in the Bible: "When the
righteous rule, the people rejoice; when the unright-
eous rule, the righteous mourn." To which I can only
add: "When the self-righteous rule, watch out."*
Donald Kaul, *Des Moines Register*

On November 23, 1980, the American Civil Liberties Union paid
$20,000 for a full-page advertisement in the Sunday *New York
Times* whose banner headline read: "IF THE MORAL MAJORITY
HAS ITS WAY, YOU'D BETTER START PRAYING." Simultaneously,
the ACLU's leaders sent a first-class mailing to their membership
with an urgent plea for funds to fight for the preservation of the
Bill of Rights.

The ACLU, founded by Rodger Baldwin, has never been
afraid of a ruckus. It has often come to the defense of unpopular
causes and groups that a lot of Americans would just as soon see
silenced. Its decision to defend the rights of the Nazi party to
march in a heavily Jewish Chicago suburb a few years ago
offended the civil libertarian instincts of a lot of members, who
staged their own protests by not renewing their membership. For
sixty years the ACLU has been America's self-appointed defender of the Bill of Rights. Former Chief Justice Earl Warren
said of the ACLU that it "has stood foursquare against the

recurring tides of hysteria that from time to time threaten freedoms everywhere. . . ."

But there was something approaching a hysterical tone in the ACLU's newspaper ad and direct-mail copy about Moral Majority. The ad in the *Times* read, in part: "Their [the Moral Majority's] agenda is clear and frightening: they mean to capture the power of government and use it to establish a nightmare of religious and political orthodoxy. . . . they are dangerously deceptive. . . . the new evangelicals are a radical anti-Bill-of-Rights movement. They seek not to conserve traditional American values, but to overthrow them."

The ACLU's assault on the Moral Majority is a rather significant departure from its carefully reasoned justification for defending Nazis. Did the ACLU overreact to the perceived threat of Moral Majority and its New Christian Right colleagues? A lot of people don't think so.

James Dunn, executive director of the Southern Baptists' Christian Life Commission in Texas, told an annual meeting of Americans United for the Separation of Church and State: "They don't want a democracy, a free people, a pluralistic society. They want a theocracy. And if you listen very carefully to the number of times the first person singular pronoun is used, you'll realize they not only want a theocracy, but every one of them wants to be Theo."

During the weeks immediately preceding and following the 1980 elections, organizations created to combat the influence of the New Christian Right proliferated. Daniel Maguire, a nationally known theologian and ethicist from Marquette University in Milwaukee, organized a group called Moral Alternatives in Politics. Maguire, who labeled the New Christian Right "religious fascism," assembled a board of directors that included such prominent figures as theologian-historian Martin Marty of the University of Chicago, Charles Curran of Catholic University, and Rabbi Balfour Brickner of the Stephen Wise Free Synagogue in New York.

Senator George McGovern saw his defeat and that of other liberal senators as the handiwork of the New Christian Right. In his view, these people are at war with the whole Judeo-Christian ethic of compassion and commitment to care for the disadvantaged. Shortly after the election McGovern announced plans for the creation of an organization called Americans for Common Sense. In Virginia, home of Jerry Falwell and Pat Robertson, a group calling itself Virginians Organized for Informed Community Expression (VOICE) was organized in Norfolk and quickly spread to other communities in that state. All over the United States there was the same kind of spontaneous reaction to the New Christian Right, suggesting that a lot of people besides the ACLU believed the nation's liberties were threatened by these born-again Christian zealots.

The most visible new organization, and possibly the organization most likely to remain in the struggle over the long haul, is a group called People for the American Way. Spearheaded by Norman Lear, creator of "All in the Family," "Maude," "Mary Hartman, Mary Hartman," and several other television sitcom successes of the 1970s, PAW assembled a board of advisers that included such prominent religious leaders as Father Theodore Hesburgh, president of the University of Notre Dame; M. William Howard, president of the National Council of Churches; Rabbi Marc Tannenbaum of the American Jewish Committee; William P. Thompson, stated clerk of the United Presbyterian Church; Bishop James K. Mathews, former presiding bishop of the United Methodist Church; and Colin Williams, former dean, Yale University School of Divinity. Also on the list were prominent magazine editors and business persons, along with former members of Congress and presidential cabinets—all in all, an impressive display of establishment clout.

People for the American Way started gaining visibility just before the election through a series of television spots featuring a variety of Learesque characters plugging religious pluralism as the American way. One featured a forklift driver who said he was proud to be a 100-percenter on the preacher's morality list but troubled by the fact that his son had missed one item on the preacher's test and his wife two. He was confident that his son was at least as good a Christian as he, and he knew for sure his wife was a "whole lot better Christian" than he. Another spot presented a man whose family is in the background arguing about a movie they have just seen on TV. He asks the viewers how Americans can be expected to agree about things as important as religion when his family can't even agree about a movie. At the conclusion of each commercial spot, sympathetic viewers are told to write to the box number on the screen or call a toll-free number for more information about People for the American Way.

Those who called or wrote received a letter, a brochure, a reprint from the *New York Times,* and a postage-paid envelope to use for sending in a contribution to help support People for the American Way. The brochure contained these statements: "There's an alarming new movement in America—the Religious New Right. A coalition of ultra-conservative political groups, spearheaded by a new breed of politically oriented electronic evangelists, the Religious New Right is using television and radio to preach a new gospel to millions across America. They fill their followers with passion of holy war. And they label those who disagree as un-American, immoral and ungodly. In effect, they are teaching people to hate, but in a 'Christian' way."

The letter, signed by Michael MacIntyre, a young Methodist minister, was toned down considerably from one Norman Lear had circulated earlier. In that letter, which Lear described as probably the most important he would ever write—even if he lived to be a thousand—he used phrases like "ominous," "extraordinary and dangerous," "single-issue zealots," "pernicious danger," and "fascism masquerading as Christianity" to describe the New Christian Right. What these people are doing, Lear wrote, "is the ultimate obscenity, the spiritual pornography of a debased religiosity."

Several prominent liberal religious and political figures expressed concern about the tone of Lear's attack and the accuracy of some of his charges, as well as surprise that such prominent persons would identify themselves with a campaign that seemed not very different in spirit and content from the mudslinging that was coming from the most vicious elements of the New Right. Some of the members of Lear's advisory committee apparently felt the same way, because the mass mailing was tempered considerably.

There was a lot of hysteria and near hysteria about the New Christian Right among editorial writers. By and large, liberal syndicated columnists had a heyday. None was probably more exercised than Nicholas von Hoffman, former sparring partner with conservative James J. Kilpatrick on the Point/Counterpoint segment of "60 Minutes." It took von Hoffman only a few days after the Dallas briefings in August to sharpen his pen and drive unrelentingly into the hearts of "these Christian Stalinists." Von Hoffman thought the time was nigh to organize the Immoral Minority. "Excluded from this fraternity of immoralists," he wrote, "would be those who mistake the not terribly well-informed creakings of their own minds for the Divinity." But von Hoffman was just getting warmed up. Here are some excerpts from his column:

We don't have enough government regulation. When these round-heads get into power, we're going to have a U.S. Moral Life Commission in Washington with federal watch and ward bailiffs empowered to mind any citizen's most intimate business.

There is the smell of Elmer Gantry about this crusade. Or of Tartuffe, Molière's pious phony who inserts himself into the household by flaunting the Bible in order to rob the master, marry his daughter and seduce his wife.

The born-again ayatollahs preaching fundamentalist pugnacity on our television are as impervious to the give-and-take rationality of sane politicians as the old boy with the X-ray eyes in Tehran.

As if they were back on "60 Minutes," Kilpatrick responded by defending Jerry Falwell and his Moral Majority, at least in a backhanded sort of way. ". . . this sawdust apostle and his God-fearing flock have every right to pursue their political aims in whatever legal way they wish," Kilpatrick wrote. But his defense of Falwell was really more an attack on "ultra-lib editors" who were attacking Falwell. "By and large," Kilpatrick admitted, "the Reverend Dr. Falwell, his brethren and sistren, give me the willies." Then, to retain the symmetry with von Hoffman's Immoral Minority, Kilpatrick said that if he ever succumbed to the urge to organize a political group, he would likely organize the Immoral Majority. Perhaps prophesying the election outcome, Kilpatrick continued, "There are more of us than there are of them."

Some of the attacks on the New Christian Right were colorful, but most were dulled by the deadpan seriousness of the critics. Political cartoonists had a field day depicting the pious "moral majority,'' but there was a distinct absence of humor in the work of most cartoonists and syndicated columnists. Mike Royko of the *Chicago Sun-Times* was an exception. He wrote a column about a friend who had a terrible nightmare that Ronald Reagan had become president and Jerry Falwell had replaced Johnny Carson as the host of late-night television. His guests, of course, included the likes of the head of the National Rifle Association.

Heated rhetoric is not unusual in political campaigns. What was unusual about the 1980 campaign was that the candidates' strongest language was reserved not for the opposition, but rather for the leadership of the New Christian Right. Jerry Falwell caught most of the heat. Except for the fact that the combatants took themselves so seriously, the battle might have lightened a campaign between two candidates between whom the real majority of Americans probably would have preferred not to have to choose. Jerry Falwell has never been known for walking away from a good fight, so when the politicians took out after him, he fought back.

On September 23, 1980, Secretary of Health and Human Services Patricia Roberts Harris made a speech in which she decried the Moral Majority as "a serious threat to the democratic process." She added, "I am beginning to fear that we could have an Ayatollah Khomeini in this country." Jerry Falwell went to Washington and called a press conference at the Department of Health and Human Services to lob a few verbal assaults back at Secretary Harris. "The truth of the matter," Falwell said in a prepared statement, "is that as long as it is a liberal group or an ineffective conservative group speaking out, Secretary Harris and others have no objection. However," he continued, "the left see this new level of involvement by the Judeo-Christian community bringing masses of new recruits to the conservative side of the spectrum and so they are desperately trying to discredit the movement."

A few days after Secretary Harris's statement, the Congressional Black Caucus appealed to blacks to mobilize in opposition to what they viewed as a "frightening" political movement aimed at "turning back the clock of hard-fought and hard-won justice for the over 25 million black Americans who live in this country." The Congressional Black Caucus also sent out signals that it might have to investigate the Moral Majority in order to identify the "powerful corporate money interests" that were bankrolling the organization. Falwell shot back: "An investigation of the people who contribute to Moral Majority will reveal that our average gift is $20 and that more than 400,000 'little people' are the backbone of the financial support. . . ." And then he challenged the Black Caucus to examine the financial records of Moral Majority. No one accepted his challenge.

In the same week independent presidential candidate John Anderson spoke out forcefully against the Moral Majority: "The political marriage of the so-called Moral Majority and the New Right is not one ordained in Heaven. It is a union which seeks to inject unbending rigidity and intolerance into church pew and polling booth alike. It is an alliance that seeks to purge from the political process ideas and ideals and those hapless souls who hold them dear." Like the great majority of Americans on election day, Falwell passed by the opportunity to endorse Anderson's position.

Most of the critics of the New Christian Right did not challenge the leaders' right to be involved in politics—such a posture would have been blatantly inconsistent with the knowledge that liberal Protestantism and Catholicism have long been politically active. What appeared illegitimate about the New Christian Right's move into politics was the *way* in which it took place.

That word, *way,* meant a lot of things to different people. To some it meant being involved without being well informed about the complexity of issues. To others it referred to the tactics—the "dirty tricks" members of the New Christian Right allegedly used. To still others, *way* referred to what these people, if they gained power, would do to violate the rights of others. And there was a strong sense that the application of "Christian principles" in evaluating a candidate constituted a violation of the meaning and implications of the principle of separation of church and state.

Predictably, much of the criticism directed at the New Christian Right during the 1980 campaign came from mainline Protestant, Catholic, and Jewish leaders and the organizations with which they were associated. In a tradition-breaking move, William Sloane Coffin, senior minister at the prestigious Riverside Church in New York, opened his sanctuary to television cameras for the first time in the history of that church as he lashed out at evangelical preachers for their association with right-wing politics. Coffin said that he would agree with the fundamentalist preachers that the Bible contains "all the answers, at least all the significant ones." But the Bible is a source of insight, inspiration, and wisdom, not a storehouse of unbending literal truths. "The Bible," Coffin stated, "is something like a mirror: if an ass peers in, you can't expect an apostle to peer out."

Later in the political campaign, Coffin, who is best known for his role as a civil rights and antiwar activist, met Jerry Falwell to debate on the "Today" and "Donahue" shows. Again, he attacked Falwell's theology as "shallow" and "simplistic": "I think deep down, he is shallow. His biblical positions are not sound biblical study. *Anybody* who has done any *real* Bible study knows you can't come up with those conclusions from the Bible. I think what he calls a simple moral issue is very complex. It is very rare to get a Christian position. You get Christians believing different things" (emphasis added).

If there is condemnation in the rhetoric of fundamentalist preachers when they chastise "modernists" or "liberals" for not accepting the Bible as the inerrant, literal truth of God, the condescension in the language of the liberals is no less real when they call fundamentalists "shallow," assert that they have not "really" studied the Bible, and therefore imply that they are "nobodies." The same tone is apparent in remarks made by the Right Reverend Paul Moore, Jr., Episcopal bishop of New York, to the 203d annual convention of the dioceses, which were reprinted on the Op-Ed page of the *New York Times*: "They [the Moral Majority] call themselves Christian Conservatives, but it is the traditional churches who merit the description of truly conservative." Elsewhere in the editorial, Moore used such phrases as "this strange breed of Christians" and "false conservatism" to characterize the "so-called Moral Majority."

The language of many of the New Christian Right leaders is strident and not to be defended. But if one examines the language of the liberals as they launched a counterattack, from the perspective of a conservative, their language is also pretty offensive. What is most offensive to conservatives is the liberals' aura of ontological superiority—the fact that they take for granted the intellectual and moral superiority of their perspective.

As the 1980 campaign built up a head of steam, so also did the attacks on the New Christian Right from the "religious establishment." Leaders from fifteen of America's largest Protestant denominations released a statement that condemned the New Christian Right as theologically and politically unsound and, by implication, un-Christian. The statement; entitled "Christian Theological Observations on the Religious Right Movement," read, in part, as follows: "There is no place in a Christian manner of political life for arrogance, manipulation, subterfuge or holding others in contempt. . . . There is no justification in a pluralistic and democratic society for demands for conformity along religious or ideological lines."

Throughout the country there were collective statements of condemnation where the New Christian Right was active. In Oklahoma, for example, the Oklahoma Conference of Churches, which represents seventeen major religious bodies, unanimously passed a resolution that cautioned against "religious partisanship which . . . threatens American religious freedom." Max E. Glenn, executive director of the Conference, further warned that making ". . . judgments about the character and motives of others is in danger of being unjust, simplistic and self-righteous." Furthermore, Glenn added, "Uncritical endorsement which ignores the humanity of candidates is dangerously naive."

Criticism of the New Christian Right by mainline Protestant, Catholic, and Jewish leadership was extensively reported by the press. What the press nearly missed, however, was the extent to which conservative evangelical church leaders raised doubts about the appropriateness of Christian involvement in partisan politics.

No one is more responsible for reshaping evangelical thought about political engagement than Carl F. H. Henry. He is the founding editor of the country's most influential evangelical journal, *Christianity Today,* and is broadly recognized as one of the foremost evangelical theologians in the United States. For more than thirty years Henry has been prodding conservative

Christians toward social and political involvement. His little book, *The Uneasy Conscience of Modern Fundamentalism* (1947), indicts evangelicals for their preoccupation with "individual sin rather than social evil." He saw evangelical Christianity divorced from the great social movements of modern times and challenged his brethren to become engaged.

Still, when the born-again politicians moved into high gear in the 1980 elections, Henry expressed "grave doubts" and caution about the surge of activity: "I've pleaded ever since *Uneasy Conscience* that evangelicals get involved. So, formally, I can do nothing but commend their getting in. But the swiftness with which they've gotten in and the identification of specific objectives troubles me. They want a quick fix, that's what troubles me most. . . . [And] when they were criticized, they backed off from particulars and said they were interested in principles. But they took the higher ground only under criticism rather than in their initial formulation of the problem. I think one of the weaknesses of evangelical Christianity is that it has leaped from one-issue and one-candidate solutions without doing all the intermediary spade work that is involved in the formulation of a political philosophy predicated on principles with its implications for platform and candidates."

Henry told those assembled at the annual meeting of the National Association of Evangelicals that he was worried about the "goose-step morality of a handful of vocal religious leaders who have suddenly become politically active." The most troubling and regrettable aspect of their involvement, Henry stated, is "the implication that one is not a morally sensitive Christian unless he shares an indicated stand on political specifics."

Like Carl Henry, Stanley Mooneyham, who heads World Vision, an organization that utilizes telethons to raise $45 million a year to feed the world's hungry, is an influential and respected man. Many denominations and independent religious organizations, as well as hundreds of individual churches, have cooperated with World Vision in carrying out various missionary endeavors. Mooneyham, too, is concerned about the motives of evangelicals who have suddenly gotten into politics. His thoughts, published in the April issue of his magazine, *World Vision,* echo the chilling reminder of Lord Acton that power corrupts and absolute power corrupts absolutely. "Political power has long been recognized as a seductive secular temptation," wrote Mooneyham. "It also must be seen as a seductive religious temptation." Sensing the mood of some of his evangelical friends in 1980, Mooneyham stated forthrightly that "it scares the daylights out of me." Then he issued a stern warning: "I see little to convince me that evangelical power—past or present—is less immune to . . . misuse than any other kind of power. . . . I am as scared of an evangelical power bloc as I am of any other. Worldly power in religious hands—Islamic or Christian—has hardened into more than one inquisition. That God has delivered us from the hands of zealous but misguided saints is all that has saved us at times."

Mooneyham doesn't exclude the possibility of harmonizing religious power and political power, but his mood is clearly cautious. Christianity, he believes, finds its strength in powerlessness and love, whereas politics acknowledges no place for love and the ends tend to justify the means.

At the far right of evangelical theological thought stand three generations of Bob Joneses who view themselves as the standard bearers of fundamental biblical truth. Bob Jones University, where their brand of literal biblical truth is taught to new generations, publishes a periodical entitled *Faith for the Family*. The September 1980 issue contained separate articles by Bob Jones, Jr., and Bob Jones III attacking Jerry Falwell for creating the Moral Majority. So eager were the Joneses to get their message out that they mailed the articles as letters to BJU "preacher boys" in early June, almost three months ahead of scheduled publication.

The Joneses had two bones to pick with Falwell and Moral Majority. First, they contended that it is not the business of the church to clean up America's morals. "Preaching Christ is our mission," wrote Bob Jones III. "When purging the country's immorality is the pulpit's objective, we have lost sight of our goals. America's problems are not moral; they are spiritual." Their second concern was that a group like Moral Majority could well foster ecumenical cooperation—a cardinal sin for doctrinal purists.

At the other end of the conservative religious spectrum stand the Southern Baptists, the largest denomination in the United States. Even before the issue of Christian involvement in politics came to a head, the Baptists were seriously divided over internal political struggles between theological conservatives and moderates. The present and immediate past presidents of the SBC, Bailey Smith and Adrian Rogers, are theological conservatives, and both have aligned themselves with the New Christian Right.

In 1976, without a lot of fanfare, Southern Baptists lined up pretty solidly behind their own Jimmy Carter. When Baptist influentials, the likes of Rogers, Smith, W. A. Criswell, and Charles Stanley, began to identify with other New Christian Right leaders in support of Reagan, other Baptist leaders went on the attack.

Jimmy Allen, another former president of the SBC, who now heads the Baptists Radio and Television Commission, led the attack by moderates. He took the occasion of an address before the American Jewish Committee to call the union of religion and right-wing politics "divisive and ultimately damaging to both religion and government." And in the Radio and Television Commission's newsletter he wrote: "Involvement in public decision-making processes on moral issues is a positive responsibility for spiritual leaders. However, the effort to create a religious party bloc vote is a dangerous one. Dependence on political power to enforce a moral point of view can lead to weakening the element of voluntary commitment."

So, from within the ranks of evangelicals, the political activists have been challenged on the grounds of principle, methods, and motive. And the attacks have been fairly widespread rather than isolated events. Criticism has spread from national denominational leaders to state and local leaders. They attack different aspects of political involvement, but there seems to be a grassroots swell of discontent over the engagement of evangelicals in politics.

The full implications of evangelical opposition to mixing religion with right-wing politics may not be clear at this early date, but some conclusions do seem fairly obvious. Most of the leaders of the New Christian Right are from the southern region of the United States. They are theologically evangelical and fundamentalist. Those involved in television ministries, particularly Jerry Falwell and James Robison, draw their audiences disproportionately from the South. Thus, even on their own home turf, where presumably they have the greatest potential to build their political strength, there is significant resistance. Part of this is based on the theological supposition, grounded in early twentieth-century fundamentalism, that man's work is to bring men to Christ, not to deal with social evils. Still another part of the resistance is grounded in some fairly strong ideas about separation of church and state. And yet another source of resistance is a strong thread of individualism that resists preachers, political parties, labor unions, or anyone else treading on one's individual right to choose—including the right to choose *not* to be concerned about politics.

This strong sense of individualism was expressed by Zola Levitt, a minor-leaguer in syndicated religious TV, in a newsletter to his supporters just before the election: "I feel sort of uncomfortable about being told how to vote. With all the talk about things called 'the Christian vote' or 'the fundamentalist stand,' I feel like I'm not getting my privilege of telling Caesar what I think. . . . I don't want to be disenfranchised by group thinking. . . . the way I think politically would surprise very few people. . . . All the same . . . I want my own chance to express [what I think]. . . ."

From almost every sector of society, and for a wide array of reasons, there has been a flood of protest about the movement of a few evangelicals into politics. But social movements are seldom silenced because of opposition. Opposition, rather, gives a movement visibility, which helps to recruit kindred souls to the cause. And being attacked often serves to solidify otherwise disparate groups into a unified front.

There is great competition for leadership in the struggle to return America to God. Even as the New Christian Right was coming together in Dallas, there was evidence that some individuals were placing social and political distance between themselves and others who were seeking leadership roles. In time, it is inevitable that they will discover differences that make a difference. Right now, they are euphoric about their successes in the 1980 elections, and they are committed to cooperation on general goals. They believe, with Jerry Falwell, that "when people begin to cooperate with what God is doing, you have an unbeatable combination.'' And the success of Moral Majority means that much of the New Christian Right leadership is going to watch carefully and take its cue from Jerry Falwell.

Jerry Falwell may have hoped that someone else would come along and pick up the leadership role the New Right coaxed him into accepting, but for the immediate foreseeable future, that role belongs to him. In considerable measure he will determine whether the New Christian Right, having tasted political power, will begin to inch toward the center of American politics, where it can build a real power base, or will fulfill the deepest fears of those who already see it as the most serious threat to democracy and individual liberties since Joseph McCarthy.

9

The Mobilization
of the Moral Majority

*For me, Moral Majority had a family beginning.
Several years ago we were having family devotions.
. . . We were going to pray for . . . our leaders and I
was sharing with the children the fact that they
probably would not know, when they became my age,
the freedom that I have known. It is very doubtful that
America will remain a free nation for another ten or
twenty years. . . . That's what I said to my family,
because I think as parents we have a right to prepare
our children. . . .*

*And the retort from my fourteen-year-old son,
Jonathan—and boys seem to have an exaggerated
opinion of dad's capabilities—was "Dad, why don't
you do something about it?" Well, I dismissed it that
night, but the next night I got the same question:
"Dad, why don't you do something about it?" Until
finally I awakened during the night hearing those
words, "Dad, why don't you do something about
it?"*

*I began to internalize the fact that I had no right to
preach that God through the gospel can change the
world, and that we ought to give Christ 100 percent
no matter what the cost, if I am not willing to do the
same. So it was from that beginning, already
bothered by all the problems in our society, that my
family-oriented spiritual burden would not allow me
to do anything but one day, June 1979, to organize
Moral Majority.*

Jerry Falwell

Jerry Falwell, like many other evangelical and fundamentalist
preachers, once took serious exception to the mixing of religion
and politics. That point of view was particularly widespread in

159

the South during the mid-1960s when northern students and clergy crossed the Mason-Dixon Line in droves to buoy up the civil rights movement.

On March 21, 1965, Jerry Falwell preached a sermon entitled "Ministers and Marchers" in which he boldly chastised clergy for their involvement in civil rights. That same day, hundreds of clergy assembled along with thousands of other civil rights workers in Selma, Alabama, for the resumption of a march on Montgomery that had earlier been interrupted by violence. Falwell told his audience that not only were the marchers engendering hate and unrest, but their methods ran contrary to a minister's calling. "Believing the Bible as I do," he said, "I would find it impossible to stop preaching the pure saving gospel of Jesus Christ, and begin doing anything else—including fighting communism, or participating in civil rights reforms. As a God-called preacher, I find that there is no time left after I give the proper time and attention to winning people to Christ. Preachers are not called to be politicians but to be soul winners." Elsewhere in that sermon Falwell argued, "Nowhere are we commissioned to reform the externals. . . . The gospel does not clean up the outside but rather regenerates the inside."

Jerry Falwell now believes he was wrong about clerical involvement in politics, and he jokes about trying to buy back copies of that sermon, which was printed as a booklet. Apparently there are plenty of other ministers whose minds have changed, too. A 1980 survey of clergy in metropolitan Charlotte, North Carolina, revealed that 90 percent of those responding felt it was their *duty* to speak out on social and political issues—and most felt the pulpit was a proper forum. Indeed, sociologists Norman B. Koller and Joseph D. Retzer discovered that the clergy talk a great deal about social and political issues. The majority of those polled indicated that during the previous year they had at least mentioned in sermons nineteen of twenty topics on the sociologists' checklist!

For a conservative southern community, it's hard to believe that this doesn't represent a radical departure from the 1960s when conservatives were so critical of liberal clergy for their involvement in civil rights. Of course, it's hard to say with certainty that the clerical community of Charlotte is representative of clergy all over the country—or even all over the South. So overwhelming is their engagement in political commentary, however, that we would be surprised to find that clergy in other communities are not following the same course. Liberal clergy have long believed it is proper to speak out on social and political issues, so if the Charlotte survey is at all typical of what is happening in the rest of the United States, the shift can be attributed to significantly greater proportions of conservative clergy speaking their minds.

In 1977 Albert Menendez published a book about voting behavior in which he concluded that evangelical Christians in this country constitute a "sleeping giant." Even before the 1980 campaign began to gear up, evangelical leaders began making bold assertions about the potential of an evangelical vote. Prophesying that the giant was about to awaken, Robert Grant, co-founder of Christian Voice, told his followers, "If Christians unite, we can do anything. We can pass any law or amendment. And that is exactly what we intend to do." Pat Robertson often expressed the same confidence to viewers of "The 700 Club": "We have enough votes to run the country. . . . And when the people say 'we've had enough,' we are going to take over the country."

The outcome of the 1980 elections persuaded many Americans that the sleeping giant had awakened and was signaling at the ballot box, "We've had enough." The surprise of the elections was not Reagan's victory, but rather the crushing defeat of many liberal leaders of Congress. The Reverend Jerry Falwell didn't waste a moment in claiming responsibility. During the campaign he had repeatedly stated that Moral Majority would register 4 million voters. Immediately after the election he claimed that in addition to having achieved that goal, Moral Majority had activated an additional 10 million church members. The Reagan landslide, he argued, could be significantly attributed to the Christian political movement led by Moral Majority. "Church people," he told a reporter, "are the secret ingredient that none of the pollsters counted on." He told another reporter on election night that "in every campaign where the station champions of Moral Majority were involved, we have not lost. We batted a thousand tonight."

The shock of the election results, plus the high visibility of Falwell and Moral Majority in the weeks preceding the election, made his claims credible. And there were quite a few defeated senators and congressmen who agreed with him. Pollster Louis Harris sanctified this interpretation of the election outcome when his post-election survey credited the "moral majority" with the margin of victory. But Harris made a blunder in his operational definition of "moral majority" that deserves to go down in the annals of polls alongside the famous 1948 *Chicago Tribune* poll that gave John Dewey a victory over Harry Truman. Yet hardly anyone noticed. The question Harris used to determine whether people belonged to the "moral majority" was : "Do you belong to, or attend in person, watch on television, listen on radio, or receive literature from any *evangelical church* or *preacher*?" If a person answered any one of these affirmatively, they were classified among the "moral majority." And in his syndicated report, Harris made reference to those people as "followers of the TV evangelical preachers."

What Harris did was to assume that all persons who are in any way associated with evangelical religion were supporters of Moral Majority and its causes. That this was not the case, however, was apparent in Harris's own data. In a poll conducted a month earlier, he used the same question but did not call evangelicals the "moral majority" in his findings. What he found then was quite different from the findings of his post-election report—and from what could be inferred from examination of Moral Majority documents.

For example, in that earlier survey only one in three white evangelicals agreed with the statement "It is impossible to be a liberal politically and also be a good Christian." And only 37 percent of them agreed with the statement "Most sex-education courses in the schools are really little more than pornography." Even on the question of abortion, which the New Christian Right is solid in identifying as murder, 45 percent of the white evangelicals in the Harris poll did not favor a constitutional amendment that would ban abortion. In short, a sizable proportion of those Lou Harris has identified as the "moral majority" don't agree at all with the "official" positions of the Moral Majority organization.

Still, there is a solid core of support for the conservative ideologies of Moral Majority and other New Christian Right groups. To rush to the judgment that all evangelical Americans have already jumped, or are about to jump, on the Moral Majority bandwagon, however, is to misjudge seriously the heterogeneous nature of the evangelical community and to misinterpret the available evidence.

Evangelicals did vote decisively for Ronald Reagan. A voter exit poll conducted by the *New York Times* and CBS showed that white "born-again" Protestants voted 61 percent for Reagan, 34 percent for Carter. The results of an ABC exit poll were very close, giving Reagan 59 percent and Carter 33 percent. That margin, however, is not dramatically out of line with support Reagan received from other sectors of society. Polls conducted throughout the presidential campaign which ascertained "born-again" status of voters showed a pretty even split between Carter and Reagan. During the last weeks of the 1980 campaign Reagan and Carter were running nip and tuck. Given the normal range of sampling error, the election was "too close to call." A pre-election poll conducted in Virginia by political scientist Larry Sabato produced results almost identical to the national pattern—an even split of evangelicals for Carter and Reagan. Then, just before election day, the undecided broke decidedly for Reagan. White evangelicals merely followed this marked shift.

Analysis of voting behavior and post-election polls all seem to point to the conclusion that an awful lot of Americans voted for a change. A *New York Times*/CBS pre- and post-election poll of the same people revealed that 20 percent of registered voters changed their minds in the last four days of the campaign, and about three-fifths of those who changed did so in a way that hurt Carter. Last-minute activities relating to the American hostages in Iran served to remind the electorate of lots of other things that had upset them about the Carter administration. But in the final analysis, it was probably the grim specter of inflation that led the majority of "undecideds" to vote their pocketbooks. A post-election Gallup survey showed no discernible ideological shift to the right. Voters were just plain mad, and anyone with any real vulnerabilities felt their wrath.

In this context, the organizational efforts of New Christian

Right groups were no doubt felt. There is real evidence of Moral Majority organization in some states. Indiana is such an example. In early October, state chairman Greg Dixon, pastor of the Indianapolis Baptist Temple, reported that Moral Majority had local chapters in all ninety-two counties in the state. On election day Senator Birch Bayh and Representative John Brademas, a twenty-two-year House veteran and majority whip, went down in defeat. There was evidence of active Moral Majority organization in other states as well. But there are important instances where liberal and moderate incumbents held onto their seats in the face of apparent organized opposition from the New Christian Right. Democratic House Majority Leader Jim Wright of Texas won despite opposition from several conservative groups and individuals, including evangelist James Robison, who lives in Wright's congressional district. Democratic Senator Alan Cranston of California easily retained his seat despite his having been targeted by Christian Voice for his zero score on its "Report Card"—and California is presumably the stronghold of Christian Voice organizational strength.

It all adds up to the conclusion that the New Christian Right flexed its youthful muscles in the 1980 election. When all the post-election analyses are completed, however, and when all the other factors that affected the election are taken into account, it may be very difficult to locate unequivocal evidence of its decisiveness.

What do we make, then, of Jerry Falwell's claims about the influence of the Moral Majority? For all the indicators of success, including the phenomenal amount of media attention, Falwell's claims about Moral Majority are like his claims about the listening audience of "The Old-Time Gospel Hour"— exaggerated.

During the campaign Falwell variously claimed 2 to 3 million members for Moral Majority, including 72,000 pastors. The numbers just don't square with the evidence. For one thing, Moral Majority doesn't really have a national membership. In October of 1980 Michael Farris, executive director of Moral Majority of Washington State, claimed that his membership of 12,000 was the largest of the fifty state chapters. By simple arithmetic, if every state had that many members, Moral Majority would be 600,000 strong—not 2 to 3 million.

By Falwell's own admission, the circulation of the *Moral Majority Report* at election time was 482,000. If Moral Majority itself had 2 to 3 million members, are we to believe that only one-fourth to one-sixth received the organization's newspaper? Neither Jerry Falwell nor his computer is that lax.

We could go on about how 72,000 pastors would represent nearly half of the Protestant evangelical pastors in the country, about how registering 4 million new voters would have required every person on the mailing list of *Moral Majority Report* in the early fall to register ten people each, about how absolutely impossible it is to determine the real numerical strength of such a fledgling yet widespread movement. But it seems obvious to us that Falwell is simply once again exercising the ministerial license for exaggeration—and once again taking the media and the public for a little ride. Only this time the stakes are a lot higher.

Jerry Falwell understands well the importance of a media image. As with the ostentatious big-spending entrepreneur, or the vivacious high-living entertainment star, the *image of success* is as important to developing a social movement as it is to promoting personal careers or business success. The appearance of success draws the media just as certainly as the hard evidence of achievement. When the media found Falwell and his Moral Majority, there was already a lot of motion. But the motion was mostly the cranking up of a social movement organization, not the motion of a well-greased, smoothly functioning machine.

The real importance of the Moral Majority and other New Christian Right organizations is not in what they accomplished during the 1980 elections, but rather in the *potential* they represent as a burgeoning social movement. There are three reasons for this. First, there is much restlessness and discontent in America today, and much of it is mobilizable in the name of Christian virtue. The number of evangelicals in America is large—very large. Second, every important social movement since the advent of television has been developed through mass communications. Marches and demonstrations are means to gain the attention of the news media and thereby bring the cause of a social movement's leaders into America's living rooms on the evening news. The New Christian Right doesn't have to draw a crowd to attract the attention of the media; they have merely to turn on their television cameras. At present the television preachers aren't reaching the audiences they claim they are, but the audiences are sufficiently large to develop powerful social movement organizations. And when they want the rest of the country to pay attention, they can use the airwaves to organize media events like Washington for Jesus and the National Affairs Briefing. The organizers of Washington for Jesus are planning approximately twenty rallies to take place in various states, commencing in spring 1981 and culminating with a return to Washington in April 1982. They continue to maintain that their effort is nonpolitical, but the strong political overtones are no less apparent now than they were during the Washington for Jesus rally.

The third factor that makes the potential of the New Christian Right so awesome is that its leaders have mastered the use of the ancillary technology of television that pivots around the computer, the foundation of which is direct mail targeted to audiences likely to be sympathetic to a cause. It is a proven way to raise big money and galvanize people in support of a cause. Toll-free telephone numbers facilitate that galvanization.

The next four years will be critical in determining whether the New Christian Right can develop a real base of political power and, if it does, shaping the manner in which that power will be exercised and deciding what goals will be pursued.

As the head of Moral Majority, no one will have a more important role in shaping the direction of the New Christian Right than Jerry Falwell. Many people see him as the personification of ultraconservative right-wing politics in America and, as such, a grave threat to our cherished liberties.

Falwell has on any number of occasions expressed views that are downright scary. And sometimes his behavior gives cause to question the sincerity of his more palatable rhetoric and whether he really understands the meaning of free speech. His concept of a debate, for example, is closer to a verbal free-for-all than a setting, governed by rules, in which both sides have the opportunity to express their views.

Falwell speaks boldly of defending the free speech of others, but in almost the same breath he makes comments that leave one with the uneasy feeling that he is prepared to withhold that right if what one speaks is morally offensive to him. On the subject of pornography, for example—and much of what Falwell would define as pornography others would consider art on the one hand and just bad taste on the other—he told a Moral Majority rally in Richmond, Virginia, "I'm for censorship of anything that is not fit for our children to see." But who is to make the decision about what is fit? And about those who produce the literature he considers pornographic, Falwell told that same meeting, "People like Hugh Hefner and Larry Flynt ought to be in the penitentiary."

Such words don't sound like the words of a man prepared to live in a pluralistic society. They also don't sound like the words of a man who says he believes in the separation of church and state, doesn't want to control government or establish a Christian republic—all viewpoints Falwell has expressed on numerous occasions.

To watch Jerry Falwell a little is to understand why a lot of people believe him to be a man for whom the ends justify any means. To watch him rather more carefully, however, *and* to understand his Baptist background, is to understand that Jerry Falwell may not really be "the most dangerous man in America," as he has been described by some of his adversaries.

Jerry Falwell was born and raised in Lynchburg, Virginia, not very far from the Thomas Road Baptist Church, which he founded and where he has spent his entire ministry. He attended school at Lynchburg College, only a few blocks away, until he had a conversion experience during his sophomore year. The only time he was ever away from Lynchburg was while he attended Baptist Bible College, a fundamentalist school in a small town in the Midwest Bible Belt.

His television program is broadcast all across the land, and he jets around the country in his own plane, but Jerry Falwell has never strayed very far psychologically, intellectually, or theologically from his Baptist roots in Lynchburg. Until recently he was a spiritual E. F. Hutton for fundamentalists: whenever he spoke, people listened; his word was gospel. But mostly he spoke only to fundamental Bible believers and other kindred spirits. As long as that was his world, no one outside it much cared what he said. Not until the late 1970s, when he began to talk politics, did the rest of the world begin to cup its ears and listen.

Much of Falwell's strident language and shoot-from-the-hip behavior may just be the result of his being a big fish in a little pond for so many years. Travel the back roads of the Bible Belt and look for big Baptist churches. Chances are that when you find one, you'll find a preacher who behaves a whole lot like Jerry Falwell. One needs to be cautious about stereotyping, but Falwell is a caricature of a successful Baptist preacher. He is intelligent, outgoing, charismatic, caring, and a little boastful. And even though success tends to go to their heads just a little, preacher boys like him love and give of themselves to their congregations, and they are in turn revered by their followers. When these Baptist ministers preach about social issues which for them are mostly private sins, they sound a whole lot like Jerry Falwell.

It wasn't until 1980 that the national press discovered Falwell. For many who were assigned to cover an event where he appeared, it was the first exposure to fundamentalist religion. Many were quick to see him in unfavorable stereotypical terms, and at least some of what Falwell said reinforced those stereotypes. The truth of the matter is that many who have written about Jerry Falwell share a disposition to which Falwell himself is not immune—namely, a profound distaste for anyone with a different world view. Few reporters, however, have been as candid in admitting their bias against Falwell and fundamentalism as was Teresa Carpenter, who did a cover feature for the *Village Voice*. Somewhat taken aback by Falwell's charm and sincerity, Carpenter wrote: "You can either give Jerry Falwell the benefit of the doubt, that is *keep an open mind*. Or you can *assume* he is a sophisticated snake oil salesman. I tend toward the latter, and that, I will be the first to admit, is a purely emotional reaction. Whenever I step within a 10-foot radius of a fundamental minister *my reason clouds over*."

As Jerry Falwell's visibility soared, the press watched and

listened ever more attentively. And on several occasions he said things that he would like to be able to take back. The first embarrassing episode occurred early in the summer of 1980 when he was nailed by the press, on a leak from the White House, for loose and careless talk about a conversation with President Carter that never really happened. At first he defended his remarks as "merely allegory," but gradually he backed away. Although he never fully recanted, he did eventually apologize—on national television.

And then there was the occasion when he defended the comment of Southern Baptist President Bailey Smith on the matter of whether God hears the prayers of Jews. He gave a theological response not unlike one a learned rabbi might have given in response to a question about the Jews' view of Jesus Christ as the Messiah. Nevertheless, Falwell agreed with Bailey Smith: "God does not hear the prayers of Jews." Shortly afterward, Falwell was honored by Israeli Prime Minister Menachem Begin, along with Senators Frank Church, Henry Jackson, and Jacob Javits, for support of Israel's right to exist. But this event passed almost unnoticed while Falwell continued to receive negative press for his defense of Bailey Smith. Falwell must surely have been confused about the press's priorities.

If 1980 was the year the national press discovered the television preacher from Lynchburg, Virginia, it may also have been the year that Jerry Falwell discovered the world to be bigger and more complex than he had previously imagined. His response to a reporter about having doubts was one of the most revealing moments in his budding role in U.S. politics during the 1980 campaign. The questioner was Marvin Kalb on "Meet the Press."

> KALB: Sir, you speak here and in much of the material that I've read as a man of considerable certainty. I just wanted to ask you, do you have any doubts?
> FALWELL: Oh, yes. I think everyone has doubts. I think we're constantly probing, learning, developing, maturing. . . . I hope there are things today that I would have a better understanding on than I had one year ago. I'll give a particular illustration. I think I'm more sensitive today to the complexity of this pluralistic society than I was maybe a year ago. I think the spotlight helps us

all to be more aware of everyone out there. I hope next year I'll be able to say the same thing.

These could easily be the words of a smooth-talking politician who knows the value of the middle of the road—if the road will take him to Washington. Or they could be the sincere reflections of a man from the Bible Belt ghetto who has discovered that Baptist preachers may not be the authority on or even understand all that is happening in the modern world. Might this possibly be a man discovering a world beyond the Thomas Road Baptist Church and people whose lives are guided by principles not frequently elucidated on "The Old-Time Gospel Hour"?

In that same interview, Kalb asked Falwell this question: ". . . when you speak of having a divine mandate to carry your message to Congress . . . I don't mean for this to be a frivolous question but you've read the Old Testament and you know that Abraham had conversations with God . . . I wonder, do you feel that you have conversations with God?"

Without hesitating for even a moment, Falwell responded: "No, I really don't." A dangerous ayatollah who takes orders directly from God and no one else? Would Falwell hide his mystic leanings to find greater acceptance? It doesn't seem likely.

Holy men who are convinced that God speaks to them have little choice but to obey His voice. No price is too great, no means illegitimate, in the pursuit of God's will. But men of God who are confined to something less than face-to-face dialog with the Almighty as their source of knowledge of His will may also be capable of discerning the limits of their own ability to know His wishes. They may even be able to accept the possibility that someone of a different persuasion has insights into God's hopes and purposes for mankind. Maybe.

A glimpse of this latter possibility was evident when Falwell met William Sloane Coffin on the Phil Donahue show. Coffin is the senior minister of perhaps the most prestigious liberal Protestant pulpit in the United States and is best known for his civil rights and antiwar activities. It is hard to imagine any clergyman being more diametrically opposed to Falwell on so many issues.

Something rather unexpected happened on "Donahue." Falwell and Coffin found themselves agreeing with each other on several issues each had presumed to be a bone of contention. Furthermore, Falwell appeared to be genuinely intrigued by and respectful of Coffin. Only occasionally did he launch into his canned lines, and on any number of occasions he listened when, on previous occasions, he had interrupted his "debating" partner. Might it just be possible that Falwell is beginning to develop respect for those with whom he disagrees?

But what about those statements regarding censorship of anything that is harmful to our children and putting Hugh Hefner and Larry Flynt in prison? We asked Falwell about that statement. What he had to say reveals the depths of his concern about pornography while it is a confession of the carelessness of his language: "I feel the pornography industry is the poison of the American spirit. And I *personally* feel that people who are profiting off the destruction of the moral values of young people are criminal in heart, if not in act. It probably is an extreme position when I say they belong in the penitentiary, and if I possessed the ability to exercise it, wouldn't. I would say that while I suppose that's an overstatement or an overreaction to the damage they're doing, I do feel that legislatively we need to *look* at the porn industry and *look* at what it's doing to our young people—not just young people, but old people as well—and establish legal guidelines that would make it criminal. It think that when we cause young people to lose all respect for the family, for morality, for ethics; when we poison their minds and hearts with this kind of garbage, we're doing them damage, we're really doing society damage."

We're not very comfortable with the cause-and-effect link that Falwell makes between pornography and the moral values and behavior of our society (a Presidential Commission on Obscenity and Pornography produced nine volumes of data that failed to establish such a relationship). But there is certainly nothing wrong or threatening to civil liberties to propose that we *look* at the effects of pornography on our society.

As for censorship, Falwell says he agrees with the Supreme Court that we should establish community standards, but insofar as the airwaves are concerned, he thinks we need national standards. He objects to the moral content of much of what comes over the national airwaves, and he does not see a violation of the rights of others in organizing pressure to alter those standards. The fear of contamination is strong. Pay television is a different matter, however. If adults want to pay to receive dirty movies in their homes, that's their business, he says. But the majority of Americans, who Falwell feels agree with him, shouldn't have to be subjected to such materials over network television. As for printed matter, he says he would like to see it on shelves where it is out of the reach of children.

A few weeks after the 1980 election Jerry Falwell wrote a short paper on "The Real Intent of Moral Majority," which stated in part: "It has never been and never will be the intent of Moral Majority to imply that those who disagree with us are the 'immoral minority.' The name of the organization was chosen because we felt it expressed an attitude held by a majority of Americans of many different religious and, in some cases, no religious backgrounds. We are not intent on forcing Christianity or any other religious faith on anyone else. We simply feel that in a pluralistic society our views have as much right to be heard and considered as anyone else's views, and it is to that end we are committed."

Is all of this just so much snake oil? Perhaps. But then perhaps Jerry Falwell is learning that when you play under the spotlight in the big tent, you'd better say what you mean because someone is going to print it and take it seriously. Jerry Falwell's views are conservative—no question about that. Many of them are, in principle, as offensive to liberals as liberals' views are offensive to Falwell and his followers. The critical question is what *means* he is willing to employ in the pursuit of his goals for America. Is he willing to play by the rules, as he says, or will the end justify the means?

The liberal establishment has more than likely overreacted to any immediate threat posed by Jerry Falwell and his Moral Majority to the civil liberties of the people of this nation. But in the final analysis, that overreaction may be for the good. It has certainly given the New Christian Right cause to reflect about what it really wants and about what means it is willing to use to achieve its goals. The reaction has also alerted a significant segment of society to the fact that its values are being challenged. And whenever something we cherish is challenged, we are forced to consider anew why it is important to us. We can hardly be a poorer people for having reexamined our values and, if they are really being threatened, protecting them.

Even if the great fears many Americans have about Moral Majority are not realized, there is still one unsettling aspect of the political involvement of the New Christian Right. At the edge of the left and the right stand spokesmen for a lunatic fringe who do hear voices or are otherwise confident that they have both special insights about what is wrong with society and a mandate to pursue their goals. The United States is currently experiencing a resurgence of Ku Klux Klan and anti-Semitic activities the likes of which we have not experienced for many years. So also are we experiencing a new boldness by religious bigots. The Office for Intellectual Freedom of the American Library Association, for example, reported a fivefold increase in attempted censorship in the month after the election. Two brothers who believe rock-'n'-roll music is the handmaiden of Satan travel the country as itinerant preachers and organize record-burning rallies. Throughout the country there are reports of renewed intolerance by religious zealots.

The leaders of the New Christian Right would like to believe that such happenings are unrelated to their social movement. But it's not that simple. The lunatic fringe may not be the constituency of the New Christian Right, but the latter's success certainly gives those who commit excesses reason to believe that their acts are acceptable and legitimate. No greater damage was done to the civil rights movement than when its leadership failed to denounce unequivocally violence committed in its name. It would be similarly dangerous for the New Christian Right to ignore the threat of the lunatics.

Jerry Falwell, James Robison, and all the other television preachers cannot stop the lunatic fringe, but they can define the boundaries of lunacy by firmly denouncing those who have no regard for or understanding of human rights in a pluralistic society. And to the extent that the televangelists do command the respect of conservative preachers in America, they can certainly help prevent the spread of madness among their ranks. The credibility of the New Christian Right may well be defined in terms of how it reacts to those who stand on the same end of the political spectrum but beyond the consensual rules of U.S. politics. Given the semiautonomous nature of Moral Majority chapters, this may well be Jerry Falwell's greatest challenge.

10

Digging In for the Struggle

The electronic Church is fostering in our midst a completely private "invisible religion." This "invisible religion" is—or ought to be—the most feared contemporary rival to church religion—and church religion is the only faith the New Testament knows.
Martin Marty

The evangelical social movement illumined by the flickering light of TV screens is now seeking to grab with gusto the power it has so long been denied. The televangelists have tasted success—and they like it. They want more and are determined to have it. The power to change America—religiously, socially, and politically—is their ambition.

But power is never given; it is always taken. Power must be taken from somebody who surely does not want to give it up. It seems clear that the practitioners of the electronic church threaten government power *over* the media and moderate evangelical and mainline religious power *in* the media. Also at issue is government power to regulate the social order and the power of moderate evangelicals and mainliners to preside over the national religious ethos.

Unless the technology that brings in the big dollars fails the televangelists, their pursuit of power will not slacken. But for every mobilization there is a countermobilization. The responses to the electronic church—from government, moderate evangelicals, mainline Protestants, Catholics, and secular groups—will do much to shape the future.

It is yet too early to gauge the muscle that will be wielded by secular groups—old established groups like the ACLU and new groups created to combat the influence of the televangelists, like People for the American Way. There are two sectors of society, however, that can certainly be counted on to wage serious struggles against the rising power of the televangelists—the established churches and various government agencies.

In the past there has never been much enthusiasm among regulators for tackling the thorny problems sometimes presented by religious broadcasters. This reluctance is likely to change, however, both because the independent sector will pressure the government to regulate and also because some of the changes the electronic church leaders would make in government, if they had the power, constitute a real threat to entrenched government bureaucracies. Mainline church leaders, on the other hand, will not hesitate to take on the televangelists, and it is very likely that established conservative churches, like the Southern Baptists, will side with them to check the power of the TV preachers.

Mainline Protestantism never used to be very concerned about the Night Riders of the high-voltage radio stations because they perceived that those preachers appealed to a different clientele. Many a liberal Protestant, in fact, had a good laugh listening to the fiery soul savers blaring forth their messages into the night from 250,000-watt station XERF across the border from Del Rio, Texas. Comedian Andy Griffith broke into show business back in the late 1940s with a hilarious caricature of a fundamentalist preacher. His routine probably wouldn't have been very funny were it not for the fact that we had heard his likeness before on the radio.

As we have seen, mainline religious groups initially were the recipients of most free time allocated by networks and local stations for public service. Not until the early 1970s, when evangelicals began buying up big hunks of the Sunday morning "religious ghetto" time, did mainline Protestants take up arms. In all arenas of social interaction, concern for one's adversaries or competitors is directly proportional to their perceived threat. By the mid-1970s it was obvious to those in Protestant communications that the evangelicals' brand of commercial religion was having devastating effects on their religious broadcasting time. Although some stations still refuse to sell time for religious programs, more and more have discovered that Sunday morning can be very profitable. Why should they give away this valuable time? They can find other slots in their broadcast schedule to fulfill their public service obligations. As the free time disappeared, so also did the programming produced by various sectors of the mainline Protestant and Catholic faiths.

By the end of the decade there was deep and growing concern that the highly successful nationwide television programs were also having adverse effects on local congregations of mainline churches. Concern was aroused, in part, because the growing success of the entrepreneurial religious broadcasters coincided with an incipient decline in mainline Protestant membership and attendance. It seemed a reasonable assumption that at least part of the difficulties they were experiencing could be attributed to the fact that some of their congregation were now getting their religion in the comfort of their homes. And to that assumption could be added another—the financial contributions of those stay-at-home Christians were being rechanneled to the cathode church.

Add to this the fact that mainliners and many evangelicals consider the theological messages of the electronic churches to be shallow and simplistic, and you have all the ingredients of a pretty good conflict. The tremors of an impending eruption were already being felt before some of the TV preachers made their entrée into politics. Some of the critiques that appeared in religious periodicals and conferences were pretty spicy. Robert Cleath, for example, wrote in *Eternity* that "most religious TV programs have become dispensers of religious junk food as marketable as the Super Whopper. . . ." Martin E. Marty, usually a calm voice, who for years has been a bridge between the conservative and liberal religious communities, decried the "completely private 'invisible religion' " being fostered by the electronic church. Few persons who attended the Consultation on the Electronic Church sponsored by the National Council of Churches in February 1980 disagreed with psychologist Robert Liebert's view that the conflict over the electronic churches "has every hallmark of an intensifying war of survival among battling Christian groups."

The TV preachers realize that the most dangerous charge that can be made against them is that they are competing with the organized churches. A little public criticism might actually be good for the electronic churches. It calls attention to them, and that may cause the curious to check them out. But those who labor in the electronic vineyard can't afford to get stuck with the criticism that they are taking people out of the pews and dollars out of the collection plates. So they can be expected to fight these charges. Their argument, of course, is that their broadcasting is meant to complement and augment the activities of the local congregations. And almost all of them can point to the fact that they make repeated appeals to their audiences to get involved in local churches.

Speaking at the 1980 convention of the National Religious Broadcasters, Jerry Falwell told his fellow broadcasters: "We must convince the pastors and laity in the churches that television is an arm of the church and not a church unto itself; that we are here to help get the unsaved into the church and work in unity one with another. We have got to get over the fear that television is an alternative to the church. It is not. It is a part of the church."

We have encountered no one who actually thinks of the electronic church as a church per se, but mainliners have worried that this movement might offer some kind of substitute for participation in local organized churches. The joining together of individuals in congregational worship and work is central to Protestant and Catholic doctrines of the "visible" church. Any movement that tends to pull people away from or weaken allegiance to a local church is inimical to mainline ecclesiastical doctrine. And there is a certain aspect of *belonging* readily detectable among many of the viewers of and contributors to the electronic church. The contributors have invested something of themselves in something larger than themselves; their giving seems to reflect a need for community, a literal "joining of the club." Questions are raised by the notions and phrases that run through the movement: "club members," "partners," "Prayer Key Family members," and other comparable terms.

Ben Armstrong certainly did not intend to touch off a storm when he coined the concept of the electric church, but that is what he did. Plainly, he considered the religious broadcasting explosion of the 1970s to be completely praiseworthy. Said

Armstrong, "In this vision, I saw the electric church as a revolutionary form of the worshipping, witnessing church that existed twenty centuries ago. . . . In the electric church, as in New Testament times, worship once against takes place in the home."

Examples of electronic congregations abound. Rex Humbard, who has often referred to himself as "your TV pastor," presents an annual communion service on television. He invites viewers to participate with their own loaves and cups in front of their TV sets. Lester Sumrall, head of the LeSea Broadcasting Network, has conducted a communion service on his television program and invited his viewers to run to the refrigerator for the necessary supplies so that they can follow along. One mainline minister reported the request of a family for a telephone hookup to a funeral parlor so that a deceased family member's favorite TV preacher could deliver a eulogy by long distance.

Mainline fears about this kind of thing are only exacerbated by Ben Armstrong's assessment in *Christian Century* of electronic church viewer-supporters: "They are really joining the electronic church. It's like joining the local church. They are loyal to it and support it with their gifts."

The leaders of the electronic churches deny any intent of competing or interfering with local congregations. Still, they are extending their influence not only by offering an array of services for their partners, but also by reaching directly into local communities. "The PTL Club" refers people to specific local congregations. So does "The 700 Club," which has teams of prayer counselors in scores of cities across the country. Robert Schuller's church is in Orange County, California. Listeners to his "Hour of Power" telecast founded a sister church in Orange County, Florida. Graduates of Jerry Falwell's independent Liberty Baptist Seminary are fanning out across the country and establishing new churches that mirror Falwellian theology.

It is not at all beyond reason to speculate that the next surge of new denominationalism in America will be the franchising of churches that meet standards laid down by the televangelists. Although there are clear differences in the theologies of Oral Roberts, James Robison, and Pat Robertson, if all three were to go into the business of franchising local congregations labeled by their respective surnames, there certainly would be a lot of confusion among prospective communicants.

Nearly every mainline spokesman has had something to say about TV religion. An examination of speeches and periodicals, however, reveals that nearly all have been saying the same things: entrepreneurial TV religion presents a dangerously abbreviated version of the Christian gospel and is a threat to the congregational Christianity of the New Testament. Additionally, many of the values displayed in the electronic church were considered inimical to the Christian ideals of self-denial and service to others. There were also considerable questions whether the electronic church was achieving success at the expense of organized churches—that "bucks and bodies" were being stolen from plates and pews of local churches.

From our hundreds of hours of viewing religious television programs, we have concluded that the critics have a point. But the crucial question remains unanswered—are local congregations losing ground to the electronic churches? The fact of the matter is that there is very little evidence of this, and what little evidence is available leads to ambiguous conclusions. For example, in 1978 the Christian Broadcasting Network released the results of a study conducted for it by Market Research Group of Detroit. A survey of 1,300 of CBN's regular contributors revealed that they gave an average of $190 per year, while another survey of *former* 700 Club Partners revealed an average annual contribution of $107.

In both surveys, the CBN contribution was estimated to be about 20 percent of the individual's total contribution to religious organizations. The implication in the news release was that the balance of giving was to local congregations. We were unable to determine whether other questions on the surveys would permit this conclusion, but we are inclined to think it is unwarranted. One source of skepticism is that in yet another survey conducted during the same time, Partners were asked about their viewing habits with respect to other religious programs. Almost half (48 percent) reported that they had watched "The PTL Club" an average of twelve times during the previous month. Nearly seven out of ten (68 percent) reported watching Oral Roberts, 60 percent watched Billy Graham, 49 percent Rex Humbard, 48 percent Jimmy Swaggart, 43 percent Robert Schuller, and 30 percent Jerry Falwell. Those who watched other programs viewed them on the average of three times per month.

All this adds up to a lot of viewing of religious television. We have no hard data, but it seems reasonable to infer that some of the contributions of these people go to other religious programs. If this is true, there is still no way of knowing whether these people are giving more, or redirecting some of their former giving from a local church. The 700 Club. Partner survey reported that nine out of ten are involved in a local church. Thirty percent say their involvement in a local church has increased, and only 2 percent report a decline as a result of their involvement in the 700 Club. That leaves about two-thirds reporting no change.

In a questionable methodological procedure, the survey asked respondents to assess the behavior of others. Eighty-six percent of the 700 Club Partners agreed with the statement "Most Christians that I know would support their local church financially first, and then ministries like CBN. . . ." And 82 percent agreed that "Ministries like CBN have actually helped increase support for local churches rather than take away support." Both statements assume knowledge of what other people do, knowledge that they cannot reasonably be expected to possess. Thus, the questions must be seen either as designed to be self-serving or as the products of careless social science research.

Such reservations about the CBN survey notwithstanding, if its returns are representative, and if the respondents correctly reported their own behavior, the net increase in local church involvement as a result of becoming involved in the 700 Club is by no means insignificant.

A study entitled "Profile of the Christian Marketplace" (PCM) conducted by Gallup for the American Research Corporation in 1980 reached different, but not altogether dissimilar, findings with respect to the effects of religious television on involvement in a local church. Among those who said they had made a personal commitment to Jesus Christ, 18 percent reported that TV viewing had increased their involvement in the local church, as compared to 9 percent who reported decreased involvement. These figures don't control for the amount of viewing, nor are we able to determine whether these people contribute to television ministries. Younger people in the PCM survey are about twice as likely as people over fifty to report that their involvement in a local church has declined as a result of watching TV religion. The results of both the CBN and PCM studies point toward a net gain for the local churches as a result of TV viewing, but the data do not permit the conclusion that this means a net increase in financial support.

The PCM survey provides the only data we are aware of that estimate the proportion of the U.S. adult population who contribute to electronic church ministries—an estimated 2.3 percent contribute to Christian television more than once a year. That figure comes out to about $3^1/2$ million contributors to all the electronic churches. When combined with information on the amount of giving per individual, that appears to be an adequate figure to account for the combined reported budgets of the electronic churches. The PCM survey asked people what their choice would be 'if they were going to contribute to *only one* organization. Churches beat out health organizations by 37 to 35 percent for the first choice, followed by the United Way with 12 percent. At the bottom of the list was religious broadcasting with 1.5 percent. Those over fifty years of age were slightly more likely to pick religious broadcasting as their first choice than were those eighteen to thirty-four, but they were significantly more likely than young people to pick churches as their first choice.

There is one other piece of information that provides insight into the effects of the electronic churches on the life of the local congregation, and that is the simple matter of when the electronic church programs are scheduled. Those who were critical of the role of the churches in the struggles for social justice in this country used to like to remind folks that 11 A.M. Sunday is the most segregated hour of the week. That may still be true, but 11 A.M. Sunday is certainly not the most popular hour for the producers of religious television programs. Most of them would prefer to be on anytime but that traditional hour of worship.

Oral Roberts has maintained his hold on top of the audience charts for more than a decade. He has done so while broadcasting on far fewer stations than some of his competition. In February 1980 only one of the 165 stations on which Oral Roberts appeared scheduled him at 11 A.M.! Only 3 percent of the time slots for the top six syndicated religious programs are on at that hour. The most important reason the electronic preachers do not broadcast at 11 A.M. Sunday is that they have learned through experience that a significant proportion of their potential audience turns off the television set and goes to church. This time slot is not profitable in terms of either audience or revenue. Between them, Kenneth Copeland and Jack Van Impe purchased new time on more than 120 stations in a brief period near the turn of this decade. Neither purchased a single 11 A.M. time slot.

Combined, this evidence doesn't clear the electronics of the charges that they are having deleterious effects on attendance and the coffers of local congregations, but it does suggest that the news is not as bad as many had imagined. The electronic churches are supported by a very small percentage of the population. Some of those people give a significant proportion of their income, and in some cases this is no doubt done at the expense of the local church. But the statistical evidence doesn't point to a wholesale robbery of the local congregations' treasuries. Where that has happened, there is probably as much room for examining the shortcomings of the local congregation in meeting the needs of its lost sheep as there is for examining the seductive techniques of the electronic churches. One North Carolina pastor wrote, "In my ministry, as I talk with those who watch and listen regularly, both active church members and nonmembers, one accusation keeps coming up: the church is failing to offer them a balanced diet, so they feel the need to supplement their spiritual diet—or replace it."

The electronic churches probably have had more negative impact on local congregations than their leaders would be willing to admit, but less than the critics contend. It is important that systematic research be conducted so that the real and alleged effects of the electronic churches can be more accurately assessed. But even if it should turn out that the electronics have no measurable effects on the life of mainline churches, the struggle will not end. It will take the mainliners a long time to get over the bitterness of having lost valuable air time to the evangelical entrepreneurs. To the extent that the airwaves are seen as a way of supplementing and bolstering the offering of the local congregation, the mainliners have lost their opportunity for outreach.

The theological disputes between the mainline and electronic church leaders will also remain a longstanding source of conflict. Mainliners have tried to reconcile their theologies with science, which in turn necessitates interpreting at least some segments of the Scriptures as theological rather than literal history. The gospel according to TV they see as a dangerously abbreviated version of the Christian message. The fundamentalists, on the other hand, give primacy to the Bible as the ultimate authority. Scriptures are the inspired and inerrant word of God not only in matters of faith but also in historical, geographical, and other secular matters. And they look upon the ''liberals'' as people who have capitulated the most essential aspects of the faith to secular humanism.

Although bound together by this fundamental belief, the televangelists do present great diversity in their theology—even though most of it is conservative. More important, though, all the central figures of the electronic church promote, whether consciously or unconsciously, a privatized faith. Belief does not involve a relationship between the believer and a fellowship of believers. Rather, it is a private affair. People construct a faith that suits their own interests and needs. When it no longer satisfies immediate needs, it is reconstructed or abandoned. This, not the protection of a specific theological doctrine, is at the heart of Martin E. Marty's concern about the ''completely private 'invisible religion' '' being fostered by the electronic churches.

Marty recognized that the creation of private religion is rather widespread in contemporary society. In an interview about the effects of the electronic churches, Marty drew an analogy between the kind of privatized secularized religion college-educated youth create and the privatized religion constructed by those who watch the electronic churches. The college-educated, he writes, ''will take a little dab of the Judaism they were brought up with, a little bit of Catholicism from their wife, a bit of Zen Buddhism they got in college, a weekend of est, a half-baked belief in astrology, a love for jogging, and a macrobiotic diet and kind of make up a religion out of it.'' Then he goes on to say: ''In a way that's not recognized, that's what's happening in these programs, too [the electronic churches]. You take a little bit of one kind of belief in the Bible, another kind of belief in the Holy Spirit, another kind of borrowing of a psychological technique of motivation, another technique from sales, and you put it together, but *you* are in control.''

Ours has become a very privatistic culture. (We prefer the concept privatism to narcissism or hedonism because it doesn't seem quite as value-laden.) But there is great irony in this. There is irony, first of all, in the concepts that Marshall McLuhan gave us about the impact of modern communications technology. We have become a global village, but we receive the messages of the village in cool, discontinuous blips. The medium is incapable of transmitting messages of any depth or complexity. We have come together in the sense that we are aware of global happenings, but inasmuch as the medium deprives us of depth, continuity, and authority to help us understand the world, we fall back upon our own resources to locate meaning. The self becomes the ultimate authority, the ultimate expression, the ultimate meaning. And the irony of the electronic churches is that although they mean to transmit a message to all the world that is unchanging through the ages, they may simply be transmitting blips—blips packed in ways that satisfy immediate needs, but blips that have little relationship to a major world religion that has survived two millennia.

At least some segments of mainline church leadership recognize these ironies. Today, however, their solutions to the dilemmas are hardly spelled out in programs or policy. There is much astir, however. In addition to their fighting with the electronics, we can expect mainliners to fight a good bit among themselves.

Some are certain to argue for head-on competition with the electronic evangelicals—to fight fire with fire. But there are several obstacles that collectively may constitute an insurmountable obstacle to this approach. The first is organization. By what authority might such an approach be undertaken? Assuming it were possible to get past the question of the efficacy of the task, the matter of who should do it could keep the project tied up in committee for years. And then there is the question of supporting religious programming. Again, if one could assume it were possible to put aside the question of the broadcasters' ''duty'' to provide free time and accept the fact that air time would have to be purchased, there is the question of how the programs would be supported.

Organizationally, the finances of Protestant denominations are transmitted upward from the local churches through the intermediate dioceses and synods. Even if the authority existed, neither denominations nor the National Council of Churches has adequate contingency funds to launch, much less sustain, a major religious programming effort. And the question of utilizing the same fund-raising methods as the evangelical electronics is certain to cause much rancor, because many mainliners view those techniques with considerable abhorrence. And if, finally, all these problems could be solved, there would still be the knotty problem of deciding who would be the star of the mainliners' cathode church. Imagine what kind of heat that would generate!

The only probable way that mainliners are going to enter the big time of the electronic churches is if one or more pastors with a local telecast receive consent from their board to syndicate and then, through luck and hard work, build an audience adequate to cover the costs of growth. In a sense that is what Robert Schuller has done. But attractive though he may be to some elements of mainline Protestantism, his heavy emphasis on "possibility thinking" is distasteful to many mainliners and he is unlikely to become "their man on the tube."

With the cost of TV time rising steadily, the obstacles to breaking into Sunday morning prime time are ominous but not impossible. And there is always the chance that a rising star will come along just at the right moment and capitalize on the misfortunes of someone on the way down. In the world of television, all stars have their ups and downs; no one survives indefinitely. Both Oral Roberts and Rex Humbard are past sixty. Both would like to pass their ministries along to their sons. As in other walks of life, however, this dream is not always realized. There may be opportunities for those of different theological orientations to work their way onto the TV gospel train.

Competition that is not head-on in nature seems a more likely option. The United Methodist Church has approved a project to raise $25 million to purchase a high-quality commercial TV station. Profits from the operation, if the project materializes, will be used for program production and possibly the purchase of other broadcasting units. The project was the brainchild of Charles Cappelman, head of CBS's Television City in Hollywood and president of the board of United Methodist Communications. Precisely what type of religious programming would be produced has yet to be clarified.

Some hint of where the mainliners may be heading may be gleaned by looking at what they have done in the past as well as what has survived from the 1960s when mainliners were much better represented in the repertoire of religious offerings. Drama with a religious message seems a likely direction. The Lutheran Church—Missouri Synod did this with considerable success for many years with a program entitled "This Is the Life." The objective of the series was to reach the unchurched through quality drama in a "natural" setting without a hard sell of religion. Tommy Thompson, executive vice-president of Religious Heritage of America, believes the Missouri Synod can attribute a significant proportion of its growth to the success of its radio and television programming.

"Insight," produced by the Paulist Fathers, is the longest-running dramatic series on television and one of the few free-air-time programs to survive the onslaught of commercial religion. Produced by Father Ellwood Keiser, the program has attracted top writers and actors who work for the minimum wage because they respect the kind of social messages communicated on the program. Many of the programs are not religious dramas per se, but they explore questions of faith and meaning.

Keiser sees television as having passed through two periods in its brief life. The first belonged to businessmen who utilized the airwaves aggressively to sell their products, the second to politicians who applied the same media concepts to sell themselves. He believes television is now moving into a third phase, which will belong to those who will use the airwaves to humanize society.

Keiser is critical of television and feels it has abdicated its responsibility and squandered much of its humanizing potential. He feels it has too frequently conveyed the message that "consumption is the meaning and fulfillment of life." Yet, there is nothing intrinsic in the logic of television that necessitates this message. The humanizing revolution Keiser now sees unfolding is being forged by many organizations and individuals—institutionalized religion being only one of many participants. He sees in contemporary programming many humanizing messages. For example: "Thematically, 'The Waltons' says that people are more important than things. 'Family' says that love and honesty are not only possible but necessary in an affluent and sophisticated family. 'All in the Family' says that bigotry is absurd, yet bigots are lovable. 'M*A*S*H' says that it is possible to retain one's human dignity in an essentially inhumane situation, especially if you have a sense of humor."

For all its critical acclaim, "Insight" has never attracted large audiences, seldom over half a million total. Russ Reid heads a highly successful marketing organization that specializes in servicing nonprofit clients. He shares Ellwood Keiser's enthusiasm for the potential of television to humanize culture, but he would like to see Christian organizations play a more than incidental role in the production of television drama. The greatest potential for getting the messages of the Christian gospel across is on evening prime time and not on the Sunday morning "ghetto" hours. He believes prime-time television is ready for quality religious drama and is already at work developing the concept. If the programs are properly done, he thinks the networks ". . . will pay us to produce the movie of the week and they'll get a sponsor for it." An expert in direct-mail fund raising, Reid thinks this is also an option for raising funds to produce religious programming, but more difficult and less satisfactory than getting the networks to pick up the tab. This way, he says, "it won't take a dime of the Lord's money."

The evangelical preachers dared to think big when they made the leap from syndication on a few stations to nationwide syndication. Whether mainliners compete head-on or in other ways, it will take no less vision, daring, and imagination to have an impact as dramatic on American culture as that of the evangelicals.

The relationship of nearly every sector of our society to government has changed rather dramatically since 1925 when evangelist Aimee Semple McPherson fired off the following angry wire to Commerce Secretary Herbert Hoover after inspectors had temporarily closed her station because it was unable to stay on its assigned frequency: "Please order your minions of

Satan to leave my station alone. You cannot expect the Almighty to abide by your wavelength nonsense. When I offer my prayers to Him I must fit into His wave reception. Open this station at once.'' Regulatory authorities have never expected the Almighty to abide by their ''wavelength nonsense,'' but they certainly have expected broadcasting stations to do so.

Today we more or less accept the legitimacy of the government's role in regulating and enforcing the law. Although we may sometimes be annoyed, even enraged, by regulations and what we perceive to be unnecessary ''meddling'' in our lives, it is hard to imagine anyone today ordering a cabinet-level official to do *anything*. Even if we thought some high-level government official were deserving of our rage, the mere thought of the power of government bureaucracies to investigate or require paperwork would surely temper our public utterances.

Not so with the television preachers. They don't like the idea of government telling them what to do any more than did Aimee Semple McPherson. And when the government does something they don't like, they let the government know—usually through their constituencies. They also maintain strong legal counsel through the aegis of the National Religious Broadcasters, whose present chief counsel is a former FCC chairman.

In 1979 the Federal Communications Commission charged PTL with soliciting money for foreign missions and spending it to pay bills for U.S. operations. Jim Bakker fought back and accused the FCC of a ''back-room witch-hunt'' and a ''fishing expedition.'' While resisting the efforts of the FCC to open his books, he regularly denounced the FCC government bureaucrats, equating them with satanic forces: ''I don't believe all the demons in hell, I don't believe all the astrologers, I don't believe all the bureaucrats in the federal government can stop God from sending revival to this generation.''

Bakker's attacks on the federal government brought tens of thousands of letters flooding into the FCC mail room. But the amount of mail generated by PTL viewers was infinitesimal compared with what evangelical Christians are capable of when they get aroused. In December 1974, Jeremy D. Lansman and Lorenzo W. Milam, two noncommercial broadcasters, filed with the FCC a petition to halt the assignment of noncommercial educational FM radio frequencies to religious groups. Viewed as a "petition against God," it brought 700,000 pieces of mail to the FCC before it was dismissed in August 1975. The dismissal of the petition, however, did not end the deluge of mail. It got worse. And worse. And worse. Somehow, the story began to spread that atheist Madalyn Murray O'Hair had petitioned the FCC to prohibit all religious broadcasting. The rumor probably had a direct lineage to the Lansman and Milam petition, but it also spawned additional rumors of its own.

Congress gave the FCC a quarter of a million dollars to combat the rumor, but it refuses to die. *By the end of 1980, the FCC had received more than 12 million pieces of mail opposing a nonexistent petition!* And the FCC continues to receive daily deliveries, ranging from several hundred to several thousand letters, depending on the swirling of the rumor.

In 1977 a bill introduced in the House of Representatives, HR-41, would have placed fund raising by religious and charitable institutions under the supervision of the U.S. Postal Service, which would have access to the financial records of the nonprofit organizations. Many organizations opposed the bill, but it was the TV preachers who spread the word and buried the House Post Office Subcommittee under letters and telephone calls. HR-41 never emerged from committee. Fund-raising broadcasters know that similar legislation could be proposed again. If that happens, it is certain to be met with a massive counterattack from the electronic churches. Given a little time to work on it, the preachers of the electronic church could probably drop a million letters on a lawmaker on a given day.

Legislators know this. Regulators know it as well. Both have learned through experience to think twice before taking on the wrath of evangelical Christians who feel they are being wronged by their government. This notwithstanding, it is inevitable that there will be future confrontations between the electronic preachers and the government, and this promises to be an important page in the history of religious broadcasting in the United States. There are several reasons why this struggle cannot be averted.

First of all, the government, under the aegis of the Federal

Communications Commission, is responsible for licensing and regulating the use of the airwaves. Broadcasting is largely a laissez-faire industry, but it is possible to get in trouble with the FCC, and over the past fifty years several radio and television preachers have. If it can be proved that a station is not operating "in the public interest, convenience, and necessity," the FCC can revoke its license. Evangelist Carl McIntire learned this in 1970 when his license to operate WXUR in Media, Pennsylvania, was revoked because of his unrelenting one-sidedness toward persons and organizations unsympathetic to his far-right political and religious views.

Except in cases where the television preachers own stations, and some of them do, the FCC's relationship to them is indirect. The FCC licenses and regulates stations, not program syndicators. The Fairness Doctrine, issued in 1963, is one of the principal means whereby the FCC oversees station activities. This directive states that when a program includes a personal attack on an individual or organization, the station must transmit the text of the broadcast to the person or group with a specific offer of time for a response. Since 1967 the station must make that offer within one week or face the possibility of a $10,000 fine for each offense.

The first real test case of this doctrine came in 1964. Evangelist Billy James Hargis, in a program aired over radio station WGCB in Red Lion, Pennsylvania, attacked author Fred J. Cook, who demanded time to reply. WGCB offered to sell him the time, or give it if Cook could show that he was unable to pay. Cook would not accept either condition and the case went to the Supreme Court. The Court affirmed the Fairness Doctrine in 1967.

In practice, the Fairness Doctrine operates usually only when somebody complains, as was the case in Dallas when James Robison made comments about homosexuals that brought a complaint to station WFAA-TV. Fearful of reprisals from the FCC, the Dallas station simply put Robison off the air. It wasn't until Robison organized a demonstration and proceeded to drag the case through the courts that WFAA-TV reinstated his program.

None of the television preachers particularly likes the Fairness

Doctrine. The politically minded among them, in particular, consider it to be an infringement of their freedom of speech. Jerry Falwell has called the Fairness Doctrine "the most unfair doctrine ever created by mortal men."

But the necessity for legal restrictions and a governmental response mechanism is illustrated by the broadcasting career of Father Coughlin in the 1930s. Pastor of a Catholic church in Royal Oak, Michigan, Coughlin gathered amazing political power all through the 1930s. He began broadcasting a Sunday afternoon children's program in 1926. On Sunday, October 30, 1930, when America was sinking into the fear and bewilderment and anger of the Great Depression, he went political. On that day Coughlin spoke to the parents, not the children, with a stern denunciation of "money changers" and "subversive socialism."

Coughlin received a flood of mail. He sounded as if he had some answers, and people wanted to know more. He kept speaking and the people kept writing, and a lot of his mail contained dollar bills. Coughlin expanded to more and more stations. His radio audience was estimated to number in the tens of millions.

He jumped on the Roosevelt bandwagon in 1932 with the slogan "Roosevelt or Ruin." He fully expected to be in Roosevelt's circle of advisers, and he offered radical economic theories about how to cure the depression. When Roosevelt accepted neither Coughlin's personal approaches nor his economic theories, Coughlin became Roosevelt's bitter enemy.

Coughlin's demagoguery, arrogance, and power continued to grow; a single speech in 1932 drew 1,200,000 letters. Computers had not been invented, but 106 clerks and four personal secretaries were able to handle his mail. Coughlin did not send letters; he only received them—and many contained those dollar bills.

Coughlin founded his own political lobbying group, the National Union for Social Justice. He established a weekly newspaper, *Social Justice*. And in 1936 he established his own political party, the Union party, with "Liberty Bill" Lemke of North Dakota as its presidential candidate and the principles of social justice as its platform. Coughlin did not expect Lemke to win, but he did expect to set the stage for an even stronger push in 1940. He boasted that he would deliver 9 million votes to Lemke, but Lemke received fewer than a tenth of those promised. Coughlin suspended the activities of the NUSJ and retired temporarily from the air.

He returned in early 1937, more strident than ever. He reconstituted his NUSJ chapters as a group of Christian clubs, then as a "Christian Front" organized into platoons. Coughlin's anti-Semitic and pro-Nazi sentiments began to emerge, and the Christian Front began to act out some of those sentiments. Coughlin's speeches and writings grew steadily more vehement and his supporters more ganglike.

The nation could no longer tolerate the Coughlin brand of fascism after the start of World War II. His newspaper mailing privileges were revoked under the Espionage Act of 1917. The Roosevelt administration, not wishing to indict a priest for sedition, persuaded Coughlin's archbishop to silence him. Coughlin's public career ended in April 1942. He lived out his days as pastor of the Shrine of the Little Flower, the Royal Oak church from which he had arisen.

Charles J. Tull has said in his book about Coughlin that he "was never a serious threat to American democracy, but the mere fact that he could win the support of so many Americans for such incredible notions should alarm any American who believes that our democratic system is worth saving."

Could another Coughlin arise? We do not think it likely, for three reasons. First, there simply are too many preachers on TV, each with a following; there were no competing radio superstars in Coughlin's time. Second, there was no Fairness Doctrine to regulate the content of broadcasting then. Third, it is not likely that the social and economic conditions of the 1930s will ever be duplicated. Coughlin arose in a time of national despair.

Still, it would be wise, as Wallace Stegner has said, ". . . to ponder the enormous following he [Coughlin] had at his peak. It would be well to consider how vague, misty, uninformed, contradictory, and insincere his program was, and yet how it won the unstinting belief of hundreds of thousands, even millions. It would be well to remember that even a people like the Americans, supposedly politically mature . . . can be brought to the point where millions of them will beg to be led. . . ."

There are two other government agencies that have an important stake in the activities of the electronic churches: the Securities and Exchange Commission and the Internal Revenue Service. The SEC has moved against Falwell and Humbard, but not for broadcasting reasons. Both sold church bonds in violation of SEC rules, but after corrective measures were agreed upon, no punitive action was taken. The IRS is concerned with seeing that the electronic preachers follow regulations that govern tax-exempt organizations. The electronic church seems to be well aware of such regulations, which are basically fairly lenient, and they follow the letter of the law.

The movement of a few television preachers into politics is almost certain to have a dramatic impact on the present relationship between religious broadcasters and the government. Tax regulations are constantly being rewritten, and there is no reason to presume that current regulations governing tax-exempt organizations are immune to reexamination. The large sums of money raised by the television preachers are currently off limits to all government agencies unless there is reason to suspect wrongdoing. Whether the Congress will continue to view these large sums of money as beyond the concern of government is questionable.

Groups that now see the television preachers as a threat to traditional American institutions and values will lead the assault and will place the electronic churches increasingly in an adversary relationship with various government agencies. The Fairness Doctrine is probably the likely point of attack for liberal groups. It would take little organized effort to make radio and television station owners as leery of, say, People for the American Way as librarians are of ultraright groups that want to burn a book for Jesus. Station owners would rather not have to deal with a barrage of complaints about the violation of the Fairness Doctrine. But they want even less to deal with the FCC looking over their shoulder. And they can be certain that the electronics will fight back if station owners lean on them too hard.

In these and other areas, perhaps yet unimagined by anyone, the government will be entangled in a series of struggles involving the electronic churches and their leadership. Generally we think of the government as a disinterested party that processes grievances between two or more other warring parties. To the extent that the electronic church leadership persists in advocating political change, it is hard to imagine that the government will be an altogether disinterested party. Government employees themselves have become a significant interest group in America. They are large in number, and inasmuch as their well-being is tied to the continuance of the government bureaucracies they run, they have a definite interest in resisting many of the changes advocated by the conservative television preachers and their followers. Before counting the electronics down and out against the onslaught of liberal forces, it would be wise to examine recent developments in California. That state's reputation for the unusual, the unorthodox, and often the bizarre is certainly well deserved when it comes to religion. California is headquarters for one-third of the more than 500 identified cults in the United States, more than the next seven states combined. One of the more incredible news stories of the 1970s was the tragedy of the People's Temple, a California group that had set up a colony in Guyana led by Jim Jones. Following a variety of leads about wrongdoing, including complaints from relatives that people were being held in Guyana against their will, California Congressman Leo Ryan flew to Jonestown to conduct a personal investigation. He and three American journalists were murdered, and thereafter more than 900 persons followed Jones in carrying out a mass suicide which had been previously rehearsed.

In October 1980 California Attorney General George Deukmejian dropped investigations against twelve religious groups, among them the Worldwide Church of God, Synanon, and the Faith Center. Herbert W. Armstrong and church treasurer Stanley Rader were under investigation for allegedly diverting up to $80 million of Worldwide Church of God funds for personal use. The church went into receivership for seven weeks in early 1979 after allegations were made that church records were being destroyed. Charles Dederich and other Synanon officers were under investigation for allegedly diverting $300,000 in solicited monies to nonchurch activities. A month earlier Dederich had been convicted of plotting to kill a lawyer with a rattlesnake but escaped imprisonment when a judge cited failing health as justification for probation. Faith Center, headed by the Reverend W. Eugene Scott, owns two California television stations that broadcast around-the-clock live and taped marathons of ''Festival of Faith.'' Scott had been accused of raising money for one purpose and spending it for another, and he had steadfastly refused to open his books for the attorney general, vowing to carry his case to the Supreme Court if necessary.

Deukmejian's reason for dropping these and nine other cases was the passage of a bill that in effect stripped the attorney general of the power to investigate and prosecute cases involving tax-exempt religious organizations. Deukmejian was accused of overreacting in dropping the suits, and the criticism appears to have some merit. Nevertheless, no one disputes the fact that the new law does significantly restrict the powers of the attorney general to investigate and prosecute. According to the new law, allegations of improper use of internal funds can be brought only by a member of the governing body of a religious group. The rank-and-file membership cannot initiate action for civil fraud.

Perhaps the most interesting aspect of this affair was the uncanny coalition that formed to support the legislation restricting the investigative powers of the government. The National Council of Churches, the American Civil Liberties Union, and a broad spectrum of liberal Protestant denominations in California joined with Herbert W. Armstrong, Charles Dederich, and Eugene Scott in favoring the legislation. Their justification, of course, was the protection of First Amendment rights.

If California is a bellwether for the ensuing struggle between secular and religious liberals, on the one hand, against conservatives led by a few television preachers, on the other, we may expect some interesting, but agonizing, alignments and realignments. When liberal groups stand up to protect the interests of groups that may be tainted, indeed downright scandalous, that action may be viewed as protection of their own interests. Sentiments for maintaining the separation of church and state and protecting First Amendment rights run high. There are a lot of people, liberal and conservative alike, who are prepared to tolerate a little fraud and abuse of liberties on behalf of a few to protect the rights of the many. Granted the validity of this proposition, it is also fairly clear that the groups supporting the California legislation were not seriously affected by any wrongdoing of the groups under investigation.

When liberals square off against the New Christian Right, they are likely to use a different scorecard. The interests of liberals are much more clearly at stake. The conservatives want to change the country in ways that threaten both material and life-style interests of nonconservatives. Furthermore, there are many who believe the conservatives are prepared to trample upon the First Amendment rights of others to get their way. The tension between protecting principles and real interests, perceived to be threatened, promises to be one of the most significant issues of this decade. The electronic churches and their leaders are destined to be in the center of the controversy.

Quo Vadis?

Of one thing there is little doubt, the evangelical community is amassing a base of potential power that dwarfs every other competing interest in American society today. A close look at the evangelical communications network . . . should convince even the skeptic that it is now the single most important cultural force in American life.

Jeremy Rifkin, *The Emerging Order*

In its infancy, modern communications technology sold us automobiles, cosmetics, soap, and beans. In its adolescence it taught us to judge political candidates by their smile and clean presentation of self. Whether we are moving rapidly toward the world of mind control depicted by George Orwell in *1984* and by Aldous Huxley in *Brave New World* isn't clear. Our world seems to possess greater quantities of complexity and ambiguity than appeared to be the case in those futuristic novels. But what does seem certain is that our consciousness will be shaped by the messages we receive through mass communications technology. The great struggle that is now taking shape is the struggle for access to and control of that technology, for with it the next great social movement will wage its wars.

The social movements of the 1960s were fought with bullhorns and human flesh. The leaders of those social movements endeavored to get a crowd large enough to attract a television camera. Thus would they gain access to the homes of America for a few moments during the newscasts. The weapons of the social movements of the 1980s will be computers that pump out direct-mail materials to audiences that have been determined to be sympathetic to the cause. Then, with the money thus raised, the messages will be transmitted to larger audiences who will remain in the comfort of their living rooms to receive them.

At present, conservatives, both political and religious, have the upper hand in the utilization of this powerful communications technology. The liberal tradition in America is largely found in the Democratic party. The Democrats have been in power for a long time and have grown lethargic. Democratic consultant Bob Keefe put it this way: "We Democrats can be likened to a car rolling downhill and going fast. Only when we got to the bottom did we find we had run out of gas awhile back." In religion, the liberals, weary from a decade of civil rights and antiwar struggles, spent a good bit of the 1970s arguing about whether the television stations had an obligation to give them free time in the public interest. While they were doing that, of course, conservative religious traditions were building their electronic empires.

The furor created by the involvement of a few television preachers in politics during the 1980 campaign did not end after the election because the televangelists are not going to wait for the next election to attempt to develop further political clout. What we are experiencing in the United States today is not the normal give-and-take of political parties that differ mainly in the mix of liberals and conservatives in their ranks. We are experiencing an ideological struggle that in some respects is related to but is not to be equated with the civil rights struggle that began in the late 1950s.

The current struggle is more about the role of government in our lives—what it may and may not do, what it should and should not do, and what it must and must not do. These concerns create a mosaic that crisscrosses traditional liberal-conservative positions. The answers any one ideological camp gives to the questions of how government may, should, and must relate to our lives creates a kaleidoscope of incredible inconsistency. It is precisely for this reason that the upper hand now held by conservatives may not be decisive.

The countermobilization of people and organizations that oppose the New Christian Right is a natural part of any social movement, as predictable as the rising and setting of the sun. And the greater the perceived threat of the right-wing Christians, the greater will be the efforts to check their political influence. What is not clear or predictable about this social movement, and the establishment's counterinsurgency, is the direction that each group will take.

To understand better the resurgence of conservative influence in the United States to date, one should focus on the New Right and its antecedents in twentieth-century conservatism. To understand where this movement is going, one needs to study carefully and watch the movements of the New Christian Right. It is the latter group that is likely to be responsible for shaping the next major developments in the conservatives' efforts to gain political power.

It is too early to know how all of this will turn out because the outcome depends very much on decisions not yet made and alliances not yet forged. The leaders of the electronic churches are only now beginning to be influential. Their role in the 1980 elections may have been exaggerated, but the role they will play in the impending struggle may be decisive.

The outcome will determine the direction of American society as we move into the twenty-first century. The struggle to determine whether we will enter the next century with determination to resolve the vexing dilemmas and problems that plague the United States and the industrial world or will drift ever closer to the abyss will be fought largely with modern communications technology. But some of the political alliances and results of the struggle may be totally unanticipated.

That most of the electronic church preachers are not now in politics is not of any great significance. Whether in politics or not, they are all searching for a broader base to support their ministries. To the extent that they succeed in their objective, they will simultaneously be adding to the foundation of a potentially powerful social movement that aspires to return the nation to God. It is important to recognize that evangelical Christians have always believed it to be their mission to transform society. What is different about the present movement is that they now possess powerful technology that can help them realize that goal.

How the electronic preachers utilize this enormous power base will have important implications for the future of this nation, indeed of our world. The potential for abuse is all too evident, but so also is the potential for constructive use.

One of the most important books of the past decade was Jeremy Rifkin's *The Emerging Order*. Along with many others, Rifkin sees America coming to the end of an epoch of unlimited growth and wealth. The United States, the world's greatest creator and consumer of resources, must take the lead in the transition from an age of expansion to a steady-state world economy. The evangelical awakening in America, Rifkin believes, is inextricably a part of the convulsions that are sending economic tremors through the industrial world.

None of this is new or particularly original. What is innovative and provocative is Rifkin's vision of Christian theology as a basis for legitimizing a new covenant that governs the relationship of man to God and man to his environment. The new covenant involves a reinterpretation of the meaning of the Genesis charge to man to take dominion over the earth. Protestant theology has interpreted that passage as license to exploit the resources of the planet. The new theology interprets the concept of dominion to mean stewardship. The earth and all that dwells therein has intrinsic value because it is God's creation.

This new theological interpretation of Genesis has gained remarkable acceptance in just the past decade or so, since we have become acutely conscious of the apparent limits of our environment. It has received greater acceptance among liberal theologians than among evangelicals, and it stands in sharp contradiction to a remarkably pristine free-enterprise theology preached by many of the television preachers.

What role then might the electronic churches play in the spreading of this new covenant theology? There are two important considerations in approaching this question. First, although there is an outside chance that Ronald Reagan will be lucky enough to experience a respite in the energy crisis, the dwindling of the world's nonrenewable energy resources is too significant for the problem to go away for very long. Second, an intrinsic feature of mass communication in the modern era is that world leaders don't have to remain locked into a consistent position. There may be limits to how much of an about-face one can get away with, but certainly there is room for significant change.

If Jerry Falwell doesn't have his finger on the pulse of the real moral majority in America, why shouldn't he gravitate toward those who could constitute the nucleus of a political consensus? When we reach the point where there is no escape from the reality of scarcity, energy as well as other resources will be defined in moral and religious terms. If the current crop of television ministers fails to preach that message, they will lose their leadership to those who will. Television shapes our values, but it mirrors them as well.

The years just ahead are going to be very dangerous and anxious times for the United States and for most of the world. Détente has come unstuck. With each passing year the Middle East becomes more explosive. Most of the Third World is a time bomb with multiple fuses. Global economic collapse could be triggered by any number of events.

Such periods in history test the character of a people. Historically, when this nation has been tested, we have discovered deep moral fibers that have their roots in our pluralistic religious doctrines and principles. Our religious heritage has never been simplistic. As America has assimilated other cultures and religious perspectives over two centuries, the complexity of her collective faith has grown, even if its public expression has weakened. The United States may well be on the verge of another great religious awakening.

During the 1960s a small group of theologians pronounced the "death of God." But as so many scholars have noted, man is by nature a religious animal and does not exist without some form of religion. "It follows," wrote Harvey Wheeler, formerly senior fellow of the Center for the Study of Democratic Institutions, "that a death of God era is also a god-building era. . . . Our time is one of the most religious periods in all history, a time in which god-building is taking place at a dizzying pace."

Eastern religions penetrated American culture in earnest during the late 1960s, and since that time we have indeed experienced a proliferation of new religious expressions. But so also has this nation experienced sustained reexamination of traditional perspectives. In all the religious ferment, there can be little question but that the growth of evangelistic faiths has been the largest, and they have had the greatest immediate effect on our culture. But it may well be premature to assume monolithic political implications from what has transpired to date.

We don't quarrel with the general proposition that there is cause for concern about the potentially regressive influence they could have on American culture. But we feel that those who are already hearing the thunderous boots of goose-stepping soldiers with swastika armbands marching up Pennsylvania Avenue are overreacting. When Thomas Jefferson founded the University of Virginia, he wrote, ". . . we are not afraid to follow the truth wherever it may lead, nor to tolerate any error so long as reason is left free to combat it." There is a great core of good and common sense in America, a moral majority capable of struggling and coming to grips with the economic, political, and moral imperatives of survival. They have survived the heavy diet of trash and pablum delivered on television since its birth. They will survive the manipulation and simplistic solutions to our problems that now are being offered by television preachers and politicians.

The struggle to reshape America will take place in front of us on our television sets. Television will not be simply the transmitter of news, but increasingly it will *be* the news as the cathode tube is utilized consciously to shape our consciousness. This will occur not only in explicitly religious programming, but in drama and investigative reporting as well. That the media seem primed, as never before, to transmit religious and moral messages may speak to the needs as well as the character of the American people.

Bibliography

Allworthy, A. W. *The Petition Against God*. Dallas: Christ the Light, 1976.

Altheide, David L., and Johnson, John M. "Counting Souls: A Study of Counseling at Evangelical Crusades." *Pacific Sociological Review* 20, no. 3 (July 1977): 323–48.

Altheide, David L., and Snow, R. P. *Media Logic*. Beverly Hills, Calif.: Sage Publications, 1979.

American Research Corporation. *Profile of the Christian Marketplace 1980*. Newport Beach, Calif.: American Research Corporation, 1980.

Archer, Gleason L. *History of Radio to 1926*. New York: American Historical Society, 1938.

Armstrong, Ben. *The Electric Church*. Nashville: Thomas Nelson Publishers, 1979.

Auchmutey, Jim. "Ernest Angley's Miracle Crusade." *Atlanta Constitution,* June 21, 1980, p. 1-B.

Barnow, Erik. *A Tower in Babel*. New York: Oxford University Press, 1966.

Carnell, Edward John. "Fundamentalism." In *A Handbook of Christian Theology,* edited by Marvin Halverson and Arthur A. Cohen. New York: World Publishing Company, 1958.

Castelli, Jim. "The Curse of the Phantom Petition." *TV Guide,* July 24, 1976.

Cavert, Samuel McCrea. *Church Cooperation and Unity in America*. New York: Association Press, 1970.

Crawford, Alan. *Thunder on the Right*. New York: Pantheon Books, 1980.

DuBourdieu, William J. "Religious Broadcasting in the United States." Ph.D. dissertation, Northwestern University, 1933.

Ellens, J. Harold. *Models of Religious Broadcasting.* Grand Rapids, Mich.: William B. Eerdmans Publishing Co., 1974.

Fessenden, Helen M. *Fessenden: Builder of Tomorrows.* New York: Coward-McCann, 1940.

Fore, William F. "The Electronic Church." *Ministry,* January 1979.

————. "A Short History of Religious Broadcasting." In *Religious Television Programs,* by A. William Bluem. New York: Hastings House, 1969.

Frady, Marshall. *Billy Graham: A Parable of American Righteousness.* Boston: Little, Brown, 1979.

Hadden, Jeffrey K. "Religion and the Construction of Social Problems." *Sociological Analysis* 41, no. 2 (Summer 1980): 99–108.

————. "Soul-Saving via Video." *Christian Century* 97, no. 20 (May 28, 1980): 609–13.

Harlow, A. F. *Old Wires and New Waves.* New York: Appleton-Century, 1936.

Horton, Donald, and Wohl, R. Richard. "Mass Communication and Para-Social Interaction." *Psychiatry* 19, no. 3 (August 1956): 215–29.

Jennings, Ralph M. "Policies and Practices in Selected National Religious Bodies As Related to Broadcasting in the Public Interest, 1920–50." Ph.D. dissertation, New York University, 1968.

Klapper, Joseph T. *The Effects of Mass Communications.* New York: Free Press, 1960.

Koller, Norman B., and Retzer, Joseph D. "The Sounds of Silence Revisited." *Sociological Analysis* 41, no. 2 (Summer 1980): 155–61.

LaHaye, Tim. *The Battle for the Mind.* Old Tappan, N.J.: Fleming H. Revell Company, 1980.

Malpus, David. Report on "Born-Again Christians." In *All Things Considered,* National Public Radio, September 4, 1980.

Marty, Martin E. *The Improper Opinion: Mass Media and the Christian Faith.* Philadelphia: Westminster Press, 1961.

Menendez, Albert J. *Religion at the Polls.* Philadelphia: Westminster Press, 1977.

Miller, Spencer, Jr. "Radio and Religion." *Annals of the American Academy of Political and Social Science* 177 (January 1935).

Neeb, Martin. "An Historical Study of American Non-Commercial AM Broadcast Stations Owned and Operated by Religious Groups, 1920–66." Ph.D. dissertation, Northwestern University, 1967.

Noonan, D. P. *The Passion of Fulton Sheen.* New York: Dodd, Mead, 1972.

Owens, Virginia Stem. *The Total Image, or Selling Jesus in the Modern Age.* Grand Rapids, Mich.: William B. Eerdmans Publishing Company, 1980.

Parker, Everett C. "Big Business in Religious Radio." *Chicago Theological Seminary Register* 34, no. 2 (March 1944).

————. "Religion on the Air in Chicago." *Chicago Theological Seminary Register* 32, no. 1 (January 1942).

Parker, Everett C.; Barry, David W.; and Smythe, Dallas W. *The Television-Radio Audience and Religion.* New York: Harper & Brothers, 1955.

Rifkin, Jeremy, with Howard, Ted. *The Emerging Order.* New York: G. P. Putnam's Sons, 1979.

Robinson, Wayne. *Oral.* Los Angeles: Action House, 1976.

Saunders, Lowell S. "The National Religious Broadcasters and the Availability of Commercial Radio Time." Ph.D. dissertation, University of Illinois, 1968.

Sholes, Jerry. *Give Me That Prime Time Religion.* New York: Hawthorn Books, 1979.

"Should Churches Be Shut Off the Air?" *Christian Century,* May 12, 1927.

Stegner, Wallace. "The Radio Priest and His Flock." In *The Aspirin Age,* edited by Isabel Leighton. New York: Simon & Schuster, 1949.

Strober, Gerald, and Tomczak, Ruth. *Jerry Falwell: Aflame for God.* Nashville: Thomas Nelson Publishers, 1979.

Taylor, Charles R. *World War III and the Destiny of America.* Nashville: Sceptre Books, 1979.

Tull, Charles J. *Father Coughlin and the New Deal.* Syracuse: Syracuse University Press, 1965.

Index